CHILDREN
WHO
MURDER

A Psychological Perspective

Robert V. Heckel and David M. Shumaker

Foreword by Honorable Eugene Arthur Moore

Westport, Connecticut
London

Library of Congress Cataloging-in-Publication Data

Heckel, Robert V.
    Children who murder : a psychological perspective / Robert V. Heckel and David M.
    Shumaker ; foreword by Eugene Arthur Moore.
        p.   cm.
    Includes bibliographical references and index.
    ISBN 0–275–96618–6 (alk. paper)
    1. Juvenile homicide—Psychological aspects.   2. Forensic psychiatry.   3. Child
psychotherapy.   I. Shumaker, David M.   II. Title.
RJ506.H65H43   2001
618.92′85844—dc21   00–042776

British Library Cataloguing in Publication Data is available.

Library of Congress Catalog Card Number: 00–042776
ISBN: 0–275–96618–6

First published in 2001

Praeger Publishers, 88 Post Road West, Westport, CT 06881
An imprint of Greenwood Publishing Group, Inc.
www.praeger.com

Printed in the United States of America

The paper used in this book complies with the
Permanent Paper Standard issued by the National
Information Standards Organization (Z39.48–1984).

10 9 8 7 6 5 4 3 2

Contents

Foreword

On January 13, 2000, in the 6th Circuit Court of the County of Oakland, Michigan, Judge Eugene Arthur Moore delivered an outstanding sentencing opinion in the case of Nathaniel Abraham, who at age 11 was charged with murder. At age 13 he was convicted of 2nd-degree murder in a case that attracted national attention and trial coverage on Court TV.

Judge Moore's opinion reflected a depth of understanding, reason, caring, and compassion in a difficult case with a series of critical issues relating to sentencing, treatment, and rehabilitation of a preteen when tried in adult court. Each of these issues Judge Moore has addressed with deep consideration for a troubled child who at the time of the offense was functioning at a 7-year level. Judge Moore did this while maintaining a strong sense of judicial responsibility, an outstanding effort.

Because of the importance of his sentencing opinion, with his permission, we have reproduced it here.

HISTORY

The trial is over and now we face an equally important decision. What should the sentence or disposition be for Nathaniel Abraham. The decision will have an enormous effect on both Nathaniel and society.

In 1999 we celebrated the 100th anniversary of the founding of the Juvenile Court in America. It started in 1899 in Cook County, Chicago. Its roots were in England during the Industrial Revolution. During the Industrial

Revolution, two groups of people joined hands to fight the abuse of children. One group opposed the criminal system treating children the same as adults when punishing those convicted of a crime. Adults and children were punished alike. The second group was concerned about using children as chattels as a form of very cheap labor. Little food—no school—large dormitories, and working 18 hours a day was common abuse of children.

The protection of children from these abuses brought about the Cook County (Chicago) Juvenile Court in America.

In Michigan in the early 1900s, the legislature decided to punish girls convicted of crimes differently than women and built the Girl's Training School at Adrian. Boy's Training School in Lansing followed shortly. This also meant punishing boys differently than men. Gradually there developed the *Parents Patria Doctrine* where the Juvenile Judge became the "substitute parent" for the child. A Juvenile Code was adopted separate from the Criminal Code. The first paragraph of the Juvenile Code mandated Juvenile Court Judges to provide for the children that come before them, "the care, custody and control that the child should have received in his own home."

To this end, the legislature created a new separate Juvenile Court—separate from the Criminal Court to ensure that the child was properly cared for. Each child was to receive "individualized treatment" necessary to change his or her behavior so the child would grow up to be a successful adult. Society was less concerned about guilt because the "court supposedly had a better world for the child than the child got in his own home."

Juvenile Court recognized that children were different from adults. They were still young, immature and not fully developed. Thus character and behavior could still be molded and they could be rehabilitated.

Rehabilitation became the byword of the Juvenile Court. Few wanted to lock up children for life. There was a recognition that if we were going to protect society from future criminal behavior by the child we had better do something to rehabilitate the child so that when released by the Juvenile Court, the child was changed. Only by doing this would you and I be protected from further criminal activity by the child.

Unfortunately, often because of inadequate resources, our Juvenile Courts failed in changing many delinquents' behavior. As a result, many people began to advocate that our Juvenile Court not "try to change a child" unless we were even more certain that the child was "guilty." Only if clearly guilty could the courts impose incarceration and even probation on a child.

Thus, in the 1960s and 1970s with the landmark cases of *Kent* and *Gault*, we found the U.S. Supreme Court ensuring that children had attorneys, the right to remain silent, guilt beyond a reasonable doubt, and many of the safeguards afforded to adults accused of a crime.

The 1980s saw a rise in juvenile crime and especially of crimes of an adult nature committed by juveniles. In response the legislature enacted tougher laws aimed at treating children more like adults and subjecting them to adult penalties. The motivation was that society expects even children to be accountable for their actions. The way to stop juvenile delinquency and criminal activity is to hold offenders accountable. This works on the theory that individuals will be deterred from future criminal behavior if they are held accountable for their actions and know that consequences will follow. Likewise, it is thought that others in society will be dissuaded from illegal actions because they see what has happened to people convicted of crimes.

Certainly, holding individuals accountable for their actions is one of the cornerstones of molding human behavior. However, at the same time, we must take a clear look at how well the adult criminal system works. The adult system does accomplish two goals.

- First it punishes criminals. When convicted, an adult criminal is held accountable for his actions. Often he is punished by probation or some term of incarceration in the jail or prison system.

- Second it keeps society safe for a period of time. While that criminal is housed, society is safe from further criminal activity by that individual. But we must look clearly and fully at the effects of incarceration.

  1. Is the criminal rehabilitated?—The answer to this question seems to be a clearly resounding "NO." Our adult penal system often does not rehabilitate the way it should.

  2. Does the criminal reoffend when released?—The answer to this question is often "YES." Our penal system has an alarmingly high recidivism rate.

  3. Is the public safe? The answer to this question seems to be twofold. The public is safe from the individual criminal for the period of incarceration. While the criminal is removed from society and placed in prison, that individual is unable to further harm society. But when this person is released what is the danger to society? The criminal, as stated, is likely to reoffend, and there is a good chance that the next crime this person commits will be more serious than the first. In essence the long term effect of incarceration in our adult criminal system seems to be that we mold more hardened criminals.

In deciding whether to impose tougher sentences on juveniles, we must also look at what are the causes of juvenile crime? This question should be debated and analyzed by everyone interested in helping children and reducing crime. It is a community problem with community solutions. No court system, in isolation, can solve this problem. Only when the community comes together and recognizes the problems and factors which contribute to crime will we be able to tackle the problem. There are many factors that contribute to criminal behavior.

We have an increasing number of children born to very young single parents who simply aren't equipped emotionally or financially to rear children. We have a generation of youth who are being bombarded by images and messages of violence. Movies, TV, music and especially video games are teaching our children violence. And to further confuse the sponge like minds of our youth, there is certainly no message of permanence or gravity. With a flick of the re-start button all the characters are alive again and the carnage can start all over. There are no lessons about compassion, compromise, empathy. No exposure to the grief of the families that are affected. Violence is made neat and clean and detached. When kids are bored they use violent games, music, and shows to occupy their time. There must be better experiences and messages for our children.

We live in one of the wealthiest counties in the entire nation. We have some of the finest juvenile programs in the country. But we must do more. Individually, and collectively many enjoy great wealth and prosperity. Why, then, can't we boast of having the best services for children in the country? Somehow we have lost our sense of social responsibility. We can't afford to live in isolation, closing our eyes to the plight of many of our youth. Children like Nathaniel can't reach out for help and be placed on a waiting list for six months. To a child, six months is a lifetime. Just as immediate consequences for one's actions are necessary, so is immediate intervention at signs of trouble. If we want to be safe from the kinds of crime that Nathaniel committed we must be prepared with our efforts and wallets to help create and fund programs to stop this tragic waste. Children, and the potential each possesses, are our most precious resource. We must collectively guard, protect, and nurture them. We need better trained parents. We need mentors. We need big brothers and sisters. We need more recreational programs and youth groups. We need more counselors for children and families. We need more foster care homes and more support for these generous families. We need better schools. Any effort that touches the life of one of our children in a positive way is a vital and indispensable piece to the puzzle in stopping juvenile delinquency and criminality. We must enlist the financial support of our privileged individuals and local corporations, as well as the individual efforts of many, to help create and fund effective programming for kids. It is only by intervening now and helping to develop mature, responsible, caring, empathic children, that we can assure a safer society. What we sow today, we will reap in the future.

Most agree that our laws were originally connected to social norms with ethical and moral justification and rationale. Within society behaviors were not randomly assigned legal values of right and wrong. Instead, we collectively believed in the moral and ethical reasons for those laws. Children must be taught the fundamental reasons for laws and rules. Learning to live in society is something that develops over an entire childhood. Children are explorers and discoverers. They have an inherent need to know why. Why is often the most repeated word a parent hears from his child. When children learn about the rules and laws of society they need real reasons to follow them. These reasons are essential for the child to feel connected to and part of society. To really understand the reason one should not kill, a child has to develop social abilities such as empathy and compassion. These are the building blocks of a cohesive society. It is only by internalizing society's norms that children, and eventually adults, will truly be guided by them and abide by them. We can't cure the problem from the outside in, we must work from the inside out.

Who are heroes for our kids? When you ask children today what they want to be in the future, do they respond—a fireman—a policeman—a doctor—a teacher. Or do we hear—a wrestler—or a sports figure—or do we hear anything at all?

Instead of increasing support for prevention programs, many said "get tough." As a result of the "get tough on kids" policy we saw changes in our "waiver" statutes. The waiver age was reduced in Michigan from 15 to 14. In addition, Prosecutors were given the discretion to bypass the Juvenile court waiver process in which the Juvenile Court Judge had a full hearing, taking testimony to measure against certain standards, in order to decide when the child should be tried. At these waiver hearings the Court looked at the child's past record, the seriousness of the crime, the child's pattern of living, and the programs available in the adult system versus the programs available in the juvenile system. Instead, for certain serious crimes, Prosecutors alone, without a hearing, could make the decision of where to try the accused child, in the Criminal Court or the Juvenile Court. Even more recently, the legislature determined that, if the Prosecutor chose a trial in the Adult Criminal Court, the child, if convicted, would have to be sentenced as an adult. No discretion was given to the sentencing Judge to decide to use the juvenile system. "Get tough" continued to be the cry of many!

Prevention and rehabilitation are the foundational elements of the juvenile system. The juvenile system recognizes that children are our most precious commodity. They are our hope for the future. If we prevent the criminal mind set from taking hold of our youth then we, in turn, prevent adult criminals from coming into existence. If we rehabilitate those youths who have committed criminal acts, we are making ourselves safe both now and in the future.

Not satisfied that we were tough enough, in the 1990s the legislature went one step further and enacted P.A. 244 of 1996 (the basic statute in the case at hand). Under this statute, the Prosecutor can elect to have the child tried in the Juvenile Court as an adult and if convicted, sentenced in one of the following three ways at the discretion of the Judge:

1. First, as a juvenile, with release at the latest at age 21.

2. Second, as an adult subject solely to adult penalties and punishment.

3. A blend sentence—Initially sentence as an adult but delay the adult sentence, first placing the child in the juvenile system. If, at age 21, the child is not rehabilitated, carry out an adult sentence. There shall be yearly reviews. The adult sentence can be imposed at any time up to age 21 if there is a violation of the juvenile sentence. Or the child can be released before age 21 if rehabilitated. If neither has occurred before age 21, there shall be a hearing. At that time the defendant may be released, if rehabilitated, or the adult sentence imposed, if not rehabilitated.

To many, this is a reasonable statute. Don't ask the Judge to look into a crystal ball today and predict five years down the road. Give the juvenile system a chance to rehabilitate. Don't predict today, at sentencing, whether the child will or will not be rehabilitated, but keep the options open. At 21, have a hearing and see if the person (at 21, now an adult) has changed for the better. If yes, release; if not, if still a danger, impose an adult sentence.

The stickler is that while the legislature placed a minimum age of 14 for judicial waiver and also set a minimum age of 14 for presecutorial automatic waiver, there was no minimum set for the statute under which Nathaniel was charged. Thus, we try a child, 11 at the time of the crime, as an adult in the Juvenile Court (now call the Family Court). We subject him to the three dispositional alternatives I listed above, including a possible sentence today of up to life in prison.

THE CASE AT HAND, NATHANIEL ABRAHAM

I have reviewed all the psychological reports, the recommendation of Mr. Hamilton the Juvenile Court Caseworker, the report of the Out of Home Screening Committee of the Juvenile Court, the report of Kathy Milliken of F.I.A., and the report of Susan Peters of Adult Corrections. I have also reviewed all the psychologicals and reports from the Prosecutor and the Defense. I have considered the testimony as part of the sentencing process. I have heard the arguments of the Prosecutor and Defense. I have heard the statements of the Ronnie Green family.

Obviously, we must deal with the law that we have. We have a child convicted of 2nd degree murder committed when he was 11 years old. The legislature has told the sentencing Judge what criteria must be weighed in making a decision about which of the three options should be used in today's sentencing:

The statute [Sec. 712A.18(18) (n)] says we must look at the "best interest" of the public in making this sentencing decision.

The *best interest of the public is to protect the public from further criminal behavior by the Defendant.*

In making the decision, the statute says the sentencing Judge must look at:

(i) The seriousness of the offense in terms of community protection, including, but not limited to, the existence of any aggravating factors recognized by the sentencing guidelines, the use of a firearm or other dangerous weapon, and the impact on any victim. Here the offense is of the most serious nature. A person was murdered. The impact upon the victim and his family is devastating. A firearm was used in the commission of the offense. Community protection dictates that a long-term program is necessary.

(ii) The juvenile's culpability . . . in committing the offense, including, but not limited to, the level of the juvenile's participation in planning and carrying out the offense and the existence of any aggravating or mitigating factors recognized by the sentencing guidelines.

Nathaniel is fully responsible, having been the person who pulled the trigger. However, his teacher, Elva Rosario, at Lincoln Middle School, is reported to have stated that Nathaniel at the time, did not understand the difference between fantasy and reality. Additionally, he was determined to be functioning between the six- and eight-year-old level in terms of emotional maturity; internalized norms for appropriate behavior, and the acceptance of responsibility for his behavior. Youngsters at this developmental age often judge their behavior strictly in terms of the immediate impact it has on them. Further, Nathaniel was tested at below average intelligence. He is also very impulsive.

(iii) The juvenile's prior record of delinquency including, but not limited to, any record of detention, any police record, any school record, or any other evidence indicating prior delinquent behavior.

This offense is not part of a repetitive conviction pattern. It is Nathaniel's first offense. It is, however, part of a pattern of antisocial behavior. Nathaniel had been noted to be engaging in delinquent behavior for about two years prior to the offense, but there was no formal intervention. While in Children's Village, his behavior has been a problem at times but has improved to some degree according to official reports; he is unlikely to disrupt the treatment of other juveniles in a treatment facility.

(iv) The juvenile's programming history, including, but not limited to, the juvenile's past willingness to participate meaningfully in available programming.

There was no effort to provide a treatment program for Nathaniel until he entered Children's Village two years ago. His mother did seek treatment for him through community mental health. He was placed on a waiting list for six months prior to the initiation of treatment. He did attend three sessions after the initial assessment. The mother indicated that a different therapist might have been more helpful as the reason she discontinued treatment. Since he has been at Children's Village Nathaniel has been seeing a therapist and has made some improvement. He needs a therapist he can trust who will help him develop self-esteem and social controls.

(v) The adequacy of the punishment or programming available in the juvenile justice system. The juvenile system is designed to provide treatment for youngsters such as Nathaniel. Programming is available to meet his psychiatric, behavioral, educational, vocational, and recreational needs. The juvenile system is also designed to provide treatment for the family. Nathaniel needs to learn that he is accountable for his behavior. He needs to be far less impulsive and more concerned for the needs of others. The programming is much more extensive and comprehensive in the juvenile system than in the adult system.

(vi) The dispositional options available for the juvenile.

The dispositional options have been identified above.

Should Nathaniel be sentenced today as an adult? If we say yes, even for this heinous crime, we have given up on the juvenile justice system. Can we be certain that between now and the time he turns 21 we can't change his behavior? Must we say today that Nathaniel, at age 13, must be put into an adult prison system? *No*, the testimony and/or reports are clear that the adult prison system is not designed for youth. It is only a last resort if the juvenile system has failed. Testimony and the psychological examination demonstrate that in the last two years, while awaiting trial, Nathaniel has made progress in the juvenile system. It is also clear that the adult system has very few treatment alternatives for a 13-year-old. In addition, at 13, Nathaniel may be subject to brutalization in prison that could destroy any hope of rehabilitation.

As I have indicated, the legislature has responded to juvenile criminal activity not by helping to prevent and rehabilitate, but rather by treating juveniles more like adults. Is this a good option? Is our adult system successfully rehabilitating people? Do our jails release productive, reformed citizens? We all know the answers to these questions. The real solution is to prevent an adult criminal population ever coming into existence. This can only be accomplished by taking advantage of the hope and promise of our youth and nurturing healthy adults.

I think the law Nathaniel has been charged under is fundamentally flawed. It is not my place to make law. I must work with the law the legislature has enacted. However, I urge the legislature to reassess this law. I urge the legislature to lean toward improving the resources and programs within the juvenile justice system rather than diverting more youth into an already failed adult system. I admonish the Juvenile Court to make sure our courts are not turning away parents who may come to us for help. In sentencing Nathaniel I have to consider the protection of our community now and in the future.

Specifically, I urge the legislature to reconsider the statute in question and set a minimum age at which a child can be charged as an adult. Is 8 too young? What about 6? The legislature, not the Prosecutor, not the Judge, not the Jury, should decide. I urge the legislature to act now. Perhaps the minimum age should be 14 as in our two waiver statutes.

THE SECOND OPTION, SENTENCE AS A JUVENILE

If Nathaniel is sentenced as a juvenile, he will be released at the very latest at age 21. Will the public be best protected if Nathaniel is released at 21? We don't know what Nathaniel will be like eight years from now. Eight more years is a long time. With the progress he has made in the last two years plus the next eight years, the juvenile justice system should be able to rehabilitate Nathaniel.

The protection of the public and the rehabilitation of the respondent are the opposite sides of the same coin. If we rehabilitate the Defendant, then the public is safe. If we don't, he may kill again.

THE THIRD OPTION, A BLENDED SENTENCE

Does Nathaniel fit the criteria that would make sense under the circumstances demanded by a blended sentence? True he did commit a heinous crime, but he is not a repeat offender. He has not failed in our juvenile programs, but rather has not been given a chance to benefit from them. Nathaniel was also an 11 year old boy who, by much of the testimony, lacked the maturity and understanding to differentiate between reality and fantasy. He is a boy who has been neglected by his home, our community, and our justice system. He represents our collective failings. He is said to have functioned at a 6–8-year-old mental and emotional level at the time he committed this crime. When they created this law, certainly the legislature was not saying that any child, no matter what his age, is capable of forming adult criminal intent and should be held accountable as an adult. To take it to the absurd, an infant could be tried as an adult under the current law.

However, if we were to impose a delayed sentence, we take everyone off the hook. Sentencing Nathaniel as a juvenile gives us eight more years to rehabilitate him. We as a community know that he will be back among us at age 21. If we are committed to preventing future criminal behavior, we will use our collective efforts and financial resources to rehabilitate him and all the other at-risk youth in our community. If we commit ourselves to this, we can ensure our safety now and in the future. The safety net of a delayed sentence removes too much of the urgency. We can't continue to see incarceration as a long-term solution. The danger is that we won't take rehabilitation seriously if we know we can utilize prison in the future. To sentence juveniles to adult prison is ignoring the possibility that we are creating a more dangerous criminal by housing juveniles with hardened adults. Adult incarceration is a vital immediate solution to danger, but it does nothing to address future criminality. We have eight years. Together we and Nathaniel can make the difference in his life and the lives of many other children in our community. Nathaniel will begin the next eight years of his life in a secure juvenile facility. Thus our immediate risk of harm from Nathaniel is alleviated. With the right programs and commitment from concerned individuals, Nate can develop and internalize the values that are necessary to be a responsible member of a civilized society.

In addition, the adult criminal sentencing guidelines provide for Nathaniel to be sentenced to prison from 8 to 25 years. If he were to fail in the juvenile system and at age 21 we were to sentence him to prison, we would have to deviate from the guidelines. The statute states he must receive credit for the 10 years he was incarcerated as a juvenile. Ten years is more than the eight-year minimum in the sentencing guidelines

Prevention, individualized treatment, rehabilitation, the bywords of the juvenile justice system, are the best we have to offer. Why should the juvenile justice system copy a failed adult correctional system? Perhaps for a few juveniles "get tough" is the only answer. But for the majority it is not. The juvenile justice system has a much higher rate of success than the adult correctional system. In order to protect society some juveniles must be sentenced as adults. But this is a small minority. Most of these children are older and are more set in their criminal pattern. For most youngsters the Juvenile Justice System is a far better alternative than the adult correctional system.

IN CONCLUSION

The option that best meets the needs of Nathaniel and the public is the juvenile system and only the juvenile system. While there is no guarantee Nathaniel will be rehabilitated by age 21, when he must leave the juvenile justice system, it is clear that 10 years should be sufficient to accomplish this goal.

It is my belief that blended sentencing is much better suited for older juveniles of 15 or 16 where there is not as much time to use the juvenile system (as there is here, with an 11-year-old), and a greater need to preserve the option of adult prison at age 21.

As I said earlier, the pendulum has swung back so that much of the public wants us to get tougher with juveniles. For some it has worked, for others it has not. Here we have dealt with the most tragic of tragedies, the killing of another human being. Fortunately, murder is a very small part of what we see in Juvenile Court. In Oakland County, less than $\frac{1}{10}$ of 1% of our juvenile cases are killings. If we don't want to throw out the baby with the bathwater, treat all youngsters more harshly, and perhaps even abolish the Juvenile Court and return to the days of the Industrial Revolution where we had one criminal court for both children and adults, we must do better with the thousands of juveniles we see every day in our Juvenile Courts. This County must be willing to pay in dollars and human energy to help prevent juvenile crime and rehabilitate our young offenders. The media, the defense bar, the Prosecutor, the Judges, Court and institutional staff, County Commissioners, volunteers and the people of our community can and must make a difference. Children are too precious to be lost because of the system's neglect and failures.

We must remind ourselves that the true victim, Mr. Ronnie Green, has been robbed of his life and has no chance of any future. In addition, we can't begin to know the kind of despair and grief that his family is going through and will continue to go through. But I believe that my decision, although it may not seem the most just to his family in terms of punishment or retribution, in the long run will give Mr. Green a legacy that will live on. Hopefully, far into the future, the Greens will be able to take some comfort in knowing that their son's death was not in vain, but rather was a wake-up call for our community and the nation that our youth are in trouble and we need to pay attention. Mr. Green's death can be the catalyst to reinvigorate help for children. His death, if our community is paying attention and commits to taking action, can affect, shape and mold the lives of countless children in the future.

Let there be no misunderstanding—Nathaniel must be accountable and responsible for his behavior. We have seen all kinds of finger pointing. Mother failed, the schools failed, the Police failed, the Court failed. Perhaps—but Nathaniel pulled the trigger. He made the decision. Thousands of children raised under similar circumstances don't kill.

THE SENTENCE THEREFORE IS AS FOLLOWS

This Court orders that Nathaniel Jamar Abraham be placed within the juvenile justice system and committed to F.I.A. for placement at Boys Training School. They shall continue to supervise the progress of Nathaniel Abraham and will conduct six-month reviews of his progress. It is further ordered that Nathaniel may not be transferred from Boys Training School without a Court Order after a hearing, with notice to the Prosecutor and Defense. This sentence shall be effective until Nathaniel reaches age 21 when this court loses jurisdiction. This shall be a treatment program involving individual and group therapy for him and his family and shall include positive role models with positive rewards for proper behavior.

THESE REMARKS I ADDRESS TO YOU, NATHANIEL ABRAHAM

Your shooting and killing of Ronnie Green has destroyed the lives of many people. You need to begin by imagining 10 times worse than you have ever felt in your life, and then imagine that feeling going on and on. This is the grief you have caused Mr. Green's family. Do you begin to understand what you have done? You clearly need to put yourself in the other person's shoes. You need to learn to think before you act. You need to look at the consequences of your behavior for yourself and for others. You have done probably the worst thing anyone can do and that is to kill another human being. You are going to have to come to terms with this before you can begin to grow as a person and develop the potential that all children possess. You need to learn to respect yourself and demand more of yourself.

You are capable of learning to value human life and potential both in those around you and in yourself. Most children see themselves as the center of the universe. Children put their own needs first. In the long run you will best have your own needs met by concerning yourself with the needs of others. You will earn respect from others, and self-respect, by treating others the way you want them to treat you.

We as a community have failed you, but you have also failed us and yourself. I will be keeping a very close eye on you and your progress. When you are able to fully understand what I am telling you, I urge you to take advantage of the help we are trying to give you. The only thing you can do to begin to repair the damage you have caused to the Green family is succeed. Don't let Mr. Green's death be in vain. Help us help you and in turn help many other children in this community. No one can do it for you. You must do it for yourself.

Nathaniel—you have the key to much of your confinement. Your behavior will determine this. If you do well you will have more privileges. If you do poorly you will lose privileges. I hope you succeed.

I schedule the six-month statutory review hearing for July 25, 2000, at 8:30 A.M.

IT IS SO ORDERED

Honorable Eugene Arthur Moore

Introduction

This book was undertaken to provide some insights into children who commit murder. We felt it important to distinguish between preteens (our subjects of study) and adolescents. The frequency of murders by preteens is low (as will be described in chapter 1). As a result, preteens are typically neglected as a focus of study or they are considered along with adolescents, despite the sharp differences in their life experiences and the causal factors involved in their cases.

Murders by adolescents have been a continuing and growing problem for law enforcement personnel, social and mental health workers, teachers, families, and friends of adolescents. Because of their high profile and the frequency of murders by adolescents, youth in this age group have been the subject of close and careful study. Many excellent books and research articles have documented and sought to account for their homicidal behavior. Adolescents themselves have communicated (albeit unwillingly at times) and have been able to articulate their intent, motives, and methods and have demonstrated at least partial awareness of the consequences of their behavior.

In child murderers access to their motives and intent is far more difficult to ascertain. Their explanations are often unclear, confusing, or even completely lacking. Awareness of consequences of their behavior is extremely limited and most often completely absent. This is not surprising, since levels of reasoning and moral judgment are in the very early stages of development. Causal relationships are mostly unformed. The conscience, which has been described as "an internalized act of moral values linked to particular emotions" (Thomas, 1997) is still in its formative stage, shaped through the observation or modeling of others and through parents' and teachers' comments, criticisms, and physical interactions such as punishment and abuse. These developmental issues are addressed in detail in chapters 4 and 7.

Literary references may not clarify underlying issues, but they have had an impact on the public's view of child murderers. This has occurred through their presence in literary works, primarily novels, plays, motion pictures, and television shows. Maxwell Anderson's *The Bad Seed*, originally a play and later several movies (1956, 1985), presents the theme of the genetic or inborn evil child who commits murder without remorse. Depression appears to be causal in Little Jude's murder of his siblings and his suicide in Hardy's *Jude the Obscure*. Stephen King's work has provided the basis for several film and television productions about killer children, for example, *Children of the Corn*. In this latter example and its sequel, motivations appear to be both genetic and cult based.

In these and other works several themes predominate: a genetic or unborn propensity for evil and hence murder; cult or peer influence; a reaction to abuse or mistreatment with a resulting angry response. Literary treatments of child murderers provide an accounting or resolution showing how the perpetrator is dealt with, often "done in" by his or her own deviousness.

A notable exception to this is the work by Sereny (1999), which describes in depth and detail the life and experiences of an 11-year-old British girl accused and convicted of murdering two young children. The work traces her early life with an abusive mother and details her subsequent experiences within correctional facilities, her treatment, and her subsequent rehabiliation and return to society. It provides an understanding of the thoughts, actions, and dynamics of a child murderer on a level not possible from clinical reports. It is a "must" read for persons who seek to understand preteens who murder. It is also important in that it offers some prospect of the treatment and rehabilitation of society's most troubling dilemma— what to do to and for children who murder. This dilemma has been amplified in this country by two cases. The first concerned Abraham, a 13-year-old male tried as an adult and convicted of murder even though he was 11 years old at the time of the incident and established as of limited abilities, functioning as a 7-year-old. The second case, being tried as of this writing, is that of a 13-year-old (Whala), also convicted of murder, who was 12 years old when the incident occurred. Like Abraham, Whala was determined to be functioning at a borderline level of ability. What options for treatment and rehabilitation are available or even possible for two children convicted of murder in court systems increasingly focused on punishment?

Unfortunately, as we will discuss in chapters 8 and 10, solutions to the issues raised in the cases of child murderers are complex, and the outcomes often unsatisfactory. Trying children as adults appears to be the intent of current legislation, but what the result of such legislation might be is unclear. At the very least these impending solutions can be viewed as increasing the options available to judicial and law enforcement bodies to prevent the premature release of "bad seeds" into the environment at ages 18 or 21. Much enacted legislation is designed as "one size fits all," however, and could thus actually reduce judges' options.

Media coverage has provided the public with an extensive and intensive examination of child murderers. Bolstered by professionals' willing to share their impressions, viewers have been exposed to what at times appears to be an information overload. It is often difficult to separate information from speculation and conjecture, causal factors from media fantasy. Two recent events, the Jonesboro, Arkansas, killings by a preteen and young teenager and the Chicago killing of a young girl supposedly by two even younger boys (7 and 8) were so widely publicized that few persons of any age were unaware of their occurrence. Our concern at this point is not to question the appropriateness or adequacy of media coverage and its impact on the conducting of criminal investigations. A larger concern is raised in the effect on judicial and law enforcement efforts to arrive at satisfactory solutions in how to deal adequately with child murderers in the Jonesboro case, and how to establish guilt or responsibility in the Chicago case. Although our work will not explore media coverage, it examines media influences as they help shape attitudes and behaviors of children. As there are may excellent in-depth studies of media impact, we will cite such efforts and limit our discussion to recognizing that it is one of many causal or contributing factors in the development of violence and murderous acts.

Chapter 4 focuses on how preteens are dealt with by the criminal justice system—by judges, lawyers, social welfare agencies, and child advocacy groups—and by families and the community at large. Although similarities exist between states, there is also considerable variability, as in determining at what age one may be tried as an adult, maximum periods for juvenile incarceration, penalties, and appropriate sites for incarceration. In Arkansas, for example, state law mandates release of the juveniles at age 18, with other options unavailable despite the concerns of victims' families, legislators, and the public. With the young boys from Chicago, later revelations offset apparent confessions with evidence that the youngsters could not have committed the crime.

Preteens represent a very small portion of pre-adults who commit murder. Their circumstances and culpability appear markedly different from those of a 17-year-old with a violent history, who though technically a minor functions as an adult, with adult levels of awareness of the seriousness and the potential consequences of his or her act. Compare this with a

9-year-old who in an act of anger smothers his crying baby sister whom he was babysitting. What levels of awareness and responsibility does he have? What consequences should he experience? Is he any less responsible than the 17-year-old? Who should determine his fate? Because of these many issues as they relate to preteen murderers, we have prepared a summary of the existing research, thoughts, ideas, possible interventions for prevention and rehabilitation, and special legal issues relating to this group. Questions abound. Answers are few and often unsatisfactory. We would like to clarify at least some of them.

ACKNOWLEDGMENTS

Most significant has been my working relationship with my co-equal co-author, David Shumaker. Important also has been the support of my wife Elizabeth, and the encouragement of my family: Belle Mead and Mark, Ken and Charlene, Bobby and Antonette and my colleagues and staff, especially Carla and Theresa.

R.V.H.

I would first and foremost thank Bob Heckel for his support and guidance; my wife, Tricia, and family, Mom and Dad Shumaker, Lisa and Dan Hurwitz, the O'Briens, Domino's, and McCarthy's; and finally Eric Schell, for his support and friendship.

D.M.S.

PART I

The Research

Chapter 1

Who Are They?

An increasing concern regarding trends in juvenile homicide has resulted in a series of excellent reviews and analyses providing a database for further study and investigation. Unfortunately, because of the structure of these approaches few statistics are currently available on our target group, preteen murderers. When we ask "Who are they, these preteens who commit murders?" we may believe the obvious answer is to be found by simple consulting of official statistics from state and federal agencies and searching through published reports in professional journals. Unfortunately, as this chapter will describe, state and federal sources often fail to discriminate between age groups for those under 18, despite some very obvious logical groupings used in descriptions of young persons: Schools, for example, separate between grade, middle, and high schools. Developmental psychologists used landmark events such as physical maturation (puberty, cognitive ability, moral reasoning, causality, etc.) to reflect different levels of functioning.

Heide (1993b), in her article on weapons used by juveniles to kill parents, indicates that the available statistical sources characteristics of the victim and the offender "are not presented according to the relationship of the victim and the offender." Descriptions of the children who kill parents and descriptions of the slain parents are not presented. Lack of in-depth data, according to her report, can in part be overcome by combining existing resources, but deficits remain. Shortcomings of existing data sets remain largely unchanged since publication of her article.

Even earlier (1974) Kathryn Adams in her critical review of the status of research on child and adolescent murderers concluded that there was much public awareness of child murderers from newspaper headlines but very little scientific study. What has been done came from diagnoses and case histories after the fact and sought common elements in each. She concluded that theorists have not agreed "upon a single underlying cause or group or course to predict and explain homicides committed by juveniles." As several of the studies that provided the basis for Adams's review are introduced in the following section, the accuracy of her assessment quickly becomes apparent. Specifically, it will be presented that early works on child homicide were plagued with methodological weaknesses (namely, very small sample sizes with a wide age range of perpetrators) and a tendency for the researcher to focus on one particular type of homicide (e.g., homicides where the victim is a parent, homicides where the victim is a stranger), resulting in a biased database.

The most appropriate starting point is a landmark work by Bender and Curran (1940) that examined preteen and adolescent homicide perpetrators from a psychoanalytic perspective. Specifically, the authors' theory held that when rivalry for the attention of a parental figure is aggravated by familial, organic, or educational factors, a child is at increased risk for committing a homicidal act. In support of this theory, the authors referred to the case histories of an 8-year-old female and a 9-year-old male who were "instrumental in the death of another child" (i.e., the exact intentions of the perpetrator were not determined), nine highly aggressive children (seven of whom were preteens), and four adolescents charged with homicide. As distinguished from many later works, this work differentiated the mechanisms behind preteen and adolescent murder, arguing that the preteen lacks a real understanding of the "immutability of the death of his victim," whereas adolescents "accept the deed as final and make an attempt to accept upon their lives and give the superficial impression of not being emotionally affected" (Bender & Curran, 1940, p. 321).

Somewhat surprisingly, little attention was devoted to this topic throughout the remainder of the 1940s and much of the 1950s until Stearns (1957) and Bender (1959) initiated a reexamination of the issue. Stearns's work will be reviewed in a later section. At this point we will focus on the work of Lauretta Bender. This later article (1959) summarized Bender's experiences with 33 children who committed murder prior to the age of 16 (21 children were less than 13 years of age) and represented an evolution in her conceptualization of this population since the 1940 essay she coauthored with Curran. In terms of major findings, Bender showed that (1) preteens preferred to drown or set fire to their victims, whereas guns were the weapon of choice for adolescents; (2) 15 out of the 33 subjects had been referred for psychiatric evaluation prior to their homicidal acts, with several receiving diagnoses for schizophrenia, epilepsy, chronic brain syndromes without epilepsy, and depression; and (3) a history of brain damage, schizophrenia, compulsive firesetting, mental retardation, unfavorable home environments, and personal life experience with a violent death increased a child's risk for committing homicide. As will be seen, although some of these findings have been replicated in more recent studies, perhaps the true legacy of Bender's work pertains to the standards she set for acceptable methodological approaches and sample sizes from which to formulate theories about this population.

The 1960s saw a continuation of the case-study approach to researching homicidal youth. During this period researchers argued that homicidal behavior was attributable either to maladaptive familial patterns resulting in one or both parents fostering the assault (Easson & Steinhilber, 1961; Hellsten & Katila, 1965), a behavioral disorder with biological and psychological origins (Woods, 1961), or a severe lack of impulse control (Smith, 1965). One of the most influential studies emerging from this period, however, is Sargent's (1962) work entitled "Children Who Kill—a Family Conspiracy?" As the title suggests, Sargent examined five cases of intrafamilial homicide committed by children between 3 and 16 years of age and, in an argument similar to that of Easson and Steinhilber (1961) and Hellsten and Katila (1965), stated that homicidal children are the agent of an adult's (usually a parent's) aggressive feelings toward the victim (usually the other parent). Overall, therefore, research conducted during the 1960s was characterized by small sample sizes, a wide scope of ages examined (3- to 21-year-olds), and an expanding range of etiological explanations for the homicide.

Several new theories purporting to explain the dynamics behind youth homicide were introduced during the 1970s. Researchers pointed toward intense self-destructive impulses (Greenberg & Blank, 1970; Malmquist, 1971)—what could best be described as psychopathic tendencies (Tooley, 1975), language and education deficits (King, 1975), and a maternal overdominant relationship (Walshe-Brennan, 1977)—as catalysts of homicidal behavior in children. Of particular interest, Duncan and Duncan (1971) developed a list of seven specific risk factors, which included (1) the intensity of a child's hostile reactions; (2) the degree of control the child has over his or her impulses; (3) the child's ability to formulate alternative solutions to difficult life situations; (4) the provocativeness of the intended victim; (5) the degree of helplessness of the intended victim; (6) the availability of weapons; and (7) a history of homicidal threats made by the would-be perpetrator. In contrast to Bender's (1959) preference for mostly biological and familial predictors of homicide in children, in their formulation of risk factors Duncan and Duncan relied more heavily upon the child's cognitive, emotional, and coping mechanisms as well as the victim's characteristics.

Interestingly, the Bender and the Duncan and Duncan lists do not share a single common predictor, which supports the assertion by Adams early research efforts in this area failed to share or synthesize information.

Thus, with Adams (1974) having so accurately assessed the state of research leading to the modern era, it would seem appropriate to conclude this section by referring to the recommendations she made for the field approximately 25 years ago. These recommendations can serve as a landmark from whence to gauge methodological advances in the field. As a first point, Adams emphasized the need for future research to draw from a much wider sample of child murderers as opposed to continuing the practice of attempting to solve the problem with a "one-cause, one-cure approach." Second, she believed that in order to predict why some children engage in extremely violent behavior, more objective and intensive studies of the child, his or her personality and environment, and context in which the aggression took place must be undertaken. Finally, she called for follow-up and longitudinal studies designed to assess the impact of the homicidal act on the child and to assess rehabilitation efforts. With these recommendations in mind, we will now turn to a discussion of recent trends in preteen homicide.

RECENT TRENDS IN PRETEEN HOMICIDE

Although considerable data are available on recent trends in juvenile homicide (for a comprehensive review, see Howell, Krisberg, & Jones, 1995), few statistics on preteen homicide are reported. In order to explain this discrepancy, it is necessary to review briefly how homicide statistics are typically reported in psychological literature. To begin, researchers usually refer to two FBI resources, the Uniform Crime Report (UCR) and an annual "Supplementary Homicide Report" (SHR), for prevalence estimates, basic demographics on perpetrators and victims, and additional circumstantial information. The UCR reports on the yearly arrests for murder and nonnegligent manslaughter by age groups and, for certain years, provides statistics on the race and sex of the perpetrator by age groups as well. The SHR allows for more in-depth analyses of homicidal behavior by generating statistics on the types of weapons used, age of oldest victim, victim-offender relationship, and number of offenders, which can be analyzed in relation to certain demographic characteristics of the perpetrator (i.e., age, sex, and race).

The usefulness of the UCR and SHR data, however, depends primarily on whether the age groups on which they report statistics mesh with the population(s) one wishes to investigate. Specifically, in some years the UCR has generated statistics where one of the age brackets includes a mix of preteens and juveniles (i.e., 10- to 14-year-olds); in contrast, the SHR has always adopted a classification scheme in which data on perpetrators 10 to 17 years of age are represented as a single unit. Considering this factor, it quickly becomes apparent that the majority of the UCR and SHR data does not allow for precise estimates of preteen homicide behavior. For example, one cannot find out how many preteens used guns to commit a homicide in 1995. Rather, the closest one can come to answering that question is by looking at how many 10– to 17–year-olds engaged in this action. These limitations have been discussed before (Heide, 1993a).

Often researchers refer to alternative data sources (i.e., psychological archival data analyses, other government resources) to circumvent the shortcomings inherent to the FBI resources. In the case of preteen homicide perpetrators, however, these secondary data sources are virtually nonexistent. This is most likely due to the difficulties inherent in isolating a large enough sample of preteen homicide perpetrators from which to explore these questions. Thus, beyond the prevalence estimates and statistics on the race and gender of perpetrators reported in the UCR, very little summary data are devoted exclusively to preteen homicide offenders.

Having discussed the limitations inherent to the UCR and SHR, the reader is asked to refer to Table 1.1 for UCR statistics on the incidence of preteen homicide according to the race and gender of the perpetrator. Table 1.1 reflects the most recent statistics on preteen homicide (encompassing the years 1994–1998). Although presentation of data on a wider range of years would have been preferable, a change in age groupings reported in the UCR between 1993 and 1994 made this a poor option. Specifically, during the early 1990s, summary statistics were available only on children between the ages of 10 and 14, thus negating the possibility of one making a precise estimate of the preteen homicide rate.

For comparison purposes, Table 1.2 represents UCR statistics between the years 1984 and 1988 reported by Ewing (1990) on preteen homicide. One caveat, information on the race of the perpetrators within this age group, was not reported by Ewing and therefore is not included in the table.

Several interesting findings emerge from these data. In terms of the overall incidence of preteen homicide, two observations can be made. First, as stated in the introduction, preteen homicide is a rare phenomenon—with none of the above-cited years reporting more than 39 arrests for this crime. Second, the incidence of preteen homicide appears to have remained relatively stable over the past 15 years. The relative stability in the annual preteen homicide rate should serve as warning for researchers inclined to group preteens into the discussion of overall trends in juvenile homicide. Preteens do not appear to have mirrored the widely reported increase in juvenile homicide spanning from the early 1980s into the mid-1990s. Since the mid-1990s, juvenile homicide appears to be on the decline. Such a lack of synthesis between preteen and juvenile homicide trends indirectly supports the argument that a different set of underlying factors is involved in preteen versus juvenile homicide.

Table 1.1
Trends and Sociodemographic Characteristics of Preteen Homicide Offenders, 1994–1998

		Gender		Race	
Year	Total	Male	Female	White	African-American
1994	39	31	8	15	24
1995	29	25	4	12	17
1996	16	14	2	6	10
1997	23	20	3	8	15
1998	22	17	5	6	16

Source: Shumaker (1998).

Table 1.2
Murder and Nonnegligent Manslaughter Arrests of Preteens by Sex, 1984–1988

		Sex	
Year	Total Arrests	Male	Female
1984	29	24	5
1985	21	17	4
1986	22	19	3
1987	39	31	3
1988	34	31	3

Source: Shumaker (1998).

Males were overrepresented in both tables. Specifically, males in the above-cited years accounted for anywhere from 80% to 91% of murders and nonnegligent manslaughters committed by preteens. Unfortunately, virtually no research has been conducted that examines (and attempts to account for) the striking differences in preteen male and female homicide rates. Therefore, focus will be limited to a discussion of SHR data on gender differences in perpetrators between the ages of 10 and 17. Prior to this review it should be noted that because of the inclusion of 13- to 17-year-olds in the SHR sample, the usefulness of these statistics is debatable. They are cited, however, with the purpose of alerting the reader to *potential* differences in the nature, as opposed to the prevalence, of homicidal acts perpetrated by pre-teen females and males. Later discussion of classification efforts, predictors, and case studies will shed light on whether these SHR statistics provide an accurate portrayal of both male and female preteen homicide.

With these limitations in mind, the author examined patterns of homicidal behavior in juvenile males (N = 12,890) and females (N = 742) over five years (1991–1995) as reported in the SHR. Overall, there were notable differences between males and females across all four circumstantial variables (i.e., weapon used, number of offenders, age of oldest victim, and victim-offender relationship). In regard to weapon type, the majority of males (81%) used guns, whereas females used "Other" types of weapons (e.g., knives, blunt objects, strangulation, and drownings) slightly more frequently (44%) than they chose guns (41%). Males were more likely to commit their offense with one or more accomplices (54%) as opposed to females, who were more likely to act alone (59%). In addition, females were more likely to murder victims their age or younger (19%) than were their male counterparts (2%). Finally, in terms of the victim-offender relationship, although both males and females were most likely to murder an acquaintance, females murdered family members at a much higher rate than did males (31% versus 5%) and were considerably less likely to murder strangers than males (15% versus 34%).

Comparing these results with earlier studies, the present analysis lends some support to the observations made by Rowley and Ewing (Rowley, Ewing, & Singer, 1987; Ewing, 1990) on the differences between males and females regarding their perpetration of intrafamilial homicide. Specifically, an analysis by Rowley, Ewing, and Singer (1987) of SHR data from 1984 also revealed that juvenile females were more likely to murder their family members than were males. In addition, Ewing has argued that youthful females are more likely to use an accomplice or accomplices when murdering a family member and are more likely to engage in "infanticide" killings (i.e., the killing of a newborn) (Ewing, 1990). Although Ewing's additional claims are intriguing, he appears to rely heavily on cases reported in the popular media for support of this hypothesis. However, the current SHR findings that juvenile females tend to commit a higher percentage of intrafamilial homicides and are more likely to murder someone their age or younger lend tentative support to Ewing's arguments.

Another trend in the UCR data that warrants discussion is the finding that African Americans were overrepresented in the present sample. This is consistent with earlier research efforts investigating racial differences in the perpetration of criminal activity among juveniles. For example, Snyder and colleagues reported that in 1992 80% of the U.S. population below the age of 18 were white and 15% were African American, but African American juveniles accounted for 49% of the arrests for violent crime (Snyder, 1994; Snyder & Sickmund, 1995). Before reaching conclusions regarding racial differences, however, it is important to note that inequality in the justice system's response to African American versus white youth charged with criminal offenses has been well documented (Jones & Krisberg, 1993; Krisberg, Schwartz, & Fishman, 1987; Pope & Feyerherm, 1993) and most likely accounts for at least some (if not all) of the racial discrepancies observed in juvenile homicide arrest statistics.

Potential differences in the nature of homicides committed by African American (N = 8,326) versus white (N = 4,958) youth were analyzed using the SHR data on juveniles (10- to 17-year-olds) arrested for murder between the years 1991 and 1995. Other racial groups were considered but did not comprise a large enough sample size to be included in the analysis. This comparison revealed few racial differences in regard to the victim-offender relationship, age of oldest victim, and number of offender variables. Both races were more likely to murder acquaintances and someone older, and both were slightly more likely to commit this crime with one or more accomplices. White and African American youth also preferred to use the same type of weapon to commit homicide. Specifically, guns were by far the weapon of choice for all races, with African Americans using guns slightly more frequently (83% of all murders) than their white counterparts (72%).

Summarizing the recent trends in preteen homicide, the following three statements appear to be true: (1) preteen homicide is rare; (2) prevalence rates have remained stable over the past 15 years; and (3) males and African Americans are overrepresented in this population. In addition, some evidence suggests that females in this age group may commit a higher rate of intrafamilial homicides and use guns to a lesser extent than do their male counterparts. These latter speculations, however, require confirmation through research that targets preteens in isolation of juvenile homicide offenders.

METHODOLOGICAL CONSIDERATIONS

Having reviewed some of the pioneering works in the field as well as recent research on trends in preteen homicide, our examination now shifts to a discussion of the methodological challenges associated with studying this phenomenon. In general, most of these issues can be addressed by asking three questions: (1) Acknowledging that preteen homicide has been an historically understudied topic, how far has the field advanced in methodology and volume of research since the Adams review in 1974?; (2) What conclusions can be drawn from studies in which only a fraction of the sample fall within the target age group or where the children in the sample are highly violent but have not committed murder? (3) What does research on juvenile homicide have to offer for the study of preteen homicide offenders?

The first question to be addressed in this section speaks directly to the observation Adams (1974) made about the benefits associated with moving beyond an exclusively "one cause—one cure" approach to researching and conceptualizing preteen and juvenile homicide. Aware of the limitations inherent to the case study design, Adams and many of her colleagues were faced with the question of whether the field would be able to isolate larger samples of juvenile homicide offenders in order to improve the generalizability of findings. Perhaps as an indirect answer to this question, as recently as the late 1980s Cornell, Benedek, and Benedek appeared to echo the sentiments of Adams concerning the state of research in the field when they said, "The small samples reported by most researchers may contribute to the diversity of opinions in the literature and undoubtedly limit the accumulation of generalizable characteristics regarding adolescents who have committed homicide" (Cornell et al., 1987a, p. 12). This opinion has been voiced by others (Rowley, Ewing, & Singer, 1987; Ewing, 1990) and raises the possibility that the study of preteen homicide offenders has not made significant methodological advances.

With the intention of casting new light on the state of preteen homicide research, the author reviewed all the psychological studies in this area since the Adams review (i.e., 1975 to the present date). Table 1.3 provides a summary of the studies reviewed and includes a description of the research design employed, number of subjects in the sample, age range of subjects, and a yes or no verdict as to whether juveniles were included in the sample. Aside from the date of the study, two other factors were considered when deciding whether a particular work would be appropriate for the present purposes. First, a study had to include at least one preteen homicide perpetrator in its sample. Several studies were excluded because they only included children 13 years of age and older or because the age range of the sample was ambiguous (e.g., Toupin & Morissette, 1990; Sendi & Blomgren, 1975). Second, because the focus was limited to psychological research studies on preteen homicide, review papers and popular media books on this subject were not included. Although every effort was made to include all studies that met the criteria, additional works may have been unintentionally excluded. Acknowledging this possibility, it is argued that the general purpose of providing the reader with a sense of the state of research in this area can be adequately achieved on the basis of the studies reported in Table 1.3.

Table 1.3 offers several clues concerning the state of research on preteen homicide. Overall, 23 studies met the inclusionary criteria. Although this figure represents a slight increase in attention over the past two decades, the continued paucity of studies delays the development of sophisticated and readily defensible models on the dynamics of preteen homicide. Perhaps one of the most telling facts is that only one study (Zagar et al., 1990) replicated the findings of an earlier investigation (Busch et al., 1990). This suggests that the field remains in an extended, preliminary stage of discovery in which several intriguing findings on the nature of preteen homicide have emerged, but relatively few have been examined thoroughly.

Table 1.3
Summary of Studies on Preteen Homicide from 1975–1998

Article	Study Design	Sample Size	Age Range	Juveniles Included
An Analysis of Adolescent Perpetrators of Homicide upon Return to the Community (Hagan, 1997)	Passive-Observational Design (Control Group)	20 subjects and 20 controls charged with other crimes	12- to 21-years-old	yes
Adolescents Who Murder (Bailey, 1996)	Descriptive Data Analysis	N = 20	5- to 18-years-old	yes
Psychopathology, Biopsychosocial Factors, Crime Characteristics of 25 homicidal youths (Myers et al., 1995)	Descriptive Data Analysis	N = 25	7- to 17-years-old	yes
Evidence of Child Maltreatment among Adolescent Parricide Offenders (Heide, 1994)	Descriptive Data Analysis	N = 7	12- to 17-years-old	yes
Parents Who Get Killed and the Children Who Kill Them (Heide, 1993)	Archival Data Analysis (SHR Statistics)	2,871 parricide cases between 1977/1986	10-years and older	yes
Weapons Used by Juveniles and Adults to Kill Parents (Heide, 1993b)	Archival Data Analysis (SHR Statistics)	2,871 parricide cases between 1977/1986	10-years and older	yes
Sororicide in Preteen Girls (Adam & Livingston, 1993)	Case Study	N = 1	10-years-old	no
Juvenile Homicide: A Growing National Problem (Cornell, 1993)	Archival Data Analysis (SHR Statistics)	1,668 juveniles and 11,012 adults arrested for homicide in 1991	10-years and older	yes
Rorschach Object Relations of Adolescents Who Committed Homicide (Greco & Cornell, 1992)	Passive-Observational Design (Control Group)	55 subjects matched with 55 controls charged with nonviolent offenses	12- to 18-years-old	yes

Article	Study Design	Sample Size	Age Range	Juveniles Included
Language Disorders in Disruptive Behavior Disordered Homicidal Youth (Myers & Mutch, 1992)	Descriptive Data Analysis	N = 8	7- to 17-years-old	yes
A Typology of Violent Delinquent Adolescents (Mezzich et al., 1991)	Descriptive Data Analysis	N = 135	12- to 19-years-old	yes
Adolescents Who Kill (Busch et al., 1990)	Passive-Observational Design (Control Group)	71 subjects matched with 71 controls charged with nonviolent offenses	10- to 17-years-old	yes
DSM-III-R Classification of Murderous Youth: Help or Hindrance? (Myers & Kemph, 1990)	Descriptive Data Analysis	N = 14 (10 who committed murder; 4 who committed a murderous act)	10- to 17-years-old	yes
Homicidal Adolescents: A Replication (Zagar et al., 1990)	Passive-Observational Design (Control Group)	30 subjects matched with 30 controls charged with nonviolent offenses	10- to 17-years-old	yes
Patterns of Homicide among Children (Goetting, 1989)	Archival Data Analysis	55 juveniles arrested for murder in Detroit between 1977 to 1984	3- to 14-years-old	yes
MMPI Profiles of Adolescents Charged with Homicide (Cornell et al., 1988)	Passive-Observational Design (Control Group)	36 subjects and 18 controls charged with larceny	12- to 19-years-old	yes
Characteristics of Adolescents Charged with Homicide: A Review of 72 Cases (Cornell et al., 1987a)	Passive-Observational Design (Control Group)	72 subjects charged with homicide admitted to the Michigan Center for Forensic Psychiatry between 1977 to 1985; 35 controls charged with larceny	12-to 18-years-old	yes
Juvenile Homicide: Prior Adjustment and a Proposed Typology (Cornell et al., 1987b)	Passive-Observational Design (Control Group)	72 juveniles charged with homicide admitted to the Michigan Center for Forensic Psychiatry between 1977 to 1985; 35 controls charged with larceny	12- to 18-years-old	yes

Table 1.3 continued

Article	Study Design	Sample Size	Age Range	Juveniles Included
Juvenile Homicide: The Need for an Interdisciplinary Approach (Rowley et al., 1987)	Archival Data Analysis (SHR Statistics)	787 juveniles arrested for homicide in 1984	10- to 17-years-old	yes
Homicidal School-Age Children: Cognitive Style and Demographic features (Petti & Davidman, 1981)	Passive-Observational Design (Control Group)	Nine homicidally aggressive children (one who murdered) matched with nine children hospitalized for other psychiatric disturbances	6- to 11-years-old	no
Therapy of a 6-year-old Who Committed Fratricide (Paluszny & McNabb, 1975)	Case Study	N = 1	6-years-old	no
The Small Assassins (Tooley, 1975)	Case Study	Two Cases	6-years-old	no
Children Who Have Murdered (Walshe-Brennan, 1975)	Descriptive Data Analysis	N = 11	10- to 15-years-old	yes

Source: Shumaker (1998).

Shifting focus from the volume of studies to the types of research designs comprising the table, the results are slightly more encouraging. In general, it appears that researchers have heeded the warnings of Adams, Cornell, and Rowley about the dangers associated with an over-reliance on the case-study approach to analyzing preteen and juvenile homicide. In fact, only 13% (N = 3) of the investigations appearing in the table were classified as case studies. The case-study approach appears to have been supplanted, in part, by descriptive data analyses (N = 7) with samples ranging from 7 to 135 subjects and a mean of 29 subjects (factoring the descriptive data analysis that included 135 subjects out of the equation, however, reduces the mean sample size to 13 subjects). The most common data source for this type of analysis was preadmission psychiatric testing on all preteen and juvenile homicide offenders admitted to a psychiatric or correctional facility over a usually extended period. In general, these descriptive data analyses are a step ahead of case studies in terms of generalizability of findings, yet they are unable to address cause-and-effect relationships and, in the present case, suffer from a relatively low sample size.

Two study designs—archival data analysis and the passive-observational design—that were not common to early investigations on preteen and juvenile homicide have been utilized in recent years. To begin, investigators used the archival approach in 22% of the studies cited in Table 1.3. However, four of the five archival analyses used SHR data and are therefore limited by the considerations discussed earlier in this chapter. In general, researchers have used this approach to compare overall trends in juvenile homicide to that of adults and to examine the general characteristics of intrafamilial homicide perpetrated by juveniles. The past 20 years have also witnessed the introduction of seven juvenile homicide studies that can be classified as passive-observational designs. The term *passive-observational design* refers to research in which the relationships among variables are systematically observed but not manipulated (Cook & Campbell, 1979). This research method can be differentiated from descriptive data analyses by its inclusion of control groups for comparison purposes. The passive-observational designs in the present analysis have, for the most part, compared preteens and juveniles who commit homicide with other juveniles who were either hospitalized for psychiatric reasons or were convicted for nonviolent offenses. Personality-testing profiles (Greco & Cornell, 1992; Cornell, Miller, & Benedek, 1988) and biopsychosocial factors (Busch et al., 1990; Zagar et al., 1990; Cornell et al., 1987a) have been the specific variables most often studied in these investigations. In summary, regarding the first question, "How far has the field advanced in terms of research methodology and volume of research?" it appears that despite a consistently low number of studies devoted to preteen homicide, researchers are making initial steps toward improving the methodological approaches used to examine this issue.

Table 1.3 is also useful in addressing part of the second question posed in this section of how to contend with studies in which only a portion of the sample falls into the target age group. For upon review, only 17% (N = 4) of the studies in the table contained a sample comprised exclusively of preteens (and three of these were case studies). To further complicate matters, it is reasonable to assume that in most studies with samples that straddle the preteen-juvenile age barrier, the bulk of the sample will consist of juveniles. For example, in a recent descriptive data analysis, Myers, Scott, Burgess, and Burgess (1995) examined the diagnostic characteristics of 25 homicidal children between the ages of 7 and 17. The mean age of the 25 subjects, however, was 14.7 years, with a standard deviation of 2.3 years. Thus, clearly juveniles were overrepresented in this sample. In addition, when considering that the Myers et al. (1995) investigation included a relatively large sample size and a lower-than-normal basal age requirement (7 years old versus the norm of either 10 or 12 years old), it is evident that even within the small pool of studies that met the criteria for inclusion in

Table 1.3, additional factors further reduce the actual number of preteen homicide offenders represented.

The researcher is faced with a similar dilemma when addressing the issue of whether studies on so-called homicidally aggressive children should be factored into an analysis of preteens who commit homicide. Studies that include a sample comprised exclusively of this population (e.g., Pfeffer, 1980; Lewis et al., 1983; Lewis et al., 1985) or with a mix of homicidally aggressive and homicide perpetrators (e.g., Petti & Davidman, 1981; Mezzich et al., 1991) are relatively common and figure prominently in the literature on youthful homicide perpetrators. In addition, there seems to be considerable variability both within and across studies concerning what constitutes homicidal aggression. For example, in the frequently cited Lewis et al. (1983) study on homicidally aggressive children, 21 of 55 children were judged to be homicidally aggressive by the investigators. However, upon review these 21 children had engaged in a considerable range of aggressive behaviors—some appearing to be more severe than others. On the less potentially fatal end of the spectrum, some of the homicidal behaviors reported included the following behaviors: "taunts older brother with knife, threatening to cut off his head"; "threatened sister with knife; slept with it under pillow"; and "hit teacher with rubber bat, stating he wanted to kill her." Without minimizing the seriousness of these behaviors, one must note that when compared to the following descriptions of other homicidal behaviors in the sample, a noticeable gap emerges: "strangled sister until she turned red; tried to choke cousin"; "set fire to couch where mother was sleeping, singed mother's hair"; "tried twice to kill mother, stood over her with hammer and turned on gas jets in house."

Thus, having described two of the more common sampling problems one confronts when studying this population, two questions remain: (1) How will the present review interpret articles with either sampling issue? (2) How can this issue be improved upon in future research efforts? In regard to the age consideration, the authors have evaluated each study faced with this issue and have attempted to assign reasonable expectations based upon the ratio of preteens versus teens. More specifically, common sense dictates that more weight be placed on the findings of a study where the sample includes at least a modest ratio of preteen homicide perpetrators as compared to a study whose sample is comprised almost exclusively of adolescents. Because of the general lack of research in this area, however, it would be premature to refuse to consider studies that gravitate to the relatively older offender. Recognizing that there may be different views on this issue, the authors have reported on the age range of samples cited in this review in order to allow readers to form their own conclusions regarding the utility of a particular study. Until there emerge more studies devoted exclusively to the younger age group, each researcher will be charged with contemplating the impact of the developmental differences across samples as they pertain to a particular work.

When considering how this issue can be remedied in future works, the authors call upon the field to make a better effort at discriminating preteens from teens in analyses, even if there are only one or two preteens in a particular sample. Currently, in an apparent effort to boost overall sample sizes, many opportunities are being missed to examine the similarities and differences between preteen and juvenile homicide offenders. Notwithstanding the difficulties inherent in obtaining a reasonable sample size to study this issue, these concerns still should not prevent researchers from conducting secondary, descriptive analyses that address the age issue.

Shifting focus, the authors have used an even greater degree of caution when incorporating into the discussion findings based on homicidally aggressive children—referring to this population only when there is a notable lack of information based on studies of preteen homicide perpetrators. Clearly, it is premature to assume that these two populations are the same in terms of their personalities, cognitive functioning, and family situation. What is required are additional studies along the lines of Sendi and Blomgren's (1975) comparative analysis of homicidal adolescents. Specifically, their investigation compared three categories of offenders: a study group of 10 adolescents who had committed homicide, 10 who had threatened or attempted homicide, and 10 hospital controls. The researchers found significant differences between the homicide perpetrators and homicidally aggressive adolescents, which indirectly supports the idea that these populations are not interchangeable. Thus, additional studies that directly compare these two groups are overdue and would serve as a guide for researchers attempting to weigh the value of a particular study.

The final question, whether studies on adolescent homicide can contribute to the present analysis, will be addressed in the same way we addressed the second question. Although there are innumerable developmental differences between a preteen and a 14–year-old that discourage one from assuming similar dynamics behind each group's homicidal actions, there are many reasons why learning more about the 14–year-old can help one achieve a better understanding of the preteen. To begin, several studies on homicidal adolescents have charted the progression of aggressive activities over the course of several years, beginning in childhood (e.g., Myers, 1994; King, 1975). Thus, these studies allow for a close examination into the prior adjustment of a homicidal adolescent and can potentially shed light upon possible critical differences between preteen and juvenile homicide offenders that cause one group to commit this crime at an earlier age. In addition, it is worthwhile to refer to studies on adolescent homicide perpetrators to see how to conceptualize and research the preteen population. That is, many of the methodological issues that plague preteen homicide research are also prominent in the adolescent literature. Therefore, as means of accelerating the learning curve, it is useful at least to be aware of how researchers have studied this slightly older population. Having provided a rationale for considering juvenile homicide research, the authors concede that a high degree of caution is required when making comparisons between these groups.

NOTE

Chapters 1 through 3 were developed from the unpublished manuscript *Children Who Murder: A Review* by David M. Shumaker (1998).

Chapter 2

What Are They Like?

CLASSIFICATION SYSTEMS AND TYPOLOGIES

To date, only a limited number of researchers studying children and adolescents who murder have attempted to construct classification systems or typologies to describe these juvenile offenders. Most of the classification systems have been developed post hoc. This has been possile when the researcher has been able to discover enough distinctions or commonalties in a sample of youthful homicide perpetrators to delineate subgroups. Still others have taken existing classification systems designed for other purposes or populations (DSM criteria, FBI typology-of-offender criteria) and examined whether these can successfully account for observed differences among youthful homicide offenders. Although they attack the issue from different angles, researchers using either approach share the belief that it is important for the field to specify underlying assumptions and to study a problem within a clearly stated conceptual framework. When considering the high degree of heterogeneity among preteen homicide offenders, a substantial value should be placed on these efforts.

Before proceeding, however, an argument against the use of classification systems should be discussed. Specifically, considering the relative infancy of the field as a whole, it could be argued that classification systems are based on insufficient data and, therefore, run the risk of prematurely shifting the focus in a direction that may not lead to the clearest understanding of this phenomenon. Any conclusions drawn from a small, diverse population gathered over time raises many questions. Although this is a legitimate concern that should remind readers about the dangers of clinging too tightly to a particular model based on a single salient behavior, murder, the authors feel that the primary goals of this discussion—to illustrate the high degree of heterogeneity among members of this population and to provide readers with a justification for how the following "predictor" section is organized—do not exceed the limits of the data. It will be argued that there are preliminary data to support the validity of each classification system introduced in this section, limited though they may be.

There have been three general approaches to classifying youthful homicide offenders. They include classification efforts based on (1) psychiatric and psychological constructs, (2) specific characteristics of the crime, or (3) the victim-offender relationship. Studies in each of these areas will be examined in an effort to determine the utility of each approach.

CLASSIFICATION EFFORTS BASED ON PSYCHIATRIC AND PSYCHOLOGICAL CONSTRUCTS

A study by Stearns (1957) can be considered the forerunner of modern efforts to classify youthful murderers within a psychiatric framework: In explaining the study's purpose, Stearns stated that "if psychiatrists are to seriously undertake a study of criminology, they must first attempt to develop some sort of classification" (Stearns, 1957, p. 303). Relying on the case histories of four adolescent males who committed murder, Stearns argued for the presence of a "clinical syndrome comparable to some of those in medicine" to explain the dynamics behind "senseless" homicides. Although many of his assertions have been questioned (for a critique, see Easson & Steinhilber, 1961), his use of a medical model to conceptualize seemingly unexplainable murders would be the perspective of choice for years to come.

Indeed, Miller and Looney (1974) used a similar model in one of the next attempts to classify youthful homicide offenders. The characteristics of their sample—10 adolescents who were diagnosed as being at high risk for homicidal behavior—are even more questionable than that of the Stearns sample. However, the classification system the authors developed merits review, in part, because it embodies several ideas emerging from other studies on this issue at the time. Drawing heavily from psychoanalytic theory, the current authors have argued for the existence of three "murder syndromes," titled (1) High Risk: Permanent (total) Dehumanization, (2) High Risk: Transient (partial) Dehumanization associated with episodic dyscontrol, and (3) Low Risk: Transient Dehumanization associated with episodic dyscontrol requiring consensual validation. In general, the authors believed that two individual factors, dehumanization and episodic dyscontrol, were the primary ingredients involved in juvenile homicide. Additionally, the majority of children in this sample were described as cold, nonempathic individuals "who show both a disinclination to value human life and an egosyntonic acceptance of violence" (Miller & Looney, 1974, p. 192). Their approach was to describe the behavior involved in murder: dehumanization and dyscontrol, and to cite them as predictors.

Approximately a year later in a popular work entitled *The Small Assassins: Clinical Notes on a Subgroup of Murderous Children,* Tooley (1975) painted a similar picture to that of Miller and Looney regarding the nature of the child homicide offender. Referring to the case histories of two 6–year-old children who had made murderous assaults on their siblings, the author described the subjects as "cool, canny far beyond their 6 years, quite well controlled and self-sufficient" (Tooley, 1975, p. 306). Motivated by a "barely suppressed wish to be rid of their younger siblings," Tooley believed the children in this sample did not suffer from a lack of reality testing or an inability to make appropriate judgments concerning social situations. Two years later Zenoff and Zients (1979) made additional arguments for the presence of such a syndrome, coining the term *nonempathic* to refer to this category of offender. Finally, Sorrells (1980) authored a work that contrasted this subpopulation with two other groups of juvenile homicide perpetrators that he labeled "prepsychotic" and "neurotically fearful." Thus, a major commonality across all these early works is the belief in a typology of youthful offender who lacks a sense of empathy, will murder either in a calculated fashion or in a fit of rage, does not suffer from obvious psychotic symptomatology, and may have a biological (syndromal) predisposition to exhibit aggressive and/or violent behavior—all characteristics commonly associated with psychopathic individuals.

In the past 10 years researchers subscribing to a psychiatric perspective have, for the most part, abandoned efforts to conceptualize preteen and juvenile homicide as a syndrome or group of syndromes with an emphasis on psychopathic traits. Rather, several attempts have been made to classify this population using DSM-III-R and DSM-IV diagnostic criteria. Perhaps the foremost study in this area was conducted by Myers and Kemph (1990) on a sample of 14 children ages 10 to 17 who had committed murder (10 subjects) or a murderous act (4 subjects). Citing a lack of a standard classification system to investigate the existence of psychiatric disorders in this population, the researchers argued that "a common diagnostic language seems essential for a collaborative effort among researchers to foster comparable research, treatment results, and prognostic studies" (Myers & Kemph, 1990, p. 240). Using the Diagnostic Interview for Children and Adolescents (DICA, DSM-III-R version) as the primary screening tool, the current authors found that in this sample the most common diagnosis was Conduct Disorder (CD) (12 of 14 subjects, 86%). In addition, although there was no evidence of psychotic symptomatology, half of the subjects received diagnoses for anxiety disorders (1 with Overanxious Disorder, 1 with Simple Phobia, and 5 with past Separation Anxiety Disorder) and psychoactive substance use dependence disorders (1 with alcohol abuse, 6 with polysubstance dependence, and 2 with cocaine dependence), while a minority of subjects received diagnoses for Oppositional Defiant Disorder (ODD) (N = 1), Attention-Deficit Hyperactivity Disorder (ADHD) (N = 2), Major Depression (MD) (N = 1), and Functional Enuresis (EU) (N = 1). The researchers concluded that the DSM-III-R could serve as a useful classification system for child and adolescent murderers because its diagnostic formulation systematically included a broader range of developmental factors than other systems had utilized.

Mezzich, Coffman, and Mezzich (1991) expanded upon this line of inquiry in their study of 135 violent delinquent adolescents (VDAs) between the ages of 12 and 19 who had committed either homicide, rape, arson, robbery, armed robbery, aggravated assault, or assault. Using cluster analytic methodology, the researchers factored nine psychiatric variables into their DSM-IV diagnostic formulation: (1) Axis I diagnoses, (2) Axis II diagnoses, (3) Axis III physical disorders, (4) Axis IV severity of psychosocial stressors, (5) Axis V highest level of adaptive functioning during the past year, (6) IQ level, (7) index of mental illness and criminality in family, (8) chronicity of delinquent history, and (9) severity and number of offenses. This approach yielded four primary clusters of VDAs that the author referred to as "Stable Behavioral Handicapped Offenders" (N = 44), "Brighter and Reactive Later Starters" (N = 27), "Early Start Frequent and Serious Offenders" (N = 45), and "Physically Ill Offenders" (N = 19). In general, each of these four groups possessed their own distinct familial, cognitive, criminal, and psychiatric backgrounds leading the authors to conclude that "violence has multifactorial etiology and is differentially expressed at various stages of development" (Mezzich et al., 1991, p. 73).

The Myers and Kemph (1990) and Mezzich et al. (1991) studies have their merits and limitations. In addition to being among the first researchers to place a priority on developing a standardized classification system of youthful homicide perpetrators, Myers and Kemph used a sample that is much more specific to the present investigation as compared to that of Mezzich and her colleagues. However, aside from its potential utility in pinpointing psychiatric conditions that might require attention during rehabilitation, a compelling rationale for why the DSM in and of itself represents a sufficient classification system is not provided by Myers and Kemph. Indeed, most researchers have conceptualized Axis I and II diagnoses as proximal causal factors involved in the perpetration of this offense (e.g., Yarvis, 1991; Malmquist, 1996) as opposed to viewing a particular diagnosis as representative of a distinct typology of youthful homicide. Myers himself appears to have recognized this limitation because the most recent classification system he has proposed (which will be discussed in the next section) relies heavily on behavioral and offense characteristics in its diagnostic formulation. The Mezzich et al. (1991) study does a better job of incorporating additional psychiatric, physical, cognitive, adaptational, familial, and historical variables. Therefore, despite the findings' limited generalizability as a result of the sample characteristics, Mezzich's attempt to move beyond Axis I disorders as the sole criteria for a classification system represents an important advance.

Overall, although preteen homicide classification systems based on DSM constructs appear to hold some promise, their effectiveness would likely increase exponentially if additional factors were incorporated into the diagnostic criteria. A quote by Malmquist (1996), in a recent work that examines homicide from a psychiatric perspective, confirms this argument. He writes,

> It is important to keep in mind that juveniles who commit homicides do not form a homogenous group anymore than do those who commit specific delinquent acts. Although it is sufficiently difficult to classify homicides legally, it is even more difficult to classify them by psychopathological states, especially when perpetrated by adolescents. . . . One possibility is that homicide is an individual act in which certain types of psychopathology may be detected and an attendant diagnosis given that *partially* explains it [italics added]. Sometimes the act is a homicide perpetrated against one family member, or it may be an act of familicide perpetrated against an entire family. In yet other situations, the act erupts in the context of a violent confrontation between two juveniles in which one is seriously injured and the other may be murdered. Another alternative is homicide perpetrated by juveniles in groups or gangs. (p. 256)

Malmquist recognizes that the field of psychology is in the best position to uncover the many personality and cognitive factors related to preteen and juvenile homicide. However, in terms of a potential limitation, Malmquist's quote highlights the need for the field to extend the parameters of its search to include a variety of contextual factors—variables that psychology and psychiatry have traditionally been reluctant to study. The next two classification systems reviewed, however, will, we hope provide a compelling rationale for the merits of focusing on contextual factors.

CLASSIFICATION EFFORTS BASED ON SPECIFIC CHARACTERISTICS OF THE OFFENSE

In recent years two notable attempts have been made to classify youthful homicide perpetrators on the basis of specific characteristics of the offense.

In part, the typologies developed by Cornell, Benedek, and Benedek (1987b) and Myers, Scott, Burgess, and Burgess (1994) appear to have been born out of frustration with the results of earlier psychiatric approaches to this issue. Specifically, Cornell and colleagues have argued that the majority of efforts in this area have not reported on the reliability of their proposed typologies, whereas Myers and colleagues have been even more blunt in their assessment of the field, stating, "In working with juvenile murderers, one soon realizes that none of the classification systems to date is adequate" (Myers et al., 1995, p. 1484). A review of each of their proposed typologies may answer the question of whether shifting focus from individual to contextual factors is a more promising approach to classifying preteen homicide offenders.

Before introducing their classification system, Cornell and colleagues (1987b) highlighted two important advantages inherent in a typology based on circumstances surrounding the offense. To begin, the authors argued that such a classification system would have greater relevance to legal decision making by virtue of its direct link to an illegal act. In addition, they felt that it would be easier to validate the typology using factors that had traditionally served as the diagnostic criteria for psychiatric classification systems (e.g., developmental and prior adjustment factors). In terms of the actual classification system studied, the authors proposed three groups of offenders: (1) *psychotic*, encompassing individuals who presented clear psychotic symptoms at the time of the offense; (2) *conflict*, encompassing nonpsychotic individuals who were engaged in an interpersonal conflict with the victim; and (3) *crime*, encompassing nonpsychotic individuals who committed the offense in the course of committing another crime.

Relying upon data from 72 children between the ages of 12 and 18 charged with homicide and a control group of 35 adolescents between the ages of 15 and 18 charged with larceny, Cornell and colleagues (1987b) argued that there was sufficient evidence to support the use of their three-group typology of juvenile homicide offenders. Overall, the authors found that very few members of their sample could be classified as psychotic at the time of the offense (N = 5); the crime group (N = 37) and conflict group (N = 30) were more heavily represented. In comparing the crime and conflict groups, it was discovered that members of the crime group were more likely to murder strangers, have an accomplice, flee the crime scene, and be intoxicated at the time of the offense. Whereas members of the conflict group were more likely to murder family members, act alone, use a weapon (usually a gun), and be caught at the crime scene. Although far more speculative, the authors found preliminary evidence to suggest that as opposed to the conflict group, members of the crime group "presented a much more consistent history of prior delinquent behavior, including poor school adjustment, prior criminal activity, and substance abuse, but a lower frequency of stressful life events prior to the offense" (Cornell et al., 1987b, p. 391).

Refering to the Cornell et al. (1987b) three-group typology as the most promising attempt to classify youthful homicide offenders up to that point in time, Myers and colleagues (1995) examined whether a classification system based on the FBI Crime Classification Manual (CCM) (Douglas, Burgess, & Burgess, 1992) could improve upon Cornell's efforts. The major advantages of the CCM was that it boasted a standard terminology for the classification of murder and included several categories of offense types to allow for a more precise classification of a particular offender. In terms of specific structure, the CCM is divided into four major categories (24 subcategories) according to motive: (1) criminal enterprise (eight subcategories); (2) personal cause (nine subcategories); (3) sexual homicide (four subcategories); and (4) group cause (three subcategories). In the study the authors interviewed a sample of 25 youth between the ages of 7 and 17 who had committed a homicide (N = 21) or a homicidal act (N = 4) in an attempt to assess the utility of the CCM as a classification system for juvenile murders.

Myers and colleagues (1995) found that all 25 children in their sample were "readily" classified according to CCM criteria and fell into one of two major categories, criminal enterprise (36%) or personal cause (64%). In regard to the specific subcategories, the vast majority (eight out of nine) of the children comprising the "criminal enterprise" category were classified under the *situational felony murder* subcategory, defined as situations where the murder was committed "during the commission of another felony because of panic, confusion, or impulse" (Myers et al., 1995, p. 1487). In contrast, children falling under the "personal cause" major category committed a greater range of crimes with the following subcategories represented: *spontaneous domestic homicide* (8% of entire sample), *staged domestic homicide* (8%), *argument murder* (12%), *conflict murder* (12%), *revenge murder* (4%), and *mixed sexual homicide* (20%). The authors concluded that overall, the CCM "proved advantageous by offering greater selection and exactness than any currently available for classifying homicides by children and adolescents," but they simultaneously called for improvements in the CCM that would allow for more precise classifications of intrafamilial, conflict, and psychotic homicides (Myers et al., 1995, pp. 1488–1489). Unfortunately, the authors did not provide information about the type of offenses committed by younger versus older children in the sample, so the only conclusion that can be derived with any certainty is that preteens in this sample engaged in only two of the four major categories of homicide (i.e., personal and criminal enterprise).

Overall, the efforts of Cornell and Myers suggest the utility of classification systems for youthful homicide perpetrators based on specific characteristics of the crime. Both studies found that children were readily classified within this type of framework and both found that there was a roughly even split between homicides arising during the course of criminal activity and those associated with interpersonal conflicts. Furthermore, in addition to the advantages cited by Cornell, Myers has pointed out that this approach to classification uses standardized terminology that may facilitate better communication between researchers, mental health professionals, law enforcement officials, and the courts—an advantage that should be considered a vital factor in future attempts to better understand this population. The shortcoming of this classification system is that by virtue of its extensive focus on the characteristics of the crime, this approach runs the risk of ignoring key developmental and psychological differences among youthful homicide offenders. Thus, there is the potential for perpetrators to become two-dimensional figures because psychological and developmental factors have less input in the diagnostic criteria. Potential solutions to this issue will be discussed at the end of the following section.

CLASSIFICATION EFFORTS BASED ON THE VICTIM-OFFENDER RELATIONSHIP

Upon first review, classification systems based on the victim-offender relationship could be considered one of several categories falling under the broader rubric of the previously discussed classification systems based on specific circumstances of the offense. Although this is true in the strictest sense, the authors have chosen to allocate this subcategory its own section. This decision parallels the trend in the field whereby children who murder a parent (this phenomenon is referred to as "parricide") or, more generally, any immediate family member are studied in isolation of the remaining pool of youthful homicide offenders. Indeed, many researchers seem to have reached the conclusion that the multitude of etiological and prognostic differences between these two groups necessitates such a distinction. The present discussion will focus on major findings and arguments in support of viewing intrafamilial homicide as a separate typology, saving an in-depth discussion of the specific etiological and prognostic differences between these groups for a later section.

From early on researchers have demonstrated a preference to study children who commit intrafamilial homicide separately from other youthful homicide perpetrators (see Scherl & Mack, 1966; Sadoff, 1971; Duncan & Duncan, 1971). An investigation by Corder, Ball, Haizlip, Rollins, and Beaumont (1976), however, can be considered the first systematic attempt to compare intrafamilial versus extrafamilial youthful homicide perpetrators. Although the age range of their sample was 13 to 18, the study merits review because of its long-term influence on the conceptualization and categorization of both preteen homicide and juvenile homicide. In terms of the specific protocol, the researchers compared the personality, familial, and environmental characteristics of 10 adolescents charged with parricide (killing of one's parent) to 10 controls charged with murdering a relative (other than their mother or father) or a close acquaintance and 10 controls charged with murdering a stranger. Overall, although the researchers found that all 30 cases suffered from a history of family disorganization characterized by "intense marital conflict, economic insecurity, parental brutality, and a lack of social or community ties," significant differences among the three groups existed. Most pertinent to the present discussion was the finding that children charged with parricide appeared to have a history of fewer social, sexual, and aggressive outlets than the two control groups in addition to exhibiting differences in the nature of their relationship with each of their parents.

Shortly after the Corder et al. (1976) study, Cormier, Angliker, Gagne, and Markus (1978) presented an argument in favor of not only discriminating intrafamilial from other types of juvenile homicide but also making a further distinction within the subgroup of intrafamilial offenders between children who commit matricide (killing of one's mother) versus patricide (killing of one's father) versus fratricide (killing of one's brother). Cormier and colleagues excluded sorroricide (killing of one's sister) from this discussion because of the especially low incidence of this type of offense. Relying upon their own data and that from 10 previous studies (resulting in an overall N of 100 cases, 27 classified as intrafamilial), the authors presented an elaborate theory grounded in psychoanalytic principles explaining the inter- and intragroup differences among the offenders. Perhaps the most enduring influence of the Cormier and Corder studies, however, rests not in the specific theories they postulated but, rather, in their general premise that the victim-offender relationship variable should serve as the basis from which to classify this population.

In recent years prominent researchers in the field have uncovered further evidence in support of classifying youthful murderers according to the victim-offender relationship. For example, Cornell et al. (1987a) found "some support" for making this distinction in their sample of 72 youth charged with murder, citing an extended history of interpersonal conflict with the victim and an increased likelihood of using a gun in the commission of the offense as key differentiating factors between intrafamilial versus other types of offenders. Rowley et al. (1987) made an even stronger argument in support of a classification system based on this variable, declaring, "The present findings with regard to theft-related homicide and multiple-offender homicide strongly suggest that there are major differences between juvenile homicides within the family and those in which the victim is unrelated to the juvenile killer. Indeed, the nature of these differences would seem to suggest further that there may be important psychological differences between juveniles who kill within the family and those who kill acquaintances or strangers" (pp. 8–9). An even more compelling source of support for this classification method can be found in the extensive research on this issue conducted by Kathleen Heide over the past 10 years. Relying on her own assessment interviews of 59 children and adolescents between the ages of 12 and 17 charged with homicide, Heide (1992) found that seven different types of offenders could be clinically identified and reliably rated. Of the small group of children in her sample who committed parricide (N = 7), all but one fit the profile of the *situationally trapped kid* typology of offender—characterized by a history of severe abuse, an extreme sense of desperation, a generally passive approach to life, and a typically good prognosis. Based upon this finding and her review of eight clinical studies on this issue, Heide has developed 12 characteristics that are salient to children and adolescents who commit parricide and has made arguments in favor of conceptualizing intrafamilial homicide perpetrators as a separate typology of offender.

Reviewing the victim-offender relationship literature as a whole, it would be difficult to argue against the utility of continuing to explore the differences between intrafamilial and other types of youthful murders. Indeed, virtually every study that has examined this issue has found evidence in support of this distinction, and the pattern of differences between intrafamilial and extrafamilial murders nicely parallels that observed between the conflict and crime homicides discussed earlier. There is, however, a potential risk to employing this classification system. Specifically, researchers may fall into a pattern of studying samples that are comprised exclusively of one type of offender (i.e., either intrafamilial or extrafamilial perpetrators). This practice does not allow for cross-typology comparisons that are necessary for the field to continue to test the validity of classification systems based on the victim-offender relationship. Therefore, future researchers in this area should aspire to construct samples approaching that of Corder and colleagues (1976) where intrafamilial, acquaintance, and stranger victim-offender relationships are represented.

Overall, a review of the three major classification efforts—those based on psychiatric and psychological constructs, specific characteristics of the offense, and the victim-offender relationship—suggests that each of these approaches can be useful in helping the researcher conceptualize and classify preteen homicide offenders. In future efforts, it is recommended that researchers continue to study the validity of recent classification efforts based on circumstances of the offense and victim-offender relationship (particularly those of Cornell, Myers, and Heide). As already discussed, the advantage of starting with a classification system based on these factors is that they allow researchers to verify their validity through an exploration into various psychiatric and psychological, developmental, cognitive, and familial constructs that have previously served as the basis for other classification efforts. Indeed, it could be discovered that one or more of the FBI's CCM subcategories of youthful homicide offenders studied by Myers are overrepresented by children possessing the psychological characteristics of one of the clusters proposed by Mezzich and colleagues, whereas youth comprising Heide's *situationally trapped kid* typology may have a considerably different psychological presentation. Preliminary evidence suggests that this may be the case, but additional research that directly compares the psychological status of preteens who commit various types of murders needs to be conducted before such a distinction can be made with any certainty. Taking these limitations into account, the chapter on prediction (chapter 3) will be able to offer only preliminary hypotheses on the nature of the relationship between psychological status and the characteristics of the offense.

Chapter 3

Who Will Kill?

Ewing's insightful 1990 book, entitled *When Children Kill: The Dynamics of Juvenile Homicide,* in which the author conducted an exhaustive review of the social science literature on juvenile homicide then available, will be cited frequently in this chapter in cases where his conclusions are in accord with those of the authors. Indeed, in his work Ewing included two chapters—one that reviewed psychological research on juvenile homicide and another that focused specifically on relatively younger offenders—that are devoted to answering a set of questions similar to those addressed here. This chapter will however, differ from Ewing's work and from other recent discussions of youthful homicide predictors (e.g., Hardwick & Rowton-Lee, 1996; Holmes & Holmes, 1994) in several important respects.

To begin, the current review will make a greater effort to uncover differences in the individual and familial predictors of preteen versus adolescent homicide. A major contributor to this process will be a systematic comparison of several preteen homicide offender case studies with a sample of adolescent homicide offender case studies. Despite the previously discussed shortcomings inherent to the case-study design, the majority of research efforts to date that have focused exclusively on preteens are, in fact, case studies. Therefore, one can argue that in order to move beyond the current understanding regarding preteen homicide, it is necessary to draw as much information as possible from these articles as opposed to ignoring this pool of data in favor of an exclusive focus on studies with larger samples comprised of a mix of preteens and adolescents or adolescents alone.

Several individual and familial variables that Ressler, Burgess, and Douglas (1988) have designated as childhood risk factors for future involvement in serial killing and sexual homicide will serve as the basis for the case-study comparison. This set of variables, first introduced in their landmark work entitled *Sexual Homicide: Patterns and Motives*, is an optimal choice for two reasons. To begin, it encapsulates the variety of behavioral, mental, and familial risk factors that have been explored by researchers studying youthful homicide offenders. The major advantage to using these criteria, however, is that they make a start at answering the extremely important prognostic question of whether some preteen murderers can be classified as budding psychopathic personalities who will be at a significant risk for committing additional serious crimes (including murder) later in adolescence and adulthood.

The present review of preteen homicide predictor research will differ from earlier efforts in three additional respects. First, the review will include an examination into whether the field has developed a set of psychological instruments that can reliably predict future homicidal behavior in children—an area of focus that has tremendous implications for prevention. Second, although the impact of several societal risk factors (e.g., guns, gangs, and media portrayal of violence) on juvenile homicide has been studied before, the present review will make a special effort to assess their relative impact on the subgroup of preteen homicide perpetrators. Finally, a disproportionately greater amount of attention will be devoted to more recent findings in this area (i.e., from 1990 to the present) in an effort to extend and refine the conclusions reached in earlier studies.

With these features in mind, the following section will begin by reviewing research findings on individual and familial predictors, followed by the aforementioned case study comparison, and concluding with a discussion of environmental predictors. Finally, the section will then outline key differences between intrafamilial and extrafamilial murderers.

INDIVIDUAL PSYCHOLOGICAL GLOBAL PREDICTORS

Discussions of individual predictors of youthful homicide have typically been divided into two parts, one focusing on preexisting personality and/or psychiatric disturbances and the other on cognitive factors. The next two sections will explore these areas and will be followed by the examination into whether there are any psychological instruments that can assist clinicians in predicting future homicidal behavior in children.

To begin, Ewing's (1990) review of 17 studies that reported on the psychological characteristics of youthful murderers resulted in his reaching the following two conclusions: (1) the majority of offenders were not psychotic at the time of the offense, and (2) there is conflicting evidence regarding the presence of other nonpsychotic disorders in this population. A handful of studies examining the incidence of psychotic symptomatology and other psychological disorders have been conducted since Ewing's review. Two such studies—one by Busch, Zagar, Hughes, Arbit, and Bussell (1990) and the other by Zagar, Arbit, Sylvies, Busch, and Hughes (1990)—have recently offered findings that speak directly to Ewing's first conclusion. These studies can be examined in unison, since the latter study followed the exact protocol and replicated every significant result of the former. In total, the authors in both studies compared the psychological, physical, cognitive, and social functioning of 101 homicidal children between 10 and 17 years of age with 101 nonviolent delinquent controls. Overall, the authors found a very low rate of psychotic symptomatology in both the subject group and the control group (3% versus 0%), a finding that offers firm support for Ewing's conclusion regarding a low incidence of psychoticism in this population. A more recent study by Myers et al. (1995), however, casts doubt upon the accuracy of this conclusion. Specifically, although none of the 21 subjects in Myers et al.'s sample met DSM-III-R diagnostic criteria for a psychotic disorder, almost three fourths (71%; 15/21) had a history of psychotic or schizophrenic symptoms, including paranoid ideation (67%), delusional thinking (10%), auditory hallucinations (29%), gustatory hallucinations (5%), and derealization (5%). At the very least the Myers et al. finding suggests the need for clinicians to investigate more closely the specific symptoms of psychotic and schizophrenic disorders and report these results. Indeed, it could be that although only a minority of preteen homicide offenders can be diagnosed with a psychotic or schizophrenic disorder, a substantially greater proportion of this population possesses a history of symptoms in this area. If this is the true state of affairs, it would help explain the pattern across studies in which there is a sense that a high rate of psychotic thinking may exist in this population; but a continuously low percentage of cases actually meet DSM criteria for such a disorder. One problem in assessing disordered thought in children is the range of permissible thought, which in adults would be regarded as delusional or at least disordered. For example, precausal thinking, animism, fantasy, and some hallucinatory experiences that are diagnostic signs in adults are often observed in normal children.

Turning attention to the issue of whether preteen homicide offenders suffer from other nonpsychotic psychological disorders, a review of early efforts in this area reveals that researchers have generally argued for the presence of either psychopathic characteristics (Tooley, 1975; Hellsten & Katila, 1965; Greenberg & Blank, 1970; Zenoff & Zients, 1979; Sorrells, 1977) or an impulse control deficiency (Miller & Looney, 1974; Smith, 1965; Woods, 1961) in this population. By contrast, as Ewing (1990) has pointed out, other researchers have failed to find significant evidence of psychological disturbances in their samples (Walshe-Brennan, 1975; Corder et al., 1976, Cornell et al., 1987a). This lack of synthesis across early research efforts has made it difficult to reach an easily defensible conclusion regarding the presence of nonpsychotic psychological disturbances in this population.

Thanks to the efforts of Busch, Zagar, Myers, and Malmquist, considerable advances have been made in this area in recent years. Although Busch and Zagar did not report on the incidence of specific psychological diagnoses, they indirectly shed light on this issue through their discussion of alcohol use and prior psychiatric hospitalization in their samples (Busch et al., 1990; Zagar et al., 1990). Specifically, the authors found that homicidal youth were significantly more likely to suffer from histories of alcohol abuse than were nonviolent controls (38% versus 24%). This result is consistent with the findings of other studies investigating the substance abuse histories of juveniles who commit homicide (see Myers et al., 1995; Cornell et al., 1987a; Corder et al., 1976) and suggests that this often-overlooked risk factor merits further attention in studies with an exclusive focus on the preteen age group. Regarding the second factor, the authors found that a relatively small percentage (7%) of both subjects and controls had received prior psychiatric treatment—indirectly suggesting a low incidence of diagnosable psychological disorders. This might, however also reflect economically or culturally determined lack of access to treatment.

Myers can be credited with conducting the most intensive investigation to date of the presence of DSM diagnoses in youthful homicide offenders (Myers & Kemph, 1990; Myers & Mutch, 1992; Myers, 1994; Myers et al., 1995). Arguably the most notable finding across all his investigations has been the high incidence of conduct disorder (ranging from 84% to 88% across studies). Upon reflection, this finding is not surprising and is consistent with the results of other modern research efforts in this area (e.g., Cornell et al., 1987a; Lewis et al., 1983; Petti & Davidman, 1981). Myers (1994) has made a connection between this trend and the high prevalence of childhood conduct disorder symptoms reported in Ressler et al.'s (1988) sample of serial killers. Indeed, when considering this factor in conjunction with the finding that children in his studies also demonstrated a high incidence of present (12% to 14%) or past (25% to 41%) ADHD, a connection can be made with current research on early identification of psychopathic characteristics in children (Frick, O'Brien, Wootton, & McBurnett, 1994; Lyman, 1996). Lyman (1996), for example, has recently presented an argument that views the co-occurrence of child conduct disorder and hyperactivity-impulsivity-attention problems (HIA) as a unique subtype of what he calls "fledgling psychopaths." Although this argument is in the earliest stages of verification, it offers clinicians and researchers a firm theoretical foothold from which to explore whether a portion of preteen homicide offenders are at risk for adult psychopathic behavior. Upon reflection, this theory also explains the consistently high rates of nonempathic attitudes and impulsive behavior reported across the earliest studies on preteen homicide offenders. For it could be that researchers have, over several decades, been identifying the same psychological characteristics in this population, but this consistency has been blurred by a variety of different labels being applied to the same set of constructs. The upcoming case study comparison will perhaps shed further light on this issue.

Malmquist (1996) has also conducted extensive investigations into the presence of nonpsychotic DSM diagnoses in youthful homicide offenders. His investigations have led him to a set of conclusions to similar that of Myers regarding the presence of psychological disorders in this population. He writes, "Apart from a few blatantly psychotic juveniles, most homicidal acts by juveniles occur in a group for whom an earlier diagnosis of conduct disorder in childhood can be made" (Malmquist, 1996, p. 265). Malmquist, however, offers an additional hypothesis that purports to explain the occurrence of impulsive behaviors in this population. Specifically, he believes that children who exhibit a history in this area in conjunction with separation anxiety disorder (SAD) may be in the formative stages of borderline personality disorder. Although speculative, this hypothesis is given indirect support through the Myers finding of a consistently high incidence of present (5% to 12%) or past (25% to 36%) SAD in his samples. Finally, another important contribution by Malmquist is his argument that depression may be far more common in youthful murderers than previously thought. Specifically, he cites a predominant sense of hopelessness in severely depressed children that is the main risk factor for future homicide and/or suicide in select cases. Overall, therefore, the work of Busch, Zagar, Myers, and Malmquist suggests the presence of conduct disorder and HIA in youthful murderers—two disorders with strong connections to psychopathic behavior. In addition, these researchers have highlighted the need for further attention to the study of polysubstance abuse, depression, enuresis, and SAD in this population.

INDIVIDUAL COGNITIVE GLOBAL PREDICTORS

Until recent years there was a notable lack of consistency across research efforts in the study of the cognitive characteristics of youthful murderers. Indeed, in his 1990 review Ewing presented conflicting evidence regarding the prevalence of mental retardation, learning disabilities, and neurological impairments among this group of offenders. Through its incorporation of more recent findings, this review will argue that matters have cleared significantly in at least two of these categories of cognitive research (i.e., learning disabilities and neurological abnormalities).

In regard to the intelligence of youthful homicide offenders, a slight majority of studies that have examined this issue have reported lower-than-normal Full Scale IQ scores with sizable standard deviations among subjects. Of particular importance, Petti and Davidman (1981) conducted an investigation comprised of nine preteens that found that the sample's Full Scale IQ scores ranged from 73 to 106 with a mean score of 89. Whereas Petti and Davidman's findings appear to be closely aligned with the results of some studies comprised of juvenile homicide offenders (see Lewis et al., 1988; Solway, Richardson, Hays, & Elion, 1981), other researchers have found little evidence of below-average intelligence (e.g., Walsh-Brennan, 1975; Bender, 1959; Malmquist, 1971). To further complicate matters, Busch and colleagues (1990) have recently found that 21% (15 out of 71) of their sample of preteen and adolescent homicide perpetrators could be classified as mentally retarded, with the average Full Scale IQ at 80 with a standard deviation of 13 points. This suggests a lower level of intellectual functioning than that reported by Petti and Davidman and extends the already considerable range of results reported in this area. Therefore, the safest conclusion regarding the intelligence of preteen murderers is that this remains an understudied area that has, to date, failed to produce consistent results.

In the next category of cognitive studies, early efforts focusing on learning disabilities in this population have reported evidence of either specific learning difficulties (Bender, 1959; Lewis et al., 1988) or general school adjustment problems (Sendi & Blomgren, 1975; Cornell et al., 1987a). These findings have been replicated in recent years. Of note, Busch and colleagues (1990) have argued that "severe educational difficulties" was one of four clusters of symptoms that differentiated their sample of youthful homicide offenders from a matched control group of nonviolent offenders. Additionally, Myers et al. (1995) found that within his sample 25 youthful homicide offenders, 76% possessed a learning disability and 86% had failed at least one school grade. Finally, in a separate investigation of eight homicidal youths between the ages of 7 and 17, Myers and Mutch (1992) found that significant language disorders were present in all subjects. Thus, presented with relatively consistent evidence of learning difficulties in this population, the next wave of research should investigate not only the etiological contributions of this factor but also, as Myers and Mutch (1992) have pointed out, the legal implications relating to a learning-disabled child's ability to understand the implications of Miranda warnings and assist in his or her defense.

Studies investigating the presence of neurological abnormalities in youthful homicide offenders constitute the final category falling under the general domain of cognitive research. Overall, there appears to be a consistently high rate of neurological abnormalities reported in this population, including evidence of epilepsy, serious head traumas, abnormal EEG findings, and other neurological deficits. Table 3.1 summarizes the findings of eight studies on preteen and juvenile homicide offenders that have re-

Table 3.1
Summary of Neurological Findings in Studies of Youthful Homicide Perpetrators

Article	Abnormal EEG Findings	Epilepsy/Seizures	Serious Head Trauma	"Other" Neurological Deficits
Adolescents Who Murder (Bailey, 1996)	5 out of 20 subjects	3 out of 20 subjects	Not reported	3 out of 20 subjects experienced a delay in reaching developmental milestones
Psychopathology, Biopsychosocial Factors, Crime Characteristics, and Classification of 25 Homicidal Youths (Myers et al., 1995)	Not reported	2 out of 21 subjects	9 out of 21 subjects	Not reported
Adolescents Who Kill (Busch et al., 1990)	Not reported	5 out of 71 subjects	9 out of 71 subjects	Not reported
Neuropsychiatric, Psychoeducational, and Family Characteristics of 14 Juveniles Condemned to Death in the United States (Lewis et al., 1983)	9 out of 14 subjects	4 out of 14 subjects	8 out of 14 subjects	Not reported
Homicidally Aggressive Young Children: Neuropsychiatric and Experimental Correlates (Lewis et al., 1983)	6 out of 21 subjects	10 out of 21 subjects	12 out of 21 subjects	17 out of 21 subjects had a history of perinatal problems
A Comparative Study of the Predictive Criteria in the Predisposition of Homicidal Adolescents (Sendi & Blomgren, 1975)	2 out of 10 subjects who had committed homicide; 6 out of 10 subjects who had attempted or threatened to commit homicide	Not reported	Not reported	Not reported
Adolescent Violence and Homicide (Woods, 1961)	2 out of two subjects	Not reported	Not reported	Not reported
Children and Adolescents Who Have Killed (Bender, 1959)	5 out of 15 subjects	3 out of 15 subjects	Not reported	Not reported

Source: Shumaker (1998).

ported abnormal neurological findings. Although not all the studies have found a significant occurrence of neurological abnormalities (e.g., Petti & Davidman, 1981; Walsh-Brennan, 1975), the recent efforts by Bailey, Myers, Busch, and Lewis, which benefit from modern assessment tools and relatively large sample sizes, offer a compelling counterargument to those who would claim an absence of neurological deficits in this population. Very little is known, however, about the exact relationship between this factor and the onset of homicidal behavior in juveniles. Overall, cognitive studies of youthful homicide offenders have found considerable evidence of learning and educational difficulties and neurological abnormalities in this population. However, there continue to be conflicting results regarding the intelligence levels of youthful murderers.

INDIVIDUAL PSYCHOLOGICAL MEASURES THAT PREDICT HOMICIDAL BEHAVIOR

The prediction of violent behavior continues to pose one of the greatest challenges to psychologists entrusted with making such decisions. In general, the majority of the research devoted to the prediction of violence has been conducted on adult mental health inpatients being considered for release (e.g., Monahan, 1988; Mulvey & Lidz, 1984). Clinical interviews, behavioral observations, and a patient's past history have typically served as the basis for a clinician's judgment of dangerousness in these studies. Unfortunately, as Lidz, Mulvey, and Gardner (1993) have recently discussed, the results of these attempts have been so dismal that over the past several years very little research has been conducted on this issue.

One factor that may be contributing to (or the result of) the low accuracy of these predictions relates to the notable absence of a reliable diagnostic measure designed specifically for this purpose (Rice & Harris, 1995). Although there are a few instruments that have been developed or borrowed with this objective in mind—including the Violence Risk Appraisal Guide (VRAG) (Harris, Rice, & Quinsey, 1993), the Statistical Information on Recidivism scale (SIR scale) (Nuffield, 1982), and the revised Psychopathy Checklist (PCL-R) (Hare, 1991)—these instruments have been used with mixed results on populations that differ from the current target population in two important respects. Specifically, they have been used with adults (as opposed to preteens) and individuals who have already committed a serious violent action that has resulted in their commitment to a correctional facility or mental institution (as opposed to individuals who have yet to commit a serious violent offense). Thus, the challenge is twofold for clinicians seeking to use a psychological instrument to predict homicidal behavior in preteens. Not only must the clinician find a measure that works, he or she must also find one that is appropriate for a much younger target age group that has yet to commit a serious offense.

To date, Cornell, Greco, and colleagues have conducted the only systematic studies of psychological testing performance of youthful homicide offenders. Their efforts, however, fall prey to the same two criticisms discussed above. Specifically, their research on the MMPI profiles (Cornell, Miller, & Benedek, 1988) and Rorschach responses (Greco & Cornell, 1992) of homicidal youth was conducted on a sample of already-incarcerated juveniles between the ages of 12 and 19. Their results have been encouraging, however, and support future research on the predictive utility of these instruments, or some adaptation thereof, in older preteens (i.e., 11- and 12-year-olds). Specifically, in regard to the MMPI, the authors found that the mean profile of their sample contained elevations on the F, Hs, Hy, and Sc scales—with individuals falling into Cornell et al.'s (1987b) *crime* typology of offender exhibiting significantly higher feelings of distress and alienation than their *conflict* typology peers.

In terms of the Rorschach results, Greco and Cornell (1992) summarized their findings thus:

This study supports the use of the Blatt et al. (1976) Differentiation scale in distinguishing subgroups of homicidal adolescents. Youth who commit murder in the context of an interpersonal conflict may have the capacity for comparatively more mature relationships, and this may facilitate their involvement in insight-oriented or interpersonally focused therapies as a component of their treatment. Youth who murder while committing another crime may have a more pervasive tendency to dehumanize others, permitting them to act on aggressive impulses when their needs are frustrated. (p. 581)

Thus, the performance of homicidal adolescents on the Rorschach also differed according to the type of homicide (*conflict* versus *crime*) committed. Although in either study the authors were unable to demonstrate significant differences between the responses of their subjects and those of a control group of nonviolent delinquents (the authors attribute the similarity to a biased referral practice whereby more seriously impaired nonviolent delinquents were referred for psychiatric evaluation), the fact that on both measures the performance of the subjects differed significantly from the norm should alert clinicians to the potential usefulness of conducting further examinations into this area.

Overall, it could be that the MMPI (adolescent form) and the Rorschach will not offer assistance to clinicians attempting to predict homicidal behavior in older preteens. What these results suggest, however, is that there are likely important measurable differences in the personality formation, perceptual processing, and coping mechanisms of children who are at risk for committing murderous acts versus those who are not. Therefore, the authors advocate the development of a screening protocol that incorporates information on the individual and familial risk factors of homicidal behavior (e.g., psychological diagnoses, cognitive functioning, and abuse histories) in conjunction with intelligence measures and objective and projective assessment devices that screen for cognitive and psychological disturbances. If the assessment revealed that the child suffered from several risk factors and his or her performance on the screening devices demonstrated marked impairment, then the clinician would have sufficient reason to be concerned about future violent behavior in that child.

FAMILIAL GLOBAL PREDICTORS

One of the most consistent findings in the literature is that the majority of youthful homicide perpetrators present with a history of adverse familial factors. Indeed, studies of children who commit parricide have the most in-depth investigations into this factor, but this finding appears to cut across both intrafamilial murders and extrafamilial murders. A review of the research indicates that eight specific adverse familial factors—physical abuse, sexual abuse, instability of caretaker situation and/or residency, absence of a father, parental alcohol or drug abuse, parental psychiatric history, parental criminal background, and violence in the home—figure prominently in the histories of youthful murderers. Table 3.2 provides the reader with a general sense of the frequency in which these factors were reported across 16 studies of preteen and adolescent homicide perpetrators that examined the familial characteristics of this population.

By far the most common adverse familial variable reported across studies was a history of physical abuse (12 out of 16 studies). Interestingly, the next most frequently cited factor was the "violence in the home" variable (7 out of 16 studies). Researchers of intrafamilial homicide have proposed sophisticated models of how physical abuse and violence in the home lead to murder (Heide, 1992; Post, 1982); these theories will be discussed later in a section devoted to homicide predictors associated with a particular type of offense. For now, the authors will focus on hypotheses that are not specific to any one type of homicide. In general, researchers have made two arguments that explain the relationship between child abuse and/or witnessing of violence and youthful homicide. One theory holds that children who live in homes where abuse and violence are commonplace fail to experience adequate "socialization" that is the product of years of nurturing and training by the child's caretaker(s). These children will, in turn, suffer from a need for immediate gratification resulting in periodic aggressive outbursts that may lead to murder in extreme cases (Corder et al., 1976). The other theory argues from the basic premise that children model what they see and experience. Therefore, if a child is abused and witnesses violence, he or she will learn that acting in an out-of-control, violent manner is to be expected (Sorrells, 1977). More recently Lewis and colleagues (1983) expanded upon this "learning theory," arguing that a combination of modeling and the presence of neurological vulnerabilities in the child increases the risk of murder in cases where that child becomes overwhelmed with the frustration of witnessing repeated violence in the household.

Unfortunately, even less is known about the connection between the remaining adverse familial variables and the onset of homicidal behavior in children. It has been suggested that a parental criminal, psychiatric, and/or substance abuse history is indicative of a familial predisposition toward maladaptive behavior (Lewis et al., 1983). Another argument is that these variables could be indicators of an unstable family environment and parenting

Table 3.2
Frequency of Adverse Familial Factors Reported in the Literature

Article (Author & Year Only)	Physical Abuse	Sexual Abuse	Instability in Home	Absent Fathers	Parental Alcohol Abuse	Parental Psychiatric History	Parental Criminal Background	Violence in Home
Bailey (1996)			●	●		●		●
Myers et al. (1995)	●	●			●			●
Heide (1992)	●	●	●		●			●
Busch et al. (1990)	●						●	
Zagar et al. (1990)	●						●	
Goetting (1989)			●	●				
Lewis et al. (1988)	●	●			●	●		
Lewis et al. (1985)	●					●		●
Lewis et al. (1983)	●			●	●	●	●	●
Post (1982)	●							
Petti & Davidman (1981)	●		●					
Sorrells (1977)			●	●	●	●		●
Corder et al. (1976)	●	●	●	●	●	●		●
Sendi & Blomgren (1975)	●	●						●
Walshe-Brennan (1975)							●	
Duncan & Duncan (1971)	●							
Total # of Studies	12	5	6	5	6	6	4	8

Note: *Indicates presence of factor in study's sample.
Source: Shumaker (1998).

practices that result in the inadequate socialization process discussed by Corder and colleagues. The challenge for the field in the future is to examine the interaction between these factors more closely in an effort to move beyond the current level of understanding. As a starting point, investigators would be well served to refer to the intensive study of familial risk factors that has occurred within the broader field of juvenile offending (e.g., Hoge, Andrews, & Leschied, 1996; Capaldi & Patterson, 1996; Farrington, 1995; Patterson, DeBaryshe, & Ramsey, 1989; Loeber & Dishion, 1983).

CASE-STUDY COMPARISON OF GLOBAL PREDICTORS

The present section will compare the behavioral, psychiatric, and familial predisposition of several preteens who have committed either homicide (N = 10) or a homicidally aggressive action (N = 1) with a larger sample of adolescents who have either committed homicide (N = 22) or a homicidally aggressive action (N = 6). The case studies used for the present analysis came from several sources. Specifically, eight articles contributed cases to the pool of preteen offenders: Paluszny and McNabb (1975) one case; Bender and Curran (1940) two cases; Bernstein (1979), one case; Sargent (1962), one case; Greenberg and Blank (1970), one case; Tooley (1975), two cases; Adam and Livingston (1993), one case; and Easson and Steinhilber (1961), two cases. Nine articles contributed cases to the pool of adolescent homicide offenders: Bender and Curran (1940), two cases; Myers (1994), three cases; Holmes and Holmes (1994), one case; Woods (1961) two cases; Smith (1965), three cases; Hellsten and Katila (1965), four cases; Russell (1979), five cases; Russell (1985), two cases; and Easson and Steinhilber (1961), six cases.

The rationale for conducting the case-study analysis was presented in an earlier section; here a few important points should be mentioned before beginning the discussion of the results. To begin, although the exact frequency of intrafamilial homicides committed by preteens is unknown, research on juvenile murders (which estimates that 10% to 20% of all murders in this population are intrafamilial) suggests that the true estimate of preteen intrafamilial homicide is much lower than is represented in the current analysis. Indeed, the fact that 63% of the preteen cases (7 out of 11) and 57% of the adolescent cases (16 out of 28) in this sample are intrafamilial potentially obscures the true picture of the modal preteen murderer. The authors have taken an initial step toward addressing this issue by comparing the intrafamilial murderers versus extrafamilial murderers in this sample using the same set of variables employed in the preteen-versus-adolescent comparison. The reader should be aware, however, that extrafamilial murderers have most likely been misrepresented in the literature as a result of the disproportionate amount of research that has been conducted on intrafamilial killers (for a more thorough discussion of this issue, refer to Ewing, 1990).

The second caution regarding the current sample concerns the considerable variability across articles regarding the focus and detail of their case descriptions. As would be expected, the majority of the authors who have contributed cases had their own causal theories of youthful homicide and focused extensively on predisposing factors that were critical components of these theories. In addition, several of the case studies included in this analysis were actually quite short in length, often giving only basic information regarding the child's family situation. These two considerations almost ensure that additional salient factors have been omitted in some of the cases. We have attempted to reduce the impact of this issue by reporting the presence of a particular factor when it is suggested in the text, rather than conclusively documented; it remains likely, nonetheless, that errors were made in the course of identifying these risk factors.

A final matter of discussion concerns the criteria used to select the specific behavioral, psychiatric, and familial variables used in the analysis. As already stated, the source for these variables is Ressler et al.'s (1988) landmark work on sexual and serial killers. In brief, the author compiled a list of childhood behavioral and familial factors that were reported in over 50% of the 39 cases constituting Ressler's sample. This resulted in a total of 26 variables. This list, however, included several factors not discussed in the preteen and adolescent case studies (i.e., compulsive masturbation, nightmares, destruction of property, poor body image, voyeurism, pornography, fetishism, admitted rape fantasies, and consenting sex). Although these factors may simply not have been indicated in this sample and this is why they were unreported, this is far from certain and future investigations would be well served to systematically study and report on these variables. Finally, to construct the most accurate comparison, four variables were added to the remaining list—one variable that represents a fusion of Ressler's childhood sexual experience variable defined as "unhealthy sexual experiences," and three factors that have commonly been reported in descriptions of youthful murders (i.e., cruelty to animals, truancy, and ruminations about murder before the event).

In terms of results, a series of chi square analyses were conducted comparing the performance of preteens and adolescents across 19 factors. Table 3.3 reports on the outcome of this analysis. Overall, both age groups indicated a high presence of adverse family and individual variables, with preteens and adolescents reporting an average of 7.5 and 6.5 risk factors per case, respectively. In addition, both groups exhibited a wide distribution of risk factors. Specifically, with the exception of the variables *truancy, unhealthy sexual experiences,* and *ruminations about murder,* at least one preteen and one adolescent experienced each of the remaining risk factors. Of particular note, both groups reported especially high levels of physical and emotional abuse and instability in the home living environment. Thus, children in both groups appear to have experienced similar family backgrounds to that of Ressler's sample of adult sexual and serial killers.

Table 3.3
Comparison of Preteen and Adolescent Case Studies

Variable	Preteens (N = 11)	Adolescents (N = 28)	Chi-Square Significance Test Probability Estimates
Family Alcohol/Drug Problems	4 (36%)	13 (46%)	0.568
Family Psychiatric Problems	6 (55%)	11 (39%)	0.387
Child Physical/Emotional Abuse	9 (82%)	21 (75%)	0.649
Unstable Residency/Home Environment	7 (64%)	20 (71%)	0.635
Domineering Mother	5 (45%)	14 (50%)	0.798
Negative Relationship with Father or Male Caretaker	10 (91%)	14 (50%)	0.018*
Child Perceives Unfair Treatment by Others	4 (36%)	9 (32%)	0.478
Child Isolated from Others	6 (55%)	9 (32%)	0.196
Lying	4 (36%)	2 (7%)	0.023*
Enuresis	3 (27%)	8 (21%)	0.935
Rebelliousness/Oppositional	8 (73%)	12 (43%)	0.093
Fire Setting	3 (27%)	1 (4%)	0.028*
Stealing	2 (18%)	9 (32%)	0.383
Cruelty to Children	9 (82%)	6 (21%)	0.001**
Fanatsy/Day-Dreaming	1 (9%)	8 (29%)	0.194
Truancy	0 (0%)	8 (29%)	0.047*
Cruelty to Animals	1 (9%)	2 (7%)	0.837
Unhealthy Sexual Experiences	0 (0%)	12 (43%)	0.009**
Ruminations about Murder	0 (0%)	9 (32%)	0.032*

Note: * $p < .05$
** $p < .01$
Source: Shumaker (1998).

Conversely, there were several key differences between preteens and adolescents in this sample. In particular, preteens were significantly more likely to have lied, been cruel and/or violent with other children, engaged in fire setting, and experienced a negative relationship with their primary male caretaker. By contrast, adolescents were significantly more likely to have been truant, experienced unhealthy sexual experiences (including sexual abuse), and ruminated about the murder. Although the methodological shortcomings of this analysis greatly reduce the external validity of these findings, a few interpretative comments are warranted.

Perhaps the most intriguing finding concerned the especially high frequency in which preteens had engaged in cruel behavior toward other children. In fact, 9 out of 11 (82%) preteens in this sample had exhibited this behavior. Although it is possible that a higher percentage of adolescents in this sample had exhibited this behavior than the 21% reported, what this finding does suggest is that one of the most reliable and easily observable predictors of homicide in preteens is whether the individual has already demonstrated a capacity to engage in unusually cruel and violent behavior toward his or her peers. Homicidal behavior in young children does not appear to occur "out of the blue"; rather, there seems to be a history of cruel and aggressive behavior that precedes these horrific actions.

The finding that preteens were significantly more likely to have experienced negative relationships with their male caretakers can best be interpreted when viewed in conjunction with the similarly high levels of physical and emotional abuse reported in this age group. Indeed, the majority of the preteens' households can best be described as unpredictable, nonempathic environments where the child was consistently at risk for witnessing or experiencing violence, usually at the hand of their primary male caretaker. Although both the *modeling* hypothesis and the *lack of appropriate socialization* hypothesis may partially explain the negative male relationship–preteen homicide connection, Post (1982) and Heide (1992) have offered an additional means through which this variable can increase a child's risk for committing murder. Specifically, both authors have discussed a phenomenon whereby children growing up in abusive family environments experience intense psychological pressure with little opportunity to release such pressure constructively, resulting in highly aggressive behavior under certain conditions. Heide and Post have argued that this pressure is an instrumental factor in intrafamilial murder; the authors believe that this factor can be extended to the discussion extrafamilial murderers as well. Indeed, children who murder strangers could suffer from a similar set of familial pressures and adverse factors, but they select a victim outside the family for other (as yet unknown) reasons.

Some credence is given to this last speculation by the finding that with the exception of the *lying* risk factor, no significant differences between intra- and extrafamilial murderers in this sample were observed (in this sample, extrafamilial murderers were significantly more likely to have lied). This is not meant to imply that important differences between these two populations are absent, although the finding does offer preliminary support to the argument that there are considerably more similarities in the developmental backgrounds of these two groups than has been thought to date.

The other significant differences between preteens and adolescents can be interpreted in a variety of ways. For example, it could be that by virtue of their increased level of independence, older children have a greater opportunity to be truant from school, thus explaining their higher rates of truancy. In addition, by the time a child reaches adolescence, the scope of troublesome behavior may have increased to such an extent that researchers are less likely to focus on relatively minor behavioral problems such as lying. This explanation accounts for the increased frequency in which preteens in this sample were reported to have engaged in lying behavior. The underlying message, however, is that there could be several subtle reasons for these observed differences.

Overall, this case-study analysis reveals that children and adolescents who murder suffer from backgrounds similar to those of Ressler's adult sample—a finding that has ominous prognostic implications for youthful murderers. Indeed, it could be that the sheer number and/or a particular combination of these risk factors has a strong bearing on whether the child will commit additional violent actions in adulthood. Alternatively, there could be a host of unknown differences between child and adult murderers that mute the impact of these adverse factors when attempting to isolate repeat homicide offenders. To date, it appears that Hagan (1997) has conducted the only systematic longitudinal investigation into the recidivism rates of youth incarcerated for homicide. Specifically, he compared postrelease offending (for periods ranging from 5 years to 15 years) of 20 homicidal adolescents between the ages of 12 and 21 with 20 controls who had committed other offenses. Although Hagan was unable to document additional homicides upon release, he found a majority of subjects engaged in criminal activity; furthermore, a sizable portion of these crimes were committed against persons. Until longitudinal studies that follow the progress of preteen murderers are conducted, the true recidivism rates in this population will continue to be a matter of speculation. The present case study comparison, however, in combination with Hagan's findings, should alert clinicians, researchers, and policymakers that there is cause for concern when attempting to predict future aggression and psychopathic behavior in this population.

ENVIRONMENTAL AND CONTEXTUAL GLOBAL PREDICTORS

There appears to be a growing consensus that today's society is generally more violent than in years past. As proof of this point, researchers and policymakers often refer to startling statistics on gun availability, gang activity, and media portrayal of violence. To date, however, little systematic research has been conducted on the relationship between each of these factors and youth homicide. Part of this could be attributable to the difficulties inherent in finding a way to measure the impact of environmental factors on individual behavior. Despite the challenges of the task, this section will review the state of research in this area and offer tentative conclusions about the relationship between these factors and preteen homicide.

As previously discussed, guns are by far the weapon of choice in juvenile homicide, with 81% of the males and 41% of the females in the previously discussed SHR sample using this weapon during the commission of their murders (for a more in-depth discussion of trends in gun usage in juvenile homicide, please refer to O'Donnell, 1995). There are, however, two problems—one methodological and the other conceptual—with studying the relationship between guns and preteen homicide. In regard to the methodological issue, as the reader might expect, little systematic research has been conducted on the prevalence of gun usage in preteen homicide. When considering research that suggests a fairly uniform increase in gun ownership and criminal activity as juveniles grow older (Bjerregaard & Lizotte, 1995; Blumstein, 1995), it would be inappropriate to assume equivalent rates of gun usage in preteen homicide.

On a conceptual level, guns are the only variable that has been defined as both a risk factor and a tool used to carry out the offense. Indeed, based upon this line of reasoning, an argument can be made to view knives, sticks, fists, or any other weapon of choice as a homicide predictor as well. What appears to explain the different perception of guns is that researchers have examined the increases in juvenile homicide, and, more specifically, gun use in juvenile homicide, and have reached a conclusion that were guns unavailable, this increase would not have occurred. Although this might be true, an argument can be made that many of these murders may have taken place via another weapon; in these cases, guns could no longer be viewed as a risk factor. These methodological and conceptual concerns are raised here to demonstrate that the connection between youthful homicide and guns may not be as straightforward as reported in the popular media and social science literature.

Because of the paucity of research on gun use in preteen homicide, most of the hypotheses about this relationship have been based upon clinical observations and/or archival data analyses. Cornell (1993) has conducted some of the most extensive investigations in this regard and has argued for at least six circumstances in which access to handguns places a child at increased risk for homicidal behavior. These include situations where (1) criminally motivated children are emboldened by carrying a handgun and graduate from low-risk crimes to much higher risk criminal behavior; (2) youth gangs seek superiority over rival gangs, and an "arms race" eventually escalates into a shooting war; (3) adult criminals encourage children to carry weapons for them so the adults will not face criminal charges if confronted by the police, resulting in the youngsters' need to act aggressively with a gun in the commission of crimes to prove their prowess to the adult; (4) youth who are the victim of abusive treatment are encouraged to retaliate after arming themselves with a gun; (5) a youth carries a gun as a sign of status but in the course of an ordinary disagreement uses the weapon to settle a dispute; and (6) in cases where a gun is readily available in the home, an emotionally disordered child reacts to a family argument in an ill-conceived, impulsive manner. Certainly there are many cases reported in the popular media to support each of these scenarios. The challenge for future researchers, however, is to investigate the frequency with which each of these cases occurs in the you+nger age group and, on the basis of those results, to closely investigate the relative impact that gun availability has upon preteen homicide.

Gangs have also been a prominent target in the search for environmental causes of the increase in youth homicide. Substantial evidence links gang involvement with homicidal behavior. On a national level, for example, 1994 the UCR classified 43% of all murders committed by juveniles (N = 1,157) as "juvenile gang killings." This finding has been confirmed in a series of regional (citywide) investigations of gang-related homicides (e.g., Rogers, 1993; Block & Block, 1993). On an individual level, Bush et al. (1990) classified 41% of the juvenile murders in their sample of 71 as having a gang-related motivation—leading the authors to specify gang membership as one of the four major risk factors of homicidal behavior in their sample.

It appears that there are a variety of ways in which gang involvement can increase a youth's risk for committing a homicide. Ewing (1990) has hypothesized four specific categories, including drug-related homicides, homicides committed in the course of other crimes (e.g., rape and robbery), gang-on-gang or internal strife homicides, and unintentional deaths of innocent bystanders. In addition, some authors have focused more specifically on the relation between illegal drug trade homicides and gang-related homicides (Blumstein, 1995); others have argued that territorial "turf" battles between rival gangs account for a high percentage of gang-related murders (Block & Block, 1993; Goldstein, 1991). Taking a different approach, Bjerregaard and Lizotte (1995) have argued that gang members are more likely to own a gun and be involved in a range of illegal activities—two risk factors that in combination greatly increases an individual's risk of committing a homicide and other serious crimes.

The few authors who have closely studied the age of gang-affiliated homicide offenders have however, found that most of these homicides are committed by relatively older juveniles. For example, Maxson, and Klein's (1996) recent study of Los Angeles gangs found that the mean age of homicide suspects in 1994 was approximately 20. Spergel (1983), who has conducted some of the most in-depth analyses of gangs, found that only 2.2% of the gang-related homicides in Chicago between the years 1978 to 1981 were committed by children under 14 years of age. Although this latter study runs a risk of being out of date, as recently as 1995 Spergel has argued that "the data are also clear that the extreme gang violence problem is due primarily to youths between 15 and 24 years of age, particularly those late in adolescent years" (Spergel, 1995, p. 42). Until additional studies of preteen involvement in gangs and gang-related homicides are conducted, the exact frequency in which this factor plays a role in preteen homicide will remain an educated guess. Currently, however, it appears that gangs play a much greater role in juvenile versus preteen homicide.

The impact of media violence on homicidal behavior in preteens is the last environmental factor that will be discussed in this section. As those who are familiar with this area of research can attest, literally hundreds of articles are devoted to the relationship between media violence and aggressive behavior. Whereas it is beyond the scope of this chapter to conduct an exhaustive review of these efforts, some general observations can be made that summarize the state of research in this area. To begin, there appears to be little doubt that viewing television violence increases a child's likelihood of acting in an aggressive manner in laboratory situations (e.g, Friedrich-Cofer & Huston, 1986; Roberts & Macoby, 1985). There is even some experimental evidence to suggest that exposure to television violence increases aggressive behavior in real-world situations (e.g., Wood, Wong, & Chachere, 1991). In addition, longitudinal correlational studies conducted in real-world settings have shown relatively high correlations between childhood viewing of television violence and later aggressive or criminal behavior (e.g., Huesmann, Eron, Lefkowitz, & Walder, 1984; Singer, Singer, & Rapaczynski, 1984). Thus, substantial data indicates that exposure to media violence can have a causal effect on aggression in children under specific conditions and may correlate with criminal behavior in adulthood.

What has been more difficult to prove, however, is a causal connection between television violence and real-world, violent criminal behavior in children. Indeed, although some authors have made the mistake of arguing for a strong causal connection between these variables based upon correlational research or a decision to equate aggression with violent behavior, it appears that there is a weak connection, at best, that can be influenced by a host of mitigating variables. As proof of this latter point, Paik and Comstock (1994) recently conducted a metaanalysis of 217 studies that investigated the relationship between television viewing and a range of antisocial behavior in children. In the study the researchers divided antisocial behavior into three categories: (1) simulated aggressive behavior (defined as using aggression machines to deliver shocks or other noxious stimuli, playing with aggressive toys, and the intention of performing an aggressive action); (2) minor aggressive behavior (defined as physical violence against an object, verbal aggression, and physical violence against a person not in the range of criminal behavior); and (3) illegal activities (defined as burglary, grand theft, and criminal violence against a person). In general, whereas the researchers found small- to medium-effect sizes for simulated aggressive behavior and minor aggressive behavior ($R^2 = .10$), they found a minimal effect size for illegal activities ($R^2 = .03$) and, more specifically, for the criminal violence against a person subcategory ($R^2 = .01$). This finding supports other research that suggests a lack of a substantial relationship between exposure to media violence and real-world, violent behavior in children (Freedman, 1984; McGuire, 1986).

Although viewing television violence may not have a substantial, unilateral impact on violent behavior in children in general, this factor may have a contributory effect on the violent behavior of children already suffering from emotional, aggressive, and/or cognitive problems. Lande (1993) has made such an argument and cites an impaired ability to critically evaluate violent programming as the main mechanism that increases this subpopulation's risk for suffering from deleterious consequences. Even this hypothesis, however, suffers from a lack of supporting evidence. For example, Godow and Sprafkin (1993) have recently conducted a series of studies on the viewing habits of a sample of children with emotional and behavioral disorders. The researchers were able to demonstrate that, in comparison to a control group of nonemotionally disturbed children, emotionally disturbed children watched more hours of aggressive television, were more likely to prefer aggressive characters, had more difficulty comprehending the unreality of the television portrayals of violence, and were more willing to hurt other children following exposure to aggressive content in laboratory situations. Surprisingly, however, the researchers found that in real-world settings, both violent and nonviolent television were equally likely to induce antisocial behavior in the subjects as compared to no television at all, leading the authors to conclude that, overall, "it is unlikely that television is a primary cause of the interpersonal conflicts experienced by children" (Godow & Sprafkin, 1993, p. 61).

Taking these results into consideration, perhaps the safest conclusion is that no demonstrable connection between exposure to television violence and homicidal behavior in preteens has been demonstrated to date. The evidence that links television violence with aggressive behavior and future criminality, however, suggests that this variable merits review in future investigations on preteen homicide. Indeed, although highly speculative, it could be that the *exposure to media violence* variable should be conceptualized as a lower-impact familial risk factor akin to that of the *physical abuse* and *witnessing of violence* variables discussed earlier. This argument has been made before in works on youthful homicide (Hardwick & Rowton-Lee, 1996; Sorrells, 1977).

PREDICTORS ACCORDING TO SPECIFIC TYPE OF OFFENSE

Because preteen homicide has received such comparatively little systematic attention in the literature, an attempt to discriminate the relative contribution of predictors according to the type of homicide rests on even shakier ground than the previous discussion of global predictors. For example, it is difficult to speculate on the etiology of preteen intrafamilial homicide when it is unclear how often mothers, fathers, and siblings are the targets of this crime. In addition, the present task revisits the issue of a lack of a standardized classification system to categorize this population. That is, this discussion could be framed within a *psychiatric, victim-offender rela-*

tionship, or *circumstances of the crime* classification system, with the potential that each approach would yield a different picture of discrepancies among offenders. Faced with these significant limitations, the present section will draw only a basic distinction between intrafamilial murders and extrafamilial murders. Upon review, there appears to be enough evidence to support a preliminary inquiry into differences among offenders based upon this framework.

As previously discussed, the field has shown a tendency to discriminate between intrafamilial youthful murderers and extrafamilial youthful murderers. Although the majority of systematic research on this issue has focused on relatively older offenders, the consistency across these works suggests that these predictors are robust and may also be at work in preteen intrafamilial homicide. The current authors were able to uncover four factors that may discriminate intrafamilial perpetrators from extrafamilial murderers. These include (1) access to a gun in the home; (2) extensive physical, emotional, and/or sexual abuse and interpersonal conflict in the household (conflict that is comparatively more severe than that of extrafamilial murderers); (3) few alternative modes of reaction to stress; and (4) a notable increase in adverse conditions in the home immediately before the murder (Corder et al., 1976; Cornell et al., 1987b; Post, 1982; Heide, 1992). Upon review, however, these factors appear to apply more closely to parricide as opposed to the murder of one's sibling. As Ewing (1990) has pointed out, it appears that by virtue of their smaller stature, preteens are more likely to murder siblings than parents. Much less is known, however, about the nature of this specific type of intrafamilial homicide, and to assume similar dynamics would be premature when it appears that several of the above-cited predictors speak to a revenge or escape motive that may not exist between siblings. Future research should therefore focus more closely on the dynamics behind preteens who murder their siblings.

Preteens who murder acquaintances or strangers appear to have more extensive histories of aggressive and violent behavior and are perhaps more likely to have experienced prior hyperactivity and impulse control deficits (Corder et al., 1976; Cornell et al., 1987b). They also are probably more likely to have engaged in other criminal activity and to have been removed from the home which, as Corder et al. (1976) have pointed out, would reduce the risk of their family members' becoming victims. Based upon these factors, extrafamilial preteen murderers appear at increased risk for exhibiting psychopathic behavior in adulthood and, more specifically, continuing to engage in serious violent crime. As this chapter's case-study analysis has demonstrated, however, the differences between intra- and extrafamilial preteen homicide offenders are more subtle than once thought and thus requires further investigation. As noted, the paucity of research on preteen extrafamilial homicide offenders is particularly troubling because extrafamilial homicides constitute majority of offenses committed by this age group.

Chapter 4

By What Means Are
They Dealt?

The long-standing philosophy regarding the differential approach to dealing with adult criminals and juvenile offenders has increasingly come under debate and question. Increase in juvenile violence has led to massive statutory and policy change. Violent cases once routinely handled within the juvenile system are now waived to criminal court or are by exclusion or prosecutorial decision initially dealt with in that setting (Grisso 1998). Originally, the juvenile court system emerged to separate children from the adult criminal justice system. The adult system had and continues to have punishment as its focus. Assumptions regarding the causes of the child's delinquent behavior influenced by developmental theorists, psychologists, sociologists, and others shifted from individual responsibility regardless of age to the more contemporary view of the delinquent child as a product of the environment (home, community, and school). Punishment for the delinquent child was superseded by a recognition that because juvenile offenders lack adult judgment and responsibility, the approach should be an individualized one focused on treatment, behavioral control, and rehabilitation. Several factors may account for the discrepancy between the helping professions (psychology, psychology social work, etc.) and court and correctional officials with regard to treatment and rehabilitation. First, the public and the media judge courts and correctional facilities on the basis of their failures, not their successes. Second, a prevailing attitude among correctional personnel is that "nothing works," an attitude supported in the professional literature. This is fed by increasing crime rates for violence, high rates of recidivism, and the increasing popularity of genetic (and thus incorrectable) theories of criminal behavior. Third, many court officers serve at the pleasure of elected officials or are themselves elected and are thus unwilling to risk public displeasure by supporting the more risky programs of treatment and rehabilitation. Finally, there is the mistrust of the helping professions, who are viewed as lacking full awareness of the difficulties in dealing with delinquents.

Processing of the child offender in the juvenile system continues to be distinctively different in almost every respect from processing in the adult court (Feld 1987). Even the physical setting utilized by juvenile courts rarely resembles adult court facilities; judges operate from the position of what is best for the welfare of the child. Unlike the adult court judge, who focuses on the commission of a criminal act with a strict observance of a formal process and rules of evidence, the juvenile judge operates in conjunction with a professional staff whose stated goals are the welfare of the child. Under optimum conditions this involves an extensive program of investigation involving assessment of the child, the family, the environment, and strategies to modify or overcome deficits and problems. Flexibility in the juvenile system permits creative and individualized solutions to many problems facing the child. It also results in unevenness because of philosophic variations in judges and their staffs and the increasingly heavy demands on overworked juvenile systems.

There has also been a shift in the types of offenses committed by juvenile offenders, with a measurable increase in violent crime. In a study by Heckel and Mandell (1971) of all incarcerated juveniles in South Carolina, 47% of boys and 5.7% of girls had committed violent crimes. Recent available figures on incarcerated juveniles reveal that 21% committed violent acts against persons (Sickmund, Snyder, & Poe-Yamagata, 1997), which represents a 98% increase between 1986 and 1995. Whatever factors may account for these marked differences and comparisons between South Carolina and other states may be of limited significance, the figures do suggest a growing problem of management both in the community and in the institutions to which juveniles are assigned. At the time of the original study the juvenile institution in South Carolina operated as an open campus model with one high-security building. Today all the facilities are encased in high-security fencing. These changes have occurred in every state and are the result of a rethinking and reexamination of the entire juvenile system approach.

Juveniles who commit murder or violent acts against others today face unsympathetic legislatures, judges, and communities. Recent highly publicized murders by preteens in Arkansas, North Carolina, South Carolina, and Colorado have resulted in legislative proposals to reverse discretionary handling of accused juvenile murderers by juvenile and family courts to move all cases to adult courts for trial. Many states have minimum ages for referral to adult courts, typically 13 to 14, but as high as 16 in some instances. Many states also have provision of referral to adult court in serious cases regardless of age. In most states, waiver to adult courts remains a discretionary decision of the court system, the prosecutor, or the judge. Even those offenses typically handled within the juvenile system can be waived to adult court and trial based on judicial opinion. Once a case is waved to adult court, return to juvenile jurisdiction may occur when the child is deemed incompetent to stand trial in adult court. Although return to juvenile jurisdiction happens infrequently, it does indicate a systemic flexibility when earlier judgments are modified by later information. Twenty-two states provide for reverse transfer; 18 states require that once a case is waived from juvenile court or when the child is convicted in adult court, all subsequent actions take place in adult court, following the concept of once an adult, always an adult (Sickmund et al., 1997).

JUDICIAL WAIVER

The transfer of juveniles to adult criminal court has remained an option in most states following the establishment of the juvenile court system. This transfer occurs in serious cases such as extreme violence or armed robbery. Sickmund, Snyder, and Poe-Yamagata (1997) indicate that 10 states had such provisions before the 1920s, and another 10 states had added such provisions by the 1940s. By 1996, 46 states and the District of Columbia had statutes allowing judicial waiver.

Waiver to criminal court is carried out in three ways: judicial waiver, in which the juvenile court judge can waive jurisdiction and transfer to adult criminal court; prosecutor discretion, in which the prosecutor has the discretion to file in either juvenile or criminal court; and legislative or statutory exclusion, in which certain serious offense are excluded from juvenile court jurisdiction.

Generally, transfer is limited by the nature of the juvenile's offense, age, and the amenability to treatment. The latter is a judicial decision because, as indicated by Sickmund, Snyder, and Poe-Yamagata (1997), most "exclusion or concurrent jurisdiction provisions" do not define or delineate amenability criteria. In many instances the seriousness of the offense (e.g. murder) places the child beyond means of treatment available under juvenile authority and requires punishment. The course of action in several high-profile murders by preteens and young adolescents promises to follow this protocol, where statutes permit waiver to criminal court.

Part of the reexamination of jurisdictional and waiver issues by state legislatures has been a modifying of the long-standing requirement of withholding names and identifying information regarding juvenile offenders.

Sickmund et al. (1997) report that by 1995 a series of legislative decisions opened court proceedings and records to public examination. Twenty-two states now have open hearings in certain cases. Thirty-nine states now permit the release of photographs and names of juvenile offenders. Eighteen states (8 recent enactments) bar the sealing or removal of certain juvenile files and records. Forty-five states (21 recent enactments) permit the release of juvenile records to law enforcement and professionals, including, in some instances, to the general public or to the victim. Finally, 47 states permit fingerprinting and 44 states allow the taking of photographs and the maintaining of an offense history (arrests, dispositions) on juveniles. Of these, 26 are reported as new or modified laws.

Given that this 1997 report is complete through 1995, it is certain that recent signal events of murder and violence by juveniles has resulted in additional legislative action and that these numbers represent an underestimate of present levels of disclosure regarding juveniles in the country.

By the end of 1996, in most states changes in and expansions of statutes pertaining to waiver, exclusions, and jurisdictions have also resulted, providing a combination of transfer provisions or options (Torbet et al., 1996; Torbet & Szymanski, 1998; Szymanski, 1998). Six states retain the traditional judicial waiver only (Arizona, California, Maine, Missouri, New Jersey, and South Dakota). Five states (Arkansas, Colorado, Michigan, New Hampshire, and Wyoming) and the District of Columbia provide both judicial waiver and concurrent jurisdiction as a means of transfer. Given events in Littleton, Colorado, in spring 1999, it is anticipated that legislative action will add an exclusionary provision to Colorado's options. Currently only five states provide for all three waiver methods (judicial, jurisdictional, and statutory): Florida, Georgia, Louisiana, Vermont, and Virginia. Legislative exclusions are the only option in Connecticut, New Mexico, and New York. Nebraska alone as the only state in which concurrent jurisdiction, with prosecutors determining where the child committing a serious crime will be placed in the legal process. Finally, the majority of states (27) provide for both judicial waiver and statutory exclusion: Alabama, Alaska, Delaware, Hawaii, Idaho, Illinois, Indiana, Iowa, Kansas, Kentucky, Maryland, Minnesota, Mississippi, Montana, Nevada, North Carolina, North Dakota, Ohio, Oklahoma, Oregon, Pennsylvania, Rhode Island, South Carolina, Utah, Washington, West Virginia, and Wisconsin.

Legislatures have been quite active in the last 15 years and especially active in the 1990s. Chief among their actions has been the lowering of age limits for judicial waiver (11 states) and exclusionary statutes (5 states). They have also expanded the list of crimes for exclusion (24) and waiver (10). Five states have added exclusion provisions for the first time. As further evidence for the increase in regulations and requirements, 9 states have established presumptive waiver provisions, which provide for the automatic transfer of children of a specified age or seriousness of offense unless they are able to support their suitability for juvenile treatment and rehabilitation.

Determining suitability for treatment and rehabilitation presents a significant opportunity for psychologists who provide the assessment to aid in judges' decision to waiver. Determining whether a child is dangerous or amenable to treatment is, according to Podkopacz and Feld (1996) one of the most difficult issues in juvenile jurisprudence. This determination is made more difficult (as forensic psychologists are keenly aware) by legislative and court assumptions that (1) there are effective treatment programs and interventions for juveniles who have committed serious offenses or who demonstrate persistent pathological symptoms, and (2) valid diagnostic tools permit the psychologist or psychiatrist to classify children's dangerousness and amenability to treatment and to provide appropriate dispositional recommendations.

Most juvenile courts, say Podkopacz and Feld (1996), make many waiver decisions based on statutory criteria related to dangerousness or amenability to treatment but lack substantive definitions of what constitutes dangerousness or treatability. For the psychologist it is not only a problem of definition but also one of measurement and prediction, as Grisso clearly states (1998). Because of the subjectivity of the definitions, the variability within what have been presented as predictors of both dangerousness and treatability and the variability within each juvenile court, the decisions demonstrate little consistency, with factors such as race complicating an already difficult decision process.

Sickmund et al. (1997) provide a series of statistics relating to the use of judicial waiver. In the 10-year period from 1985 through 1994, there was a 71% increase nationwide in numbers of cases waived. There was a shift occurring in 1992 in which the majority of waived juveniles had committed person offenses rather than the traditionally high property crimes. Numbers of children waived grew from an annual averages of 7,200 to 12,300. In this same 10-year period the increase of waived juveniles was greatest for those under 16, by 1994 doubling 1985 levels. There is little doubt that as judicial attitudes harden regarding serious juvenile offenses, waiving to criminal court will be the mode rather than the exception.

CHANGES IN DISPOSITION OF VIOLENT JUVENILES

Much of our discussion of waiver thus far has focused on all juvenile offenses judged to be serious (e.g., murder or attempted murder). At this point we will examine in greater depth the factors affecting juveniles who engage in violent behavior and other crimes against persons. The aforementioned trend to criminalize increasing areas of juvenile delinquent behavior is perhaps best illustrated in the judicial response to violent acts. In these instances the trend has been to view punishment, accountability, and public safety as primary concerns, outweighing concerns for treatment and rehabilitation (Sickmund et al., 1997). Dispositions are increasingly based on the nature of the offense. Dispositions thus tend to be determinate and proportional to that offense.

As part of the continued monitoring and control of juvenile offenders, statutory changes by state legislators have set mandatory minimum periods of incarceration for violent offenders (16 states) and raised the maximum age jurisdiction to 21 in most states. Accompanying these changes has been one that will ultimately have the most profound impact on juvenile dispositions—the use of blended sentences, which combines juvenile sentences with additional sentences to be carried out in adult correctional settings. By the end of 1995, 16 states provided for blended sentences. Table 4.1, from Sickmund et al. (1997), provides a clear descriptive picture of various blends available and identifies the states offering those options by 1995.

Following the tragedy in Jonesboro, Arkansas, in which a preteen and a young teenager murdered classmates and a teacher, public outcry and legislator outrage promise revision of juvenile statutes that provide for release of juvenile offenders by age 18 regardless of offense. At this writing it appears that modifications will involve both exclusions and the option of blended sentencing (Sue Madison, Arkansas state representative, personal communication, 1999).

Despite these changes, the great majority of cases continue to be dealt with in juvenile court settings. Sickmund et al. report that 86% of juvenile cases referred by law enforcement were directed to juvenile court. The remaining 14% came from schools, parents, probation officers, and victims. Some cases of violence by younger juveniles may remain in the jurisdiction of the juvenile system, particularly if the offenders are deemed too young or lack sufficient competence to assist in their own defense.

COMPETENCE ISSUES

A significant aspect of the decision to waive the child offender to criminal court rests with the issue of competence to stand trial. Three factors are central to this: (1) Does the child understand the charges and the procedures involved? (2) Is the child able to participate and assist in his or her own defense? (3) Is the child able to respond appropriately to Miranda warnings and to understand what is involved in the waiving of Miranda rights? We will deal with Miranda extensively in chapter 7 thus will limit our discussion here.

Grisso has extensively discussed and described competency issues in two or three works (1988, 1997, 1998) providing clear guidelines for evaluation and assessment. Although most issues pertain to adolescents rather than preteens, with increasing frequency they are applied to the younger group, especially when violence is involved.

Table 4.1
Blended Sentencing Options

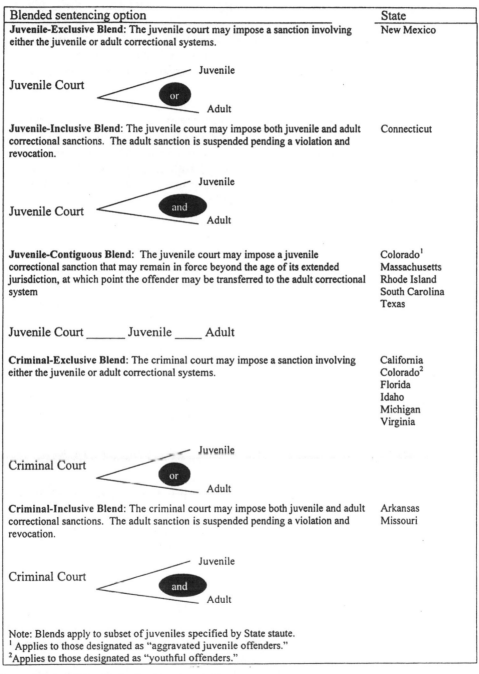

Blended sentencing option	State
Juvenile-Exclusive Blend: The juvenile court may impose a sanction involving either the juvenile or adult correctional systems.	New Mexico
Juvenile-Inclusive Blend: The juvenile court may impose both juvenile and adult correctional sanctions. The adult sanction is suspended pending a violation and revocation.	Connecticut
Juvenile-Contiguous Blend: The juvenile court may impose a juvenile correctional sanction that may remain in force beyond the age of its extended jurisdiction, at which point the offender may be transferred to the adult correctional system	Colorado[1] Massachusetts Rhode Island South Carolina Texas
Criminal-Exclusive Blend: The criminal court may impose a sanction involving either the juvenile or adult correctional systems.	California Colorado[2] Florida Idaho Michigan Virginia
Criminal-Inclusive Blend: The criminal court may impose both juvenile and adult correctional sanctions. The adult sanction is suspended pending a violation and revocation.	Arkansas Missouri

Note: Blends apply to subset of juveniles specified by State staute.
[1] Applies to those designated as "aggravated juvenile offenders."
[2] Applies to those designated as "youthful offenders."

Source: Sickmund, Snyder, & Poe-Yamagata (1997).

For those children tried in adult courts, incompetence to stand trial continues to focus on two causes, mental illness and mental retardation. When the level of impairment is judged sufficient, court proceedings are delayed until the defendant is able, through treatment, to recover sufficiently to continue the trial. In some instances years may be involved; in other cases the person may never be restored to competency and may never resume the trial process; under these circumstances charges may eventually be dismissed.

Grisso raises the issue of as yet undeveloped capacities in the case of pre-teens and young juveniles who may present normal development but who, as a result of immaturity, are unable to meet competency requirements. The seriousness of their offense has placed them in criminal court, where guilt or innocence is determined by evidence. Immaturity in development may be considered irrelevant in that determination, as was true in the British case of Mary, described by Sereny (1999).

Competency in the Juvenile System

For much of the history of the juvenile court, competency to stand trial was not an issue. The stated goal of the juvenile system was rehabilitation and treatment, not punishment. As a result, issues related to due process, legal representation, and ability to participate in an adequate defense were rarely addressed. Once a youthful offender was waived to criminal court, those issues became central but were problems to be addressed by that court system.

This process underwent change in the 1960s with the U.S. Supreme Court decisions that ruled that juveniles were entitled to many of the rights of due process afforded adult defendants, which included (Grisso 1998) the right to legal representation and, implicitly, the requirement of competence to stand trial.

In the intervening years extensive revisions in laws relating to judicial waiver and statutory exclusion lowered age limits and broadened the number of serious offense. With the advent of blended sentences, even children who remain in juvenile court could face extended sentences, which would keep them incarcerated for many years once they reach adult status. This has been the result of juvenile courts' becoming increasingly similar to criminal courts in their proceedings. Most striking is the shift to punishment as a part of the sentence or outcome. New statutes cited earlier in this chapter reflect these changes.

RISK TO OTHERS

Another significant concern when dealing with juvenile offenders is their potential for presenting a risk to others. When their offense has been a violent one—assault, attempted murder or murder, and sex offenses—most juvenile courts assume that the child represents a high risk. Where possible, the present response is to waive the child to criminal court. Even when the offender is retained in the juvenile court system, the possibility that the child may pose an immediate threat to others or repeat the criminal behavior at some future time, as well as the potential for reducing that threat through some form of treatment or remediation, plays a significant role in how the court will deal with the child. As in our discussion in chapter 7 on assessment of risk, the psychological examiner has the opportunity to play a critical role in this decision.

Grisso (1998) lists factors in the assessment of the risk of harm to others that apply to preteen offenders' need for secure pretrial detention; degree of security needed during treatment and rehabilitation; whether rehabilitative and treatment efforts have reduced risk; and whether a need exists to extend juvenile court custody.

Cases such as that of the two Jonesboro children, aged 11 and 13 at the time of the murder of four schoolmates and a teacher at the Westside Middle School, present a particular dilemma for the judicial system. Arkansas law prohibits waiving of children under 14 to criminal court. State law does not offer the opportunity for blended sentencing but does provide for continued juvenile oversight from age 18 to 21, but only if facilities are available to keep youth offenders separate from adult incarcerates. Lacking such facilities or arrangements, the youth must be released at age 18 with their records cleansed of all convictions.

A further issue in this case relates to the availability of adequate and appropriate treatment for child murderers and the very real question of how to assess rehabilitation. Lacking substantive measures, the court and the psychologist are forced be rely on their best judgment, which is again, heavily dependent on past behavior and present assessment data.

The value of self-reports of shame and sorrow for their acts of murder offer little proof of the real motivations or intents of the children who murder. As we have indicated, from legal counsel, family, and other juveniles the child quickly learns the desired response. Mitchell Johnson for example, the 14-year-old in the Jonesboro case, has already read a statement to the courts expressing his remorse for the killings. "As I've sat in jail I've had a chance to think and to the judge and all who I've affected I am sorry. If I could go back and change what happened I would change it. I thought we were going to shoot over their heads. I didn't think anybody was going to get hurt. I am sorry. I have also asked God for forgiveness and that He will heal the lives of the people I have hurt by my actions."

In this statement the offender has said the appropriate things indicating sorrow, guilt, remorse, and calling on God for forgiveness. The governor, police officials, and judge, though not completely discounting such pronouncements as well as possible pleas of temporary insanity, feel that rehabilitation and treatment represent insufficient measures in such a serious case. No measures exist that can verify the degree to which an individual "means" or feels these emotions. Skilled examiners have developed non-verbal cues (eye contact, nervous movements, body positioning, etc.) helpful in determining insincerity and lying. These examiners are quick to admit that there are juvenile and adult offenders who provide none of these cues and appear totally sincere even though guilty.

As a result of the Jonesboro incident, in 1999 the Arkansas legislature initiated a series of bills to further control use of firearms (Arkansas House Bill 1543 and 2234) and to provide a facility to house juvenile offenders between the ages of 18 and 21 (Arkansas House Bill 1316). Other states have similar and additional proposals awaiting legislative action.

On the national level 20 bills have been presented relating to school violence, with more anticipated following the murders at Columbine High School in Littleton, Colorado on March 24, 1999. During the week of March 10, 1999, the U.S. senate rejected proposed legislation and then reversed itself to enact major changes relating to gun purchases, requiring background checks by unlicensed gun dealers making sales at gun shows. The Senate also began action on bills restricting the banning of importation of large-capacity ammunition clips for assault weapons, increasing penalties for juvenile gun offenses, and banning semiautomatic assault weapons such as grenade launchers, AK-47s, or Uzis by juveniles. Whether these proposals become law or not, it is clear that on the state and national levels violent or potentially violent juveniles face greatly increased sentencing, restrictions regarding firearms, and a juvenile and criminal justice system demanding greater control and exacting higher levels of punishment when offenses occur. The violent juvenile, regardless of age, now faces penalties far greater than any imposed since the advent of the juvenile court system.

As indicated here children who are charged with murder, attempted murder, or extreme violence will almost invariably be directed to criminal court whether by judicial waiver, statutory exclusion, or prosecutional discretion. By the time this work is released, likely no state will mandate that these offenses be dealt with in juvenile court if the offender falls below the state's minimum age for criminal court (as indicated earlier, typically 13 or 14 years of age but excluding in some instances to age 16).

CHANGES IN INITIAL CONTACTS WITH JUVENILE SUSPECTS

Until recently juveniles suspected of committing a criminal act were often dealt with informally. Miranda rights were rarely used, and other due process considerations were thought to be unnecessary. Rarely were juveniles retained in custody, unless parents or guardians were not reached. The police and juvenile authorities took on the role of parent surrogates, assuming that juveniles were unable to take responsibility for or fully understand the implications or consequences of their behavior.

Statutory and policy changes have, however, moved to a policy of zero tolerance in cases of threatened violence, violence, or the possession of weapons. Even the latter has been redefined, with several cases of students being suspended for taking a household knife to school. Both police and school authorities employ great caution in dealing with juveniles exhibiting violent potential.

School systems enforcing zero tolerance typically suspend juvenile offenders and, then direct them to alternative school settings. Because alternative school facilities are lacking, suspension may be long term or even permanent. When confronted by violence or potential violence, school officials no longer deal with the issue as an internal problem. Once police are called, the violent child enters the juvenile court system. Older children may move directly into the criminal court system.

Alternative school placement has existed for many years but it experienced its greatest early growth during the cultural revolution of the late 1960s and early 1970s. Growth was limited in the intervening years, but a resurgence occurred in the 1990s as a part of the attempt to deal with problem children in the school system. Rather than simply suspend juveniles and thus let them loose on the streets, placing problem youth in an alternative school ideally provides closer supervision, smaller classes, therapeutic measures, and alternative teaching approaches designed to reach this special population. In this setting psychologists, social workers, nurses, and specially trained teachers from the staff provide a therapeutic environment and a learning setting tailored to the special needs of the student.

Although measures of success for alternative schools are difficult to assess, several markers are available: Return of juveniles to regular schools, graduation counts, and, new versus past record of juveniles' difficulty within the school and community have all been considered in assessing their efforts. Alternative schools represent both a solution and a preventive measure and will be addressed in the chapter on prevention.

SUMMARY

There have been sweeping changes in how society deals with juvenile offenders. This has occurred at all levels. The legislative level has seen revisions in disclosure, making juvenile offenders more identifiable; the lowering of age limits for waiving to criminal court; exclusions that remove extended incarceration beyond the juvenile years in serious cases; and juvenile gun access restrictions. These changes form a growing movement for greater control of juvenile offenders and lower tolerance for their offenses. These changes have also influenced dispositions by judges, prosecutors, police, and juvenile authorities. Will the measures prove effective in controlling violence? It appears unlikely, since the majority of changes speak only to how the juvenile offender is dealt with, not to how to create greater awareness and self-control in the child. Restriction on access to guns will, of course, limit the child's legal access to guns. Unfortunately, though, many of the gun-related offenses by juveniles were committed with stolen and illegally obtained weapons.

PART II

Developmental Issues

Chapter 5

Moral Development

In this chapter our goal is to assess how moral development and moral reasoning relate to the factors research studies have identified as predictive of children who murder. What is the role of morality in the method of murder? Is it possible to have normal moral development, yet exhibit violent behavior? How do abusive families and environments prevent children from attaining appropriate moral responses as they develop? Can children be born with "something left out," preventing normal moral growth? Even more surprising, how can a child experience the overwhelming impact of an unstable family and an unhealthy environment, yet fail to show violent behavior and demonstrate high levels of moral development?

Moral development plays a key role in circumstances that cause or permit the child to commit murder. Whether murderous behavior stems from uncontrollable violence, dehumanization of the victim, or a lack of empathy, at its heart rest moral issues. Psychologists generally agree on the component parts of morality or moral behavior. They also agree that there are distinct stages or phases in moral development. These stages are distinguished by the degree to which the child is able to demonstrate internalization of moral values as a guiding principle for behavior as opposed to showing behavior that is governed by external forces, typically caregivers, family members, or teachers. This transition, from the primitive actions of the young child (typically to age 3) who observes few rules to the adult who is able to demonstrate the highest levels of morality involving abstract moral principles, is a long and arduous process in which many fail to reach the highest levels.

In examining the behavior of children who murder, we have sought to understand the form their moral development has taken, and to compare it with the development of children who have not committed violent acts. In doing this we may determine what is present and, perhaps more important, what has been left out or what has failed to develop as expected. First we will define moral development and describe what psychologists have identified as its component parts. Following this we will outline several popular theories of moral development.

A DEFINITION OF MORAL DEVELOPMENT

According to Thomas (1997), "Moral development refers to changes in the system by which people make moral decisions." He further amplifies this by describing *moral reasoning* as the way in which one thinks or reasons about moral issues. *Moral behavior* is described as how one acts when required to render moral decisions. These definitions provide us the opportunity to examine moral issues by using a behavioral model with few limiting assumptions.

Thomas like the authors, also supports the view, that no moral values or behaviors are inborn or innate. Lest this be seen as rejection of the possibility of a "bad seed," we suggest that such children represent a group whose experiences have resulted in a deficit or failure to incorporate moral principles or rules. Thus for this group a cognitive processing problem prevents the child from developing appropriate moral reasoning. Critics of this explanation ask why the deficit is so specific when other cognitive processes are functioning at near normal, normal, or even superior levels? This is an important question that reinforces the notion that nonbiological factors appear to be salient in the formation of the moral judgment of preteen murders. Most researchers, however, agree that the "bad seed" explanation applies to only a very small fraction preteen murders.

Thomas provides two other dimensions in his approach: The child has the capacity for self-punishment and self-reward, to experience shame and guilt, and to feel satisfaction and pride. These components are necessary to form a conscience, a key element in the several models we will describe. Finally, he describes the necessity in the lives of children to experience a "constant stream of moral encounters." These experiences, large or small, exert influence on moral development and come from many sources: television, newspapers, family, neighbors, peers, and so on. Indeed, these direct experiences and the observations of the dramatic interplay of others are stored in long-term memory and become part of the moral reasoning decision process. The child who views moral behaviors that are improper, destructive, exploitive, violent, and/or disregard the rights of others may incorporate these as appropriate responses when facing moral decisions. Children in destructive and impoverished environments may experience few promoral models of behavior, limiting the incorporation of positive experiences. Whereas an impoverished environment and social context may regulate the degree to which a child experiences negative moral examples, high echelons of society may equally provide a disregard for the right of others and reduce their humanity. Accounts of murders by advantaged juveniles abound in the professional literature and in media reports. The juveniles from Littleton, Colorado, for example, both came from upper-middle-class backgrounds.

Thomas suggests the importance of context in how persons apply moral principles. This is increasingly true as children mature. The moral absolutes, which occur early in the developmental process, become conditional. The ranking of moral imperatives is both culturally and individually determined by how situations are perceived. This provides for a wide range of responses and justifications by even young children.

Part of this variability is related to positions taken by children on a series of moral universals or imperatives, which Thomas has delineated. Of particular concern is the child's view on each of these issues. At least as regards most older preteens, it is our view not that they lack moral judgment, but that on the critical issues we will describe they have chosen an alternative response, finding the culturally desired response faulty or lacking meaning or utility in their own situation. As often occurs, there is a suspension of the socially desired response because of the context. For example, the moral principle of having regard for human life, in which care and protection of others is the desired response, is suspended because of anger and/or perceived personal threat; murder is the result. A similar outcome might occur under conditions where the child murderer dehumanizes the victim or where the victim merely obstructed attainment of a desired goal (e.g., "I killed her because she made me stay in my room and wouldn't let me go out to play with my friends").

Other principles—honesty, evenhanded justice, respect for property, obedience to authority, loyalty and faithfulness, responsibility, empathy and altruism, self-preservation, self-determination, appropriate sexual relations, and social order—have appropriate and desirable social consequences and represent higher moral reasoning. Each has an opposite or negative number, however. Each negative exception to these basic 12 principles represents potential sources of difficulty for the child when interacting with society. Certainly there are families and subcultures in which operating within positive moral measures would be to the child's disadvantage. Negative values are challenged when the child comes in contact with schools, the larger community, and other families.

In the following paragraphs we will examine the implications and consequences of engaging in or failing to engage in the aforementioned moral principles and consider how their absence may relate to violent acts. We will also reflect age and maturational differences in each. In this discussion we draw heavily on Thomas's description of "widely held moral principles." As will be seen, there is a clear absence or breakdown of accepted behavior. This may be attributable to a failure to incorporate these principles at an appropriate age, which reflects a lower level of development or, under extreme stress, an act outside the normal or customary range of behavior.

1. *Regard for human life.* Paramount among issues when studying children who murder are those concerning the value of human life. Ideally, everyone values human life and seeks to protect it. Under what conditions can this value be disregarded and others harmed, violated, or exploited? In our subject population it is important to understand whether murder is an act of dehumanization or a desperate action taken in an untenable situation. Does their act represent a loss of control, or is it a manifestation of violence in response to a blocking of their goals? Most case studies of preteen murderers, including the early work of Bender and Curran (1940) and the more recent reports by Heide (1992) and Ewing (1990), indicate that situational anger and impulsivity appear to be primary causes. Another factor to consider in younger children is their lack of awareness of the finality of death or of the consequences of a serious violent act. Because young children's level of moral development is in many instances at the lowest level, stage 1—or under stress reduced to that level—consideration of the rights of others and regard for human life is still unformed.

2. *Honesty.* All cultures and religions teach and support the importance of honesty. Even in earliest years, the learning of language is accompanied by moral instruction emphasizing honesty and obedience. Some children observe honesty within the family; others, only with peers. Yet others practice honesty only when it is advantageous. The rewarding and shaping of honesty is complex and rarely perfectly achieved. The cultural and subcultural model is one of selective truth. Few children escape that knowledge.

3. *Respect for property.* Early in the developmental process in our culture we stress individual property rights. Children are taught to respect the distinction between "yours" and "mine." Indeed, property rights are a major source of sibling and intrafamilial conflicts. With the advent of school, these rights of ownership and possession are frequently challenged when one child attempts to take something belonging to another. Children have been assaulted and in some instances murdered because they failed to give up a toy, money, or other possessions.

4. *Obedience to authority.* Examination of the histories of child murderers reveals extensive evidence supporting their difficulties in dealing with authority. This is so even in the very young, with suggestions from preschool and elementary years supporting these findings. Parental reports indicate

that problems with obedience began early and increased steadily into adolescence. Few exceptions exist, though in some instances failure to obey resulted in withdrawal rather than confrontation, the more typical form of rebellion. Paradigms for disobedience are rich in the literature on behavior modification, with demonstrated successful interventions for modification of this behavior discussed in the chapter on treatment. Unfortunately, timely interventions are rare, and the durability of treatment is limited by both a lack of professionals and family resistance to treatment.

In its most primitive form, the child fails to recognize or acknowledge the authority of others and may disregard their control of rewards and punishment. Later it may take the form of apparent conformity or obedience when all other options are blocked. Self-serving behaviors are preeminent, and, once again, theorists and researchers have identified the underlying factors as family discord, peer influences (especially with adolescents), and modeling of asocial and autosocial family members.

5. *Loyalty and faithfulness*. Interestingly, in this moral principle the valuing of support for others in both word and deed is often evidenced in violent and murderous children in the form of group loyalty to their peer groups. This is especially salient in members of adolescent and preadolescent groups. The Jonesboro and Littleton murders, highlighted in the news, suggest the importance of peer influence in a leader-follower model in the commission of the murder by adolescents and preadolescents. Loyalty to a peer, coupled with a desire for revenge and the dehumanization of the victim, represents a powerful force that frequently ends in extreme violence: murder, attempted murder, or assault.

The particular moral value of group or peer loyalty and faithfulness appears to develop more fully than other values perhaps because it is a learned survival value or perhaps because it enables the individual to obtain rewards in an otherwise unrewarding environment.

6. *Responsibility*. Responsibility, like loyalty, has significant modifying factors. Ideally, in appropriate moral development each child develops a motivation to fulfill obligations to others and to society that are acquired and determined by interactions with family, the community, the school, and culturally determined roles. In normal development this involves carrying out tasks, respecting the rights of others, and upholding the principles of one's social group.

In cases where the subculture is a delinquent or asocial subculture or where the family fails to support or recognize the values of the culture, the child may show responsibility, but not to society at large. For example, hierarchical delinquent subcultures require members to be responsible in specific ways and exact severe penalties for failure to carry out obligations and duties.

7. *Empathy and altruism*. A recurrent theme in the writings of researchers and clinicians is that children of violence and murder dehumanize their

victims and lack of empathy for their rights and views. In his description of compassionate caring, Thomas (1997) uses a six-level classification in which at the lowest level of functioning the individual "feels no sympathy for others . . . in need, and feels no pleasure at others success." Children functioning at this level are egocentric, lack empathy, have a low regard for humans and animals, showing histories in which they have abused both. This level of functioning is contrasted with the early emergence of empathy in normal development, which can appear in the preschool years, especially in response to others distress. By the elementary school years empathy and altruism (Whiting & Edwards, 1988) appear with much higher frequency. Researchers have dealt extensively with the acquisition process, advancing several theories in this regard, which we address later in this chapter.

8. *Self-preservation*. Heide (1992) describes a number of factors in cases of parricide that suggest that the child kills as a means of self-protection or preservation. A fear of violence from the parent, escalating violence in the home, a feeling of helplessness, and an inability to escape threaten the survival of the child. Murder as a defensive act has been adjudicated in various ways, occasionally charged as murder, sometimes as involuntary manslaughter, or even under lesser charges depending on the state, the age of the child, and public pressure. A review of case reports by Ewing (1990) suggests that self-preservation is also a significant factor in extrafamilial murder.

9. *Self-determination*. The right of individuals to determine how they should live their lives becomes an increasingly important issue as children reach adolescence. Homicide as a result of conflict between parents and children regarding privileges, rules, and regulations is significant in parricides, but it is much less frequent in preteens.

The process of establishing the right to self-determination is deeply imbedded in the developmental process, with the family central in this. Ideally, self-determination is learned through demonstrations of achievement and competence. In many families issues of control block any attempt by the child to experience self-determination. In dysfunctional families inconsistency and variability may reduce the child's opportunity to experience self-determination and begin the conflicts resulting in violence by late preteens and adolescence.

10. *Social order*. In Thomas's description of the principle of social order, he emphasizes the concept of harmony with others in order to maintain solidarity, positive relationships, and social order. This appears to require appropriate models of behavior within the family and within the community. As described by Garbarino (1992), Heide (1992), and Samenow (1989), the disharmony in the families and communities of violent child offenders reflects a lack of concern for the importance of a regard for "the greater good." Instead, what is seen in juvenile murderers is egocentricity, a desire for immediate gratification, and a disregard or lack of awareness of the rules of

society. Concern for social order is acquired early in the developmental process. Failure to incorporate this value begins a pattern of self-serving behaviors and provides fertile ground for the modal diagnosis of antisocial personality seen in child murderers.

Modifying each of these moral principles are factors related to the learning process. The most relevant of these we highlighted (for a more complete list see Thomas, 1997). These values appear quite early in the developmental process, and their absence in even preteen murderers is regarded as significant. Factors such as age, ability to determine right or wrong regarding one's behavior, group or gang membership, and intent may modify universal moral principles. Even in normal development, acquisition and modification occur over many years. Whether awareness of consequences is significant in affecting the behavior of preteens is questionable. Recent incidents involving older preteens suggest that the preteens never considered the consequence of their actions. Rather, anger and resentment appear to have been the motive force.

In our view these represent the salient moral issues and principles affecting the behavior of children and are specifically relevant to those children who have committed murder. In the following section we will examine the theoretical approaches psychologists use to explain how moral judgments are formed and how they develop.

THEORETICAL APPROACHES TO MORAL DEVELOPMENT

In this section we will discuss four theoretical approaches to understanding moral development and consider the issues raised in our discussion of Thomas's approach. First and best known is the work of Piaget, extended and expanded by Kohlberg, which has been described as a *cognitive developmental approach*. Second is the *psychoanalytic approach*, which has had a number of contributors and has been influential in shaping approaches, at least historically. Third is the *behavioral approach*, which involves social learning and shaping. A fourth approach, suggested by Eisenberg and Murphy (1995) and developed by Lepper (1983) is based on the attributions children make regarding their behavior and motivations, and how the attributions in turn shape moral values and behavior. This is the *attributional approach*. We will attempt to amplify the aspects of each theory as it relates to children who murder but we will also address issues as they relate to all children.

Cognitive Developmental Approaches

In examining cognitive developmental approaches to moral development, two names are most prominent: Piaget and Kohlberg. Their approaches focus on stages of moral development, with Kohlberg's theories more recent and sophisticated than those of Piaget.

Piaget

In Piaget's approach the child goes through three stages preceded by the premoral period, occurring in the first five years and marked by a lack of awareness and understanding of the moral rules of society. The first stage, typically found in children between 6 and 10 years of age, is described as heteronomous morality or moral realism. This is marked by the view that moral rules are absolute and inflexible, with authority figures in unquestioned control. Violations of rules demand punishment. Extenuation and special circumstances play little or no role in the child's view. For normal children the view is of a just world. It is less clear, however, that children who murder share a worldview in which others are fair, caring, or considerate.

For Piaget, the older preteen reaches the stage of moral relativism or autonomous morality. This second stage occurs for most children by age 10 or 11. Rules become less rigid, with special circumstances and individual needs resulting in an abridging or modifying of the rules. A child may acknowledge that a violent act was wrong but feel justified by the fact that "he hit me first."

The intent of the actor now plays a significant role in judgments regarding the seriousness of an act and the level and type of punishment to be applied. Evaluators of Piaget's approach feel that although he underestimated the complexity and moral capacities of children, many of his observations are important in understanding children in Western cultures. He recognized the importance of intelligence and cognitive skills in advancing moral development. Later researchers found that children were often much more discriminating in their judgments than Piaget imagined. Even young children, for example, made distinctions between moral rules such as lying or stealing and social-conventional rules such as, not saying please. Older children in the heteronomous stage (6–10), though ordinarily respecting adult authority regarding moral issues, may question parental decisions that impinge on their personal space.

Piaget proposed a third phase of moral development, namely, moral relativisim or autonomous morality, in which the child develops an understanding of the arbitrary nature of rules and begins to see that these rules are open to question and challenge. Context and circumstance allow the modification of what for the younger child had been absolute rules. Punishment for transgressions also undergoes modification. Punishment is adjusted to fit the offense. Subsequent changes in moral growth occur through a combination of experience and cognitive growth.

Piaget saw parents as the primary source of the child's learning moral principles. He also spoke to factors that slow or impede this development, especially when a child is faced with authoritarian, dogmatic parental attitudes. He included four factors as determinants of moral development: inherited potential, environmental experiences, social transmission (social learning), and a balance between these areas that he called *equilibration*. Because Piaget focused primarily on the early stages of development, the preteen years, it remained for Kohlberg to extend the upper levels of moral development.

Kohlberg's Approach

Kohlberg (1984) accepted Piaget's position of discrete and discontinuous stages in moral development. His approach, however, differed in several important aspects. First, unlike Piaget he saw moral development continuing to evolve through adolescence and the early adult years rather than ending development in the preteen years. He also described three stages of development each consisting of two levels. Each stage is viewed as building on the previous stages with higher levels (of reasoning) requiring additional cognitive abilities.

Underlying these stages and modifying them are, according to Thomas (1997), "(a) the individuals level of logical reasoning, (b) motivation, (c) opportunities to assume social roles, and (d) the dominant justice structure of the social groups and institutions with which the individual interact." Kohlberg's stages and levels are as follows:

Level 1: Preconventional Morality. In this earliest stage the child has not internalized moral values, and responses are in reaction to rules imposed by authority figures who control rewards and punishments.

Stage 1. The child at this point is highly egocentric. Obedience to authority is to avoid punishment.

Stage 2. Instrumental hedonism. The child's moral behavior is to conform in order to receive reward or reach a desired goal. The child may respond to the needs of others, but behavior follows a pattern of doing for others in the expectation of personal gain.

Level 2: Conventional Morality. The maintenance of social order and approval from others is the dominant theme of this level. Added to material gain and punishment are verbal rewards (praise) and punishment (blame). The rights of others play a significant role in moral judgments.

Stage 3. In this stage the child seeks approval from others. Being regarded as "good" by others is the prime motivating force.

Stage 4. In stage 4, regarded as the law-and-order phase, the child accepts a rigid interpretation of right and wrong with little or no recognition of extenuation. One obeys because it "is the law" and the law maintains social order.

Level 3: Principled (Postconventional) Morality. Persons reaching this level of moral development are able to apply rules of justice and fairness that transcend personal issues and legal authority to serve the needs of individuals and society.

Stage 5. Democratically accepted law plays a major role in this stage. Laws express the will of the majority, and those laws that serve human rights should be followed. Conversely, those that do not serve these ends are worthy of dissent.

Stage 6. Principles of Conscience. This highest level of morality involves the development in the individual of a personal set of ethical principles based on universal principles of ethics and justice and consideration of the rights of all.

Much if not all observable behavior of children who murder is at the lowest levels (level 1) of moral development, where little or no internalization of moral values has occurred. One could conceive of a situation in which murder occurs as the result of an altruistic motive to save a mother (or father) and siblings. This is reported in the literature (Heide, 1992) but is rare.

Like Piaget's theories, Kohlberg's work has been extensively examined and described. Even his harshest critics acknowledge the importance of his contributions. Although not accepting the "invariance" of stages, they agree that sequential stages do describe much of observed moral development with age correlated with level of moral reasoning and cognitive development. Kohlberg recognized the importance of social experience through peer interactions, family education, and cultural experiences affecting and modifying moral development. Gilligan (1982) has stressed gender differences in modifying perceptions and responses.

Of greatest importance is to determine whether there exists a relationship between moral development (or lack there of) and criminal behavior, especially that involving aggression and violence. Without indication of some connection, there is little reason to conceptualize moral development as a predictor. Instead, more investigative effort could be placed on parental and environmental factors. In our view, although limited or impaired moral judgment may be the result of parental and environmental deficits, it may well represent a key element in determining whether children will act homicidally or divert their anger to a less violent level. Can children who reach a level of regard for the rights of others suspend this value and act violently? Several early studies using Kohlberg's model connected moral reasoning with criminality and delinquency (Rest, 1997; Blasi, 1980; Jennings, Kilkenny, & Kohlberg, 1983). More recently studies by Palmer and Hollin (1998) Gibbs, Basinger, and Fuller (1992), and Eisenberg and Murphy (1995) have provided additional support for deficits in moral reasoning correlated with incidences of delinquent behavior.

The Psychoanalytic Approach

A detailed discussion of Freudian and later analytic theory seems inappropriate for this work. There are aspects of analytic theory that can, however, be offered to explain the behavior of children who murder and those whose violence suggests murderous potential. Although direct research evidence is lacking in support of analytic percepts, the wealth of clinical observation relating to the analytic interpretation of child behavior requires examination rather than dismissal.

Of primary importance in the psychodynamic approach to child behavior is the interaction between parents and children. This interaction is not merely a process of shaping and reinforcing; rather, it is a process in which innate strivings of an aggressive and sexual nature in the child are controlled and socialized by the parents. This is accomplished by the giving and withholding of love and affection. Implicit in the psychoanalytic approach is the innate nature of the forces driving the child's behavior. Because of the renewed interest in biologically driven behaviors, psychoanalytic constructs have undergone reexamination. In this model of socialization the child learns to control his rage and sexual impulses, first out of fear (castration anxiety) and then in a more positive response by identifying with the parents and by internalizing (introjecting) their values. This process is common to other theoretical approaches and is described as social learning or modeling. The taking on of parental values is seen as forming the superego, the conscience of the child. Given the dysfunctional aspects of families of children who murder (e.g., Heide, 1992), it is possible to infer an imperfect forming of the superego, or one lacking essential components. For example, families in which violence is condoned or in which other persons are dehumanized by parental figures may detrimentally affect superego development.

Normal development in this model assumes that the child directs his or her innate sexual impulses toward the opposite-sex parent. This is thwarted however, by fears of punishment (castration, rejection) by the same-sex parent. By identifying with the same-sex parent, taking on their behaviors, beliefs, and attitudes, the threat is presumably reduced. Further, once a rival of the same-sex parent, the child turns this anger inward; this is the basis of the development of feelings of guilt. The validity of this model of normal development is in part supported by many studies in which most adults report most conflict with the same-sex parent regardless of how close they feel to the parent.

It is possible to envision a case of parricide in which a young male from an advantaged background (lacking many of the markers for violence), developmentally arrested in the oedipal stage, overly close to his mother, would murder his father for presumed (or real) abuse of the mother. Such a case would parallel the original slaying by Oedipus of his father, who in his arrogance attempted to force Oedipus from the road. Oedipus reacted with violence, refusing to yield or to bow down to his father, although he was unaware that this man was his natural father. Thus, at least by inference, we consider the dynamic explanation to have merit in such a case. Many dynamic explanations of behavior translate readily into a behavioral framework, and we will consider similar instances of murder from those perspectives. Further inferences of a dynamic nature can be made in the instances of suicide when reading Heide's work on parricide. Although Heide (1992) does not present dynamic interpretations of cases, examination of the historical data presented can be recast in that form.

How valuable to our purposes is the psychoanalytic approach? As with the other approaches to be described, it merely provides a conceptual framework within which to operate. No single theoretical approach is built solidly on research establishing clear cause-and-effect relationships.

The most fruitful of the psychoanalytically based approaches has been the work on attachment. This combines analytic theory as presented by Bowlby (1988) with strong supporting research by developmental psychologists and psychiatrists, especially the work of Ainsworth, Sroufe, Rutter, and Main. They have clearly established a relationship between adjustment and the type and degree of attachment between parent (or caregiver) and child. Four basic patterns of attachment have been described: secure, resistant, avoidant, and disorganized; these patterns have also been (1) described by Bartholomew and Horowitz (1991) as Secure, preoccupied (resistant) and (2) Dismissing (avoidant) and fearful (disorganized). Attachment style in children who commit murder and other violent acts has yet to be established, although such a style will almost certainly be found. Data from child murderers strongly emphasize the dysfunctional and unsupportive family as part of their developmental pattern.

When applied to children who murder (or even to today's children in general), psychoanalytic theory lacks an adequate conceptual framework for explaining moral development in cases of single-parent families, issues related to divorce, geographic mobility, and both parents working outside the home, as well as other issues unique to contemporary society. Lacking normal oedipal conflicts, do children today lack adequate superego development? More importantly, can children raised in a single-parent environment learn to control their aggressive impulses adequately or are they more likely to act out aggressive impulses and thus be more likely to commit murder? Modification of psychoanalytic theory developed in the strong and stable patriarchal system of the Victorian era has occurred slowly, despite efforts of neo-Freudians such as Karen Horney and Alfred Adler, who focused on the family and the environment in explaining the formation of children's behavior. Contemporary psychoanalytic writers have incorporated various aspects of social learning and behavioral constructs, but a comprehensive theory has yet to emerge although dynamically based attachment theorists should provide one in the near future.

Behavioral Approaches

Chief among the behavioral approaches to moral development is social learning or modeling and shaping through the giving or the withholding of reinforcement. In social learning, moral development, as with other learned behaviors, occurs as the result of observing the behavior of others, observing the rewards and punishments befalling the actor, incorporating those behaviors in one's behavioral repertoire through imitation. Although in many ways similar to identification in psychoanalytic approaches, social learning approaches rely much more heavily on the notion of reinforcement and punishment. For psychoanalytic theory, the chief behavior model is a controlling of active impulses. For social learning, it is a process of shaping a pliable and more passive organism through external forces, primarily the parents.

Parents do not represent the only source of this learning, however. The child draws on many sources and is shaped not only by reinforcement, its withdrawal and punishment, but also by the promise of reinforcement or the fear of disapproval and punishment. The child learns with some difficulty that certain responses, available to older siblings and adults, may not be permitted. Understanding age-related privilege is a difficult concept to incorporate that often serves as a source of conflict in the home, in school, and in the community.

The process whereby externally imposed moral principles are internalized self-sanctions (a behavioral description of the conscience or superego) is less clear. In the former instance parents and others impose social sanctions (e.g., disapproval, restrictions, or isolation). In the case of self-imposed sanctions children behave morally because doing so results in self-satisfaction. Failure to do so results in negative self-evaluation. It is not clear from present behavioral theory whether this follows a traditional learning acquisition model or how the imposed behavior is taken on to form the self-sanctioning and self-regulatory system in the morally developing child. Also unclear are what factors determine how the child may selectively incorporate moral principles—accepting some, yet ignoring others.

All approaches generally agree on the importance of parents and other high-contact persons in the child's life, since they are the source of the greatest amount of information to be learned. Schools may provide some of this learning, but the moral guides to behavior (e.g., the 12 discussed earlier in this chapter) are assumed to be present when the child enters school. Peer relationships may modify and abridge moral values, but in normal children these values are present by the time children have access to peer social groups.

A significant disparity between the behavioral approach as presented by Bandura and the cognitive developmental approach represented by Kohlberg is the question of continuity of moral developmental stages. In Kohlberg's view there exist progressive stages of moral development, which is virtually invariant. The child's thinking about moral issues evolves, with each new stage replacing earlier and more primitive levels of reasoning. Growth occurs successively through each stage in order, although a child's moral thought may become arrested at any of the levels. The child's regression to earlier decision-making processes is interpreted as "transitional disequilibrium," rather than as a refutation of the stage theory.

Bandura (1991) rejects the concept of discontinuous stages. He sees greater variability and contextual differences in moral judgments in which persons may exhibit markedly different levels of moral development. Individuals do not abandon earlier levels of moral development when they are able to demonstrate a higher level or stage. Instead, the earlier patterns remain, and under stress or extreme circumstances they may become the dominant response. As we have indicated, a child may in one situation show strong loyalty and selfless sacrifice for friends or family, yet in another situation he or she may commit murder when angered. These represent two very different developmental levels, but they do not appear inconsistent when moral behavior is modified through emotion. Thomas (1997) describes five modifiers that can alter the level of moral development in the individual: needs and drives, identified options, available alternative responses, likely consequences, and feasibility. Again, the level of arousal plays a significant role. Judgments under stress (arousal) generally follow the Yerkes-Dotson U-shaped function in which under conditions of high arousal individual judgments become limited or narrowed and the ability to recognize and consider options other than violence (and murder) may be overlooked or ignored.

Eisenberg and Murphy's Attributional Approach

Nancy Eisenberg and Bridget Murphy (1995) have carefully examined existing theories and supporting research and found important contributions from all. They advocate research to expand our understanding of the attributions of children, how they make inferences about their own motivations and moral decisions, and how these attributions influence internalization of moral values and behaviors.

Hoffman (1988) and Lepper (1983) have extensively researched how the child moves from the initially imposed external moral values from parents and others to an internalized and personal set of moral principles. Internalization is fostered by techniques used in disciplinary situations that may create arousal (but not anger) and are instructive and informative. Specifically, these training opportunities allow the child to process information and focus on consequences of the behavior in question, rather than on the parent as disciplinarian. Lepper (1983) adds the potential for some small choice for the child in the decision process, making suggestions rather than arbitrary statements, and modeling desired responses. Under these circumstances the child is open to internalizing parental messages. In contrasts, punishment and withholding of affection are viewed as blocks to internalization.

Eisenberg and Murphy have concentrated their efforts on developing an effective working model of children's moral development and moral behavior beyond presently existing theories. They recognize the importance of the parents' role in the child's moral development and responses to other persons. Unlike behavioral approaches, which describe children as "passive recipients of moral values," Eisenberg and Murphy's attributional approach finds support for the position that children are active and selective participants in the acquisition of moral values. What emerges as the child's moral values are the result of an interactive process (primarily with parents) modified by cognitions, temperament, and contextual perceptions of parent and child.

In their summary Eisenberg and Murphy (1995) point out several limitations of current theory: (1) prosocial behaviors are better understood than behaviors that violate moral values; (2) the role of mothers is more studied than that of fathers; and (3) middle-class white children are the basis of most research. Despite these limitations, they conclude, "moral children" have prosocial parental models who are emotionally warm and supporting, who use a reasoned rather than a passive approach, and who permit children to share in the family decision process with moral issues. Through their actions these parental models promote the internalizing of moral values, stressing concern and caring about others.

CONCLUSIONS

The act of murder represents the lowest level of moral development, whether by regression to an earlier or stage, or through failure to reach a level in which the rights of others are given consideration. The actions of most preteen murderers are marked by anger, impulsivity, revenge, dehumanization, and self-serving motives. Awareness of the implications of their act and the likely consequences are often completely absent in the preteen murderer. In rare instances where the act was one of self-protection or protection for an abused parent or siblings, the moral level is less clear. Does the murder represent a desperate act for the good of society and family (a possible Kohlberg stage 5), or is it a more primitive response? Certainly when coached by defense lawyers, other juvenile offenders, or even counselors, the child may express the highest motives. It is difficult for the observer to determine whether the action was based on empathic or altruistic motives or whether the act was self-serving and amoral or immoral.

Many questions remain unanswered. Research on the acquisition of moral behaviors and their place in the developmental process is in its infancy even though it has been the focus of several researchers for many years. The relationship between moral development and violence is even less developed and understood. Genetic advantages and limitations to cognitive development and their role in violent behavior have been the subject of much speculation but limited supported findings. Future research should not only focus on a deficit approach in seeking what is wrong but also assess why some children have learned to make prosocial responses, even those who may reside in dysfunctional environments.

In this chapter we have not attempted to present a complete picture of the many dimensions of moral development. Our goal has been to describe what we feel is a significant but often overlooked aspect of deficit in the behavior and cognitions of violent children. Further, we believe fuller understanding of moral values and their acquisition will provide additional tools for the professional involved in the assessment, treatment, and rehabilitation of violent and murderous children.

Chapter 6

The Changing Family

The family has undergone dramatic change over the past 30 years. Data gathered from various services such as U.S. Bureau of the Census and the Department of Labor and from a variety of authors clearly document this transformation. For example, the latest census statistics show an increased number of females in the workforce, with over half of married women with children under age 6 working outside the home, as compared with 12% in 1950; a high divorce rate, with up to half of present marriages ending in divorce and resulting in single-parent families; increased numbers of unmarried parents; and an astonishing estimate indicating that 60% of children born in the 1980s and 1990s will experience a period in which they will be part of a single-parent family. Each change in the nature and structure of the family has potential for reducing parental control and parents' awareness of their children's activities, resulting in increased risk for delinquency. Given these changes in the family, approaches and interventions to curb, control, or prevent delinquency and violence require reexamination and revision.

Simplistic solutions that call for a restoration of family values and enduring two-parent relationships represent an ideal, what must be an impossible dream. The once-supportive extended family no longer exists for many families, and responsibility resides in increasing numbers on single parents. Even intact families are experiencing stress; many have both parents working outside the home, thus limiting the effectiveness of even dedicated parents. Are we suggesting that we abandon efforts to restore the family? Of course not. Restoring the family to its former role and function would, however, require adequate training and education for marriage and parenting, adequate and positive role models, extensive community and family support systems to aid the family and the marriage, and the teaching of moral values emphasizing empathy, compassion, and caring for others. Unfortunately, the means for achieving each of these desired goals are largely lacking. Understanding some of the changes that have occurred in the family may, however, guide us toward solutions or remedies designed to reduce or prevent violence in juveniles.

It is important to emphasize that changes in the family are not limited to those that relegate the family caretaker status. Other factors reported as affecting the family include increased urbanization, population mobility, and declining affordable housing for poorer families. Perhaps most significant, the family has been affected by a decline in the sense of community, where once the community operated as part of an extended family, supporting parents in their supervision and regulation of the behavior of the neighborhood children.

The range of societal ills cited as caused by changes in the family today has increased as compared with earlier generations: Not only are there increases in the incidence of juvenile crime, especially increases in violence, but also though to be the result of changes in the family are poor school performance, low self-esteem, a lack of empathy and concern for others, increases in the use of drugs and alcohol, and gang membership. In this chapter we will offer comparisons and commentary on how the family has changed in this century, identifying what has been lost as a result of these changes and what behaviors of children in our society are a result of these changes. We will first address population changes that have dramatically altered the context and the environment in which the family functions.

POPULATION CHANGES

In 1940 America was primarily a country of farms, small towns, low mobility, and extended families. The nation's population was 132 million, with the majority living in those small towns and rural areas. The population was 151 million in 1950; 179 million in 1960; 203 million in 1970; 226 million in 1980; 248 million in 1990; with a projected 274 milion in the census of 2000, Rural and urban percentages for these years show a steady decline from a dominant agrarian culture to an urban economy. These data provide a clear statement of the massive changes occurring over this 60-year period. Doubling of the population, massive migration from rural areas to urban centers, and the expansion of small towns to urban centers are only the obvious and visible signs of change.

Farm life and industry so significant a part of our early history declined from approximately 6 million farms in 1940 to 1.9 million farms by 1990. Farm size, conversely, has grown from an average of 174 acres per farm to 469 acres by 1990 reflecting a movement from individually operated farms to multifarm corporate enterprises. In all, these shifts have resulted in 75% of our nation living in urban areas. These changes have consequences for the family, especially affecting child-rearing practices and community interactions. These take the form of crowding, restrictive use of public and private space, weakening of extended family support systems, the anonymity of large urban areas, the movement from small neighborhood schools with modest class size and an attitude of in loco parentis to huge, impersonal school systems with rigid structure and an erosion of supporting enriching activities and their buffering effects for some children. These population changes have been accompanied by other major changes such as media impact and availability and the changing role of sport video games. These changes pale when compared with the growing influence and impact of the internet. Largely unregulated, the internet provides easy access to pornography, chatrooms on any subject imaginable, information from cults and groups, and instruction on the making of bombs and other destructive devices. With access available to virtually all schoolchildren through school, libraries, and many homes, control and regulation will be necessary, but workable solutions have yet to be described, with implementation years away.

THE IMPACT OF THE MEDIA ON THE FAMILY

When America was a country of small towns and extended families, social rules, roles, and control were derived from interpersonal communication, interaction with others, and especially interaction with people who had significance in each child's life: family members, relatives, neighbors, teachers, coaches, and others. Media provided inputs in a very limited manner compared to its massive availability today. In 1940 television was not generally available and radio was limited, with much of the programming family oriented. Radio listening was often a "family" experience with multigenerational gatherings to listen to the limited offerings. Some areas were served by only one station. Even urban areas often had no more than three networks with only limited additional local programming. Children were offered a range of programs with heroic and inspirational figures (Jack Armstrong, Skippy, Tom Mix, Orphan Annie, the Lone Ranger, Buck Rogers, and many others) that combated evil and sought to do good, with limited violence and never any killing. Virtue was rewarded, but never excessively. In contrast, today radio consists of music targeted to specific tastes and interests and a few talk shows (mainly sports and special interests).

Most of the research on the impact of media on the behavior of children has been focused on television. Television is a prominent and likely target in today's society, with typical viewing time for preteens between 24 and 28 hours per week on the average and the suggestion of much higher rates for children who have limited supervision (Andreasen, 1990). Even more specific have been efforts to demonstrate that the viewing of television violence incites children to violent behavior (e.g., Hughes & Hasbrook, 1996). Like comic books, video games, and certain types of music, the search for explanations for children's violence often seek those that are external to the dynamics of the family. Television programming is extremely diverse, of variable quality, and only occasionally inspirational and informative. Popular programs with children have ranged from *Beavis and Butthead* through action cartoons extolling violence or a pondering of purchasable products, to mindless sitcoms, to high-end programs that actually do educate and stimulate, although how often children view the latter is uncertain.

This trend is not new. Each decade in our culture has found explanation for children's violence in the media. To date empirical evidence is largely lacking, regardless of the medium cited. Most arguments are the rational explanations of informed observers. These views should be examined, not discounted, by careful research. Often those views find support, but on examination some findings are counterintuitive and no effects are found. Media do not act alone. They are affected by situational and contextual factors, further modified by individual needs and dispositions. Exposure to media violence for an embittered angry child, humiliated by an insensitive, uncaring teacher or parent may result in a very different outcome than that for a child living in a supportive environment with caring peers and adults. Both children may be stimulated by the media, whether television, magazine, or newspaper. One child may be moved to an aggressive or copycat act, whereas the other may perhaps ask the question, "Why would anyone do something like that?"

Media influences in the prewar and early postwar years are even less understood than current media influences. Comic books existed then but had yet to display the unrestrained violence, murder, and explicit sexuality rampant in 1970s media. Magazines for boys and girls provided a moral tone, "regular" heroes, and the opportunity to participate with other children in their club or organization. Magazines such as *Boys Life*, *Girls Life*, and *Open Road for Boys* represented special groups (e.g., scouting), and for the child, formed a moral link with parents, schools, and the community. Even children from financially limited families could sell subscriptions to earn subscriptions, cash, and prizes for themselves.

Many of the books available to children were inspirational and full of adventurous undertakings of travel, exploration, and achievement. Series for boys and girls such as Nancy Drew, the Hardy Boys, the Motor Boat Boys, as well as many lesser-known series, provided a steady stream of reading material for the preteen and adolescent. Analysts who have examined these works have indicated that they were a significant factor in determining role-appropriate behavior for earlier generations. The range of books and magazines available to young people was more limited than it is today. Libraries, schools, and parents did much of the screening of appropriate reading material. In addition, financial constraints limited the discretionary funds available to all but a very few well-to-do children.

This is not to suggest that salacious material did not exist during the early postwar period. Such works have always been available, even in ancient Rome. For children in the early postwar period supplies were limited and quality often poor. Materials were more likely to be suggestive, rather than explicit. Those more formal works—books, particularly—were subject to censorship and banning. Possession of such material led to school expulsion and to due consequences administered by concerned parents.

What may be concluded from the many research efforts on media and violence? Many authors argue that increases in television viewing rates are coincident with or have led to a dramatic increase in violence. Other authors have found a differential effect dependent on the viewing content. For example, in their study of the impact of prosocial or violent programming, Wiegman, Kuttschreuter, and Baarda (1992) found no effect from positive programs but they did see a relationship between aggression and violent programs. When corrections were applied for level of a priori violence and intelligence, however, these effects disappeared. In our estimation this is much the case in all the research—viewing violence on TV *can* produce violent behavior, but only in certain individuals and only in certain situations or contexts.

Important? Yes. Causal? Unlikely. Contributory? Without question. The fuller answer lies more deeply in the family and the community.

SPORT AND THE FAMILY

The role of sport in the development of the child and the family's involvement presents a picture that may appear confusing and contradictory. Today most sports activities for children are highly organized with heavy adult involvement. Children are extensively arrayed with well-maintained fields, uniforms, equipment, and in many settings adults' exhortations demanding that their child must win. Family spectators and their impact on players have been described in many articles. The work of Murphy (1999) is particularly informative in its discussion of negative consequences of family overinvolvement, results of poor coaching, and the potential for harm to the less successful child. Other studies have indicated that success in sport results in a lower incidence of delinquent behavior in young males (see discussion of interventions in chapter 9).

During the depression years and those immediately following World War II, sport for preteens was seldom highly organized and only rarely had adult supervision, although adult support and approval was frequently the case. Children on their own initiative formed teams, arranged games, found vacant lots, decided on who would play each position, and even arranged for substitutions. Flawed perhaps, but that model enabled preteens to develop solutions relating to leadership and interpersonal conflict and issues, as well as to find ways to communicate effectively and above all to have fun. In today's model, rules are often imposed and controlled by adults. Children may experience little leadership opportunity or personal responsibility. Even the children's stated goals regarding sport, learning new skills, having fun, and being with friends (Gill, Gross, and Huddleston, 1983) are often reflective of adult values: "Win at any cost" or "more playing time for my child." Though speculative, it could be argued that this reduction in opportunities to exercise personal responsibility and leadership has robbed at-risk children of opportunities to enjoy the protective power of a positive sporting experience.

VIDEO GAMES

Another suspect in the expression of violence and dehumanization of others are the current series of video games. Actually "game" does not describe the interaction. A better descriptive title would be video mortal combat, based on the actions and outcomes for many popular games favored by teens and preteens. Today's "games" are a far cry from the popular Pacman of 20 years ago, in options, complexity, and lethality.

Inferring that enjoying and playing video games exhalts violence and dehumanization seems both logical and valid. Unfortunately, evidence that this is actually the case is largely lacking. Two recent reviews (Dill & Dill, 1998; Griffiths, 1999) describe a lack of empirical support for the idea that playing video games increases violent behavior. Of 32 articles reviewed from 1992 to the present, none provided support for measurable behavioral change (more aggression) from video game play. One study (VanSchie & Wiegman, 1997) did find that extensive video game play lowered prosocial behaviors.

Without supporting data we are inclined to question those cases in which defendants blamed their actions on the influence of video games (an external explanation) rather than on some internally determined expression of rage, disappointment, or frustration. Until researchers provide this support, we may feel convinced of the negative influence of video games but lacking the evidence, cannot support this explanation.

What we are able to affirm is that the video game-addicted child spends inordinate amounts of time, energy, and money on an activity that is almost devoid of prosocial behaviors and lessens real contact with others. This activity, when coupled with the other major waking activity, television viewing, can mean that many children develop fewer social skills and prosocial values. Further, this form of isolation reduces the opportunity to practice and use the rudimentary social skills of the preteen. Without extensive practice, social behaviors remain underdeveloped, further isolating the child from peer relationships.

In the extreme, the reality experienced by the child may be the reality of the game. The behaviors experienced in the game may become the dominant skills when interacting with others. The possibility of being unable to distinguish between the game and real life is a theme exploited in several popular motion pictures, such as *Matrix* and the earlier *Tron*.

POSITIVE OUTCOMES FROM CHANGE

We would be remiss if we focused only on the negative changes that have occurred as the contemporary family has evolved. Some of these positive changes may function to lessen violence in children, others may have no impact, and yet others may have unintended negative consequences. Consider a situation in which a single parent is able through effort to attain professional training and a position with sufficient income to move her family from an area of high crime and delinquency to a "safe" neighborhood, only to have other problems arise because of excessive demands on her time. In earlier generations she might have been denied access to a profession and forced to remain in an undesirable neighborhood. All this is to say that social change presents and creates new challenges and problems that require new and creative solutions.

Ours has been a culture on the move, sidetracked only by the depression years and World War II. Positive change has been inevitable. Through advances in technology coupled with an abundance of raw materials, the culture has been transformed. Families have been able to generate a sufficient return for their labors so that not only have basic needs been met, but families can afford luxuries, vacations, education, fulfillment of some dreams, and their "place in the sun."

The process has not been easy. It has taken many generations of struggle and many battles centered on equality of opportunity (sexual, racial, and ethnic), a fair wage for services, and freedom of access. Despite areas and pockets of disadvantage in our country today—inner city areas, Appalachia, glass ceilings faced by some—the United States has never had so many well-to-do and wealthy persons as today. Current statistics indicate that there are more millionaires per capita in the United States than at any other time in history. In our early history most families were locked into a system of relative deprivation, working long hours for limited wages or facing the uncertainties of making a living through farming. Benefits that most persons today accept as their due—vacations, retirement pay, medical

care, sick leave, overtime, due process of law, and the right to file griev-
ances—were simply not available. Child labor, a continuing problem in
Third World countries, was virtually eliminated in this county early in this
century. No one has captured the essence of the destructive force of child
labor than the photographer Lewis Hine, described in *Lewis W. Hine and the
American Social Conscience* by Judith Maria Gutman (1967).

Throughout the 1920s, 1930s, 1940s, and 1950s except for the depression
years, most American families improved their lifestyles. They joined clubs
and organizations in great numbers. Animal namesake organizations—Elks, Eagles, Lions—and others such as the Masons, Oddfellows,
Goodfellas, and various women's clubs all provided new outlets for the
family, though not at the expense of the family. By the 1970s their influence
waned, and today these clubs are found in few communities. Some no longer exist. Even strong patriotic groups like the Veterans of Foreign Wars
(VFW) and the American Legion are closing their doors from a lack of interest and support.

What has been the cost to the family of these changes? The major effect
has been the removal of organizational support of family and community
values. Although churches still provide that function, in earlier times
church was just one part of a network of prosocially directed activities to
which most families subscribed, especially in very small towns and rural
areas. The social clubs have been supersceded or replaced by a complexity
of services, events, and activities made possible by our increasingly affluent society, but not for all. The gap between the advantaged and disadvantaged has been publicized and discussed in the media, with income levels,
housing, health care, and educational opportunity markedly different for
the haves and the have-nots.

For the affluent, activities and entertainment have become increasingly
individualized and centered within the household—multiple TV sets,
video games, and swimming pools. Other activities take place outside the
home in controlled environments: private schools, country clubs, camps,
and arranged activities, typically without the participation of the parent.
Affluence has permitted families to delegate the difficult and sometimes
onerous task of childrearing to others willing to provide services for a fee.

This model of parenting was recently underscored in Littleton, Colorado, where homicidal juveniles were able to amass weaponry, dangerous
materials, and hate literature without parental awareness, concern, or supervision. The big four factors of effective parenting include supervision,
acceptance, affection, and consistency. It appears that Littleton parents
erred on too little supervision and, if possible, too much acceptance of their
children's judgment and maturity.

Was affluence a causal factor? Only insofar as it can serve as a means for
parents to abrogate their responsibility to provide a home environment that

builds empathy, human concerns, and respect and provide the means for appropriate moral development.

For the less affluent or single-parent families the needs are the same, but the means for achieving the goals more difficult. At present the model for low-and middle-income families is for both parents to be employed. This permits an income level that provides for material goals like those of the affluent—multiple vehicles, boats, recreational sports, multiple TVs and up-scale vacations. Entertainment needs are greatly enhanced but supervision of children and their activities, which build family cohesiveness, is often reduced.

For the single parent, most often a female, meeting basic needs may require a second job, further reducing childcare and supervision. Children raised in environments of relative deprivation are at higher risk for developing many of the contributing factors to violent behavior: low self-esteem, lack of appropriate role models, poor school performance, or exclusion from certain groups or organizations based on social class or from activities because of financial limitations. These and other factors can create levels of resentment and anger that may, under stress, result in violence. Empathy and care for others is difficult to achieve when the disadvantaged child experiences rejection and neglect from peers and adults.

THE EXTENDED FAMILY

The extended family is a magnificent support system. It provides love, attention, social control, and caring and fills many needs that might otherwise go unfilled for family members. It also, at times, fills needs when they don't exist and provides controls where none are desired or needed. Several generations have experienced the decline of the extended family. This decline has resulted in the loss of undesirable and unwanted elements of family control that for generations in this culture forced those unable to tolerate them to rebel and break with the family. Unfortunately, also lost were the stabilizing controls and the long process of developing prosocial behavior in a supportive environment.

What are some of the gains to families who have moved away from the extended family? This is best answered by examining the problems faced by families who, in today's culture, remain part of extended families. These persons are often members of racial or ethnic minorities in this country who, for a variety of reasons, have maintained the extended family. Although some portions of all ethnic groups have retained an identity and a tie with their heritage, some groups have been more successful in keeping persons in their "clan." Those who have maintained their culture are most often Greek, Italian, Polish, Chinese, and a series of newer groups for India, Lebanon, Syria, and other Arab states, as well as a number of families who moved into this country as a result of American withdrawal from Vietnam.

Still undergoing culture shock individuals in the latter group have not resolved the many problems of their encounters with the American culture. The former groups, however, have been established in the United States over many generations and have firmly implanted their culture and their model of the extended family in this country. Orientals, like blacks, can attain memberships in the community at large , but their racial identity continues to limit their full participation in all cultural opportunities available to whites.

In clinical interviews, young persons who live within extended families report interference in the affairs of their nuclear family by members of the extended family. Husbands and wives report that they can not quarrel without intervention by other family members, and the rearing of their children is commented upon, corrected, or at times even usurped by senior family members. Not only do parents get into the act, but so do uncles, aunts, cousins, and older brothers and sisters. This is especially true when several families occupy the same house. In many cases informants said that those who are not under the domination of an extended family cannot appreciate the problems they face.

A major gain for the nuclear family, as compared with the extended family, is the ability for young persons to make independent decisions free from the advice, suggestions, and control of older family members. Granted, in many instances the decisions made by the group or by a patriarch represent better decisions. This does not, however, replace the desire on the part of many young to "make it on their own" in the best American tradition. Often, in our culture, individuals look forward to the right to make their own mistakes. They are willing to risk limited success or even failure, but they reserve the right to do it on their own. This desire is seen even in the very young. One should not confuse this desire for independence with the independence sought by unregulated and unsupervised children lacking in social awareness and moral values.

Children from healthy extended families are beneficiaries of a strong moral climate stressing family and cultural values. Their seeking independence from family controls is not a sign of rebellion and disregard for cultural rules and standards. Rather, it is indicative of their desire to make their own judgments and decisions as adults. It is not surprising that children from these extended family models have consistently been underrepresented in all crime statistics.

Independence from extended family control has had far-reaching effects. With the loss of support from of the larger family, the nuclear family has faced increased demands for maintaining order and control of the children. When coupled with the previously mentioned changes—namely both parents being employed, single-parent families, a gap in childcare and child-rearing—problems have developed that have to date resulted in no successful solutions for many children at risk. We must emphasize that being at risk is not limited to socially and economically disadvantaged children but extends through all socioeconomic levels. In our discussion of the losses to the child from changes in the family, we learn that the training, moral development, and social supports that once shaped the behavior of most children in positive and prosocial directions have been eroded, neglected, and often given over to external sources unable or incapable of providing the level of coherence necessary to shape the child or to provide the consistency and caring for their external efforts to be successful.

LOSS OF THE EXTENDED FAMILY

In addition, as previously mentioned, children raised in the nuclear family geographically distanced from extended family influences and family friends often experience greater personal freedom in decision making and have unsupervised time. This has resulted in more time spent watching TV, playing video games, and "hanging out." It has also reduced the time spent by adults in instructing, shaping, and modifying the behavior of children to conform to the requirements of the family and society. Drawing heavily on peers for their behavioral models, children in today's nuclear families lack a source of the wisdom of experience, and perhaps most important, their decisions and judgments are more often determined by impulse and immediate need rather than experience. Behavioral consequences may be dimly perceived or lacking entirely. For example, young murderers have been reported as having little or no understanding of the finality of death. Children who are members of a multigenerational extended family learn early of death and its finality. One of the authors, for example, grew up in an extended family, learning at age 3 that Grandpa was gone and would not return. Was death well understood? Unlikely. What was understood was the loss and the finality of that loss. Witnessing the grief of family members over a period of time made an undeniable impression, vivid to this day. In contrast, children today report little experience with many aspects of functioning in the context of an extended family, its problems and wisdom gained from a multiplicity of caring relatives.

MOBILITY

In today's highly mobile population families do not often have a clear identification with any one community. Even when families claims ties to a specific metropolitan areas of the country, they may relate only to a highly encapsulated suburb or even a ghetto. They may have only limited involvement or recognition of the total community. Prime examples are the suburbs occupied by upper-middle-class, managerial, or professional persons. In many instances they and their families will live in the suburban community (which may be 20 to 30 miles from downtown) for a period of two to four years, moving on after that time to another community that is much the same in every respect, with only the names and addresses changed. When interviewed, these suburban gypsies speak of living in an urban area, but they have no roots, no family, and no sense of connection to these communities. This phenomenon describes an extremely high percentage of middle-class people in our country and may be seen in the deadly reality of suburbs such as Littleton, Colorado.

Many such communities lack supporting persons with a significant concern for members of other families. These communities are frequently located thousands of miles from family members who might be able to assist and provide such support to their isolated relatives. With little investment in a community they know they will leave, parents and children alike are forced to depend increasingly on the media; on external, rather impersonal support systems such as country clubs and temporary social groups; and on movies and commercial recreational activities. With less-advantaged families the problems are similar, though further complicated by inadequate housing and poverty. As we have seen in the works of Sampson, Elliott, and others, problems are even more difficult to deal with if resources and informal support systems are inadequate or missing.

With the decline of intimacy within communities there has been a disappearance of many venerable social institutions that once served to bring people together, to entertain them, and to enable them to renew acquaintances. They were less intense, short-term events that derived their special meaning because of the spectator's ties and links to the participants. Parades and special holding events are excellent examples of once popular activities that now occur infrequently, if at all, and then only as a symbol to special interest groups.

THE CHURCH AND THE FAMILY

The church was historically the focal point for many activities. Today only a limited number of organized churches offer a full, enriching program of church activities directed to their members. These activities, which include schooling, are provided throughout the week as well as on Sunday, with a high level of demand for participation by those who would be members. Other churches, when they have participation, have it on a much more limited basis.

We would be remiss in failing to mention countercultural and extremist groups that have sought to indoctrinate children and adults into their special beliefs, such as those headed by David Koresh at Waco or Jim Jones. Various other groups, like the Satanists, have appealed to persons feeling adrift in today's complex society. For most persons in our culture religion has always offered direction and guidance. Consider the typical activities of most churches in an earlier period of this century by focusing on one small midwestern Presbyterian church, a summary of whose activities is provided through the recollections of a businessman about his life in the small town in which he was raised.

> We had many things going on in our church all the time. Everybody went to Sunday school and, later that day, everybody went to church, including the little ones who spent most of their time wiggling and trying to whisper. We were all back at church that evening, that's when we had the young people's meeting—Christian Endeavor, I think it was called. We didn't have an evening service on Sunday because the preacher was at another church. During the week there were other things. Monday nights there were Girl Scouts, Tuesday nights Boy Scouts, Wednesday nights Family Prayer. It was not unusual to have social events, like a covered-dish supper, at least once a month, sponsored by the women of the church. Other times during the day the women got together for some of their Circle meetings. The men had a baseball team, which played in the Church League. There was also a Youth Church Baseball League, which, during the summer, took up several nights a week. There was also Bible study classes for those who were going to join the church. On top of that, about once (and sometimes twice) a year there would be a period of renewal and additional preachers would come in for what some of the other churches would call "revival meetings." We didn't call them that.

Small town churches encouraged a level of involvement that provided tremendous support to each person, whether he was part of an extended family or not. This form of nonfamily support has virtually disappeared and has not been replaced. Nowhere in our current social structure, with the exceptions noted, is there provided the closeness, the intimacy, and the emotional support of the churches of earlier times.

The function of the church for many children in earlier times was instructional and directed toward the development of prosocial behavior and moral values. This was true in both urban and rural areas, and at all economic levels. It represented a cultural ethic of concern, involvement, and responsibility. There were exceptions, of course, and delinquency was no stranger. Deviance and delinquency rarely went unnoticed, however, and were even more rarely ignored. The growth of affluence, urbanization, mobility, and the disappearance of many social organizations has led to the lower levels of community involvement and the care and monitoring of the young.

PARENTING

In our discussion thus far we have focused on the cultural context of the family and changes that have occurred affecting the structure and function of the family of today. Other issues relating to the family are also highly significant in producing delinquent and violent children. These relate to parenting styles and the presence or absence of meaningful and secure attachments. (To treat both topics in appropriate depth sufficient to set forth guidelines for effective parenting is beyond the scope of this work. Excellent research based publications are available for those who would seek greater understanding.) For our purposes we would note that researchers have identified those factors that enhance family stability, lessen the possibility of delinquency, and aid in the development of prosocial behavior. Early research by Maccoby and Martin (1983) led to their conclusion that two dimensions were of significance in effective familial parenting: parental warmth and parental control. Warmth is on a warmth-hostility continuum with the desired parental response one of affection, attention, and encouragement. This is contrasted with parents who are hostile and unresponsive, neglectful, and punitive, with little display of caring or love.

The other dimension relates to parental control, with the least effective approach being one of overrestriction, excessive rules, and punishment or fear of punishment playing an important role. At the other extreme overly permissive parenting fails to provide the support and structure necessary for the development of appropriate social behavior. Closely related to this dimension has been Baumrind's (1971) work on parenting style, which contrasts authoritarian, authoritative, and permissive approaches with a desired balance effected most often by the authoritative approach. Unlike the other two, the authoritative parent provides caring, control, and structure but with flexibility allowing the child selected choices and freedoms.

Familial parenting patterns lead to marked differences in the types of attachment formed by the child to their caregiver. This area offers promise of additional insights into the parenting styles, which may inhibit or foster violence in children. However, research efforts to date have not demonstrated a clear look between attachment style and violence, though logic suggests that children who are secure in the attachment to caregivers would be unlikely coordinates for violence. More likely those children who avoid or resist primary attachments to caregivers might well lack concern and empathy for others and, under provocation, exhibit a violent response.

SUMMARY

Are there clear and affirmative qualities that families should have to prevent delinquency and violence? We say yes, recognizing that there are a number of possible variations of intact nuclear families, extended families, blended families, and single-parent families that contain the necessary elements for the successful raising of nonviolent, nondelinquent children. These qualities or attitudes, when bolstered by communities rich in formal and informal support systems in which the child is encouraged to participate, provide an environment that affords protection, nurturance, and a climate for personal growth. Both aspects must be present: a strong family support system in an environment rich in formal and informal social controls. Lacking either places the child in a high-risk category.

As we have indicated in this chapter as well as in the chapter on prevention, research has shown that the financial means of the family is not the critical variable. Children of wealth who lack appropriate family controls and guidance and live in a community low in cohesion with few formal or informal controls may be as deadly as the economically poor community that also lacks appropriate controls. Littleton, Colorado, may represent a prime example of a wealthy suburban community relatively low in family-imposed controls and little sense of community and organized support systems.

We have examined the advantages and perils of single-parent families, as well as the advantages and disadvantages of multigenerational families (extended families). We have also observed changes occasioned by shifts in available occupations, population growth, and developing technology. Despite cultural change, economic changes, and population growth, nine preeminent factors remain necessary for fostering healthy, nonviolent children and adolescents. Without ranking in order of importance, they are

1. The absence of experienced or observed family violence;
2. The absence of abuse—physical, verbal, or sexual;
3. Consistent, firm, fair, loving parental care;
4. Absence of drug and alcohol abuse by parent or parents;
5. Absence of mental illness or disturbance in parents;
6. Relatively stable and supportive home environment;
7. Relatively stable and supportive community environment;
8. Encouragement and provision for social participation and interaction;
9. Availability of appropriate and stable role models.

Many if not all supportive behaviors of the violent child stem from defects or deficits in those nine requirements for successful adjustment. Although not guaranteed to produce violence and murder, absence of these supports places a child at risk and creates a need for appropriate interventions.

PART III

Assessment and Interventions

Chapter 7

Assessment

Adolescent murderers are referred with increasing frequency to criminal court. Where once waiving to adult court procedures occurred only rarely in the past, there has been a major shift in policy regarding murder. Although the impact has centered on adolescents, it has carried over to preteens as well.

The mandate of juvenile courts and instructions was historically one of rehabilitation and restoration to society. Miranda rights, due process, legal representation, and jury trials were not deemed necessary as the court sought to fulfill these goals. Children who murder now face a society and court system expressing a "zero tolerance" philosophy and a desire for accountability that requires penalties for serious crimes similar to those determined for adult offenders. To date no preteens waived to criminal court have been sentenced to death. Adolescents as young as 17 years of age are currently awaiting execution, and in a recent case a young person who committed murder at 15 was executed.

The assessment process is difficult with adolescents. It presents even greater difficulties when the juvenile is a preteen. Heide (1992), Grisso (1998), Hoge and Andrews (1996), and Sattler (1998) present extensive and valuable information on the techniques, resources, and issues when assessing juveniles. Although much of their presentation is focused on adolescent offenders, many of the techniques and issues also apply to preteen murderers. We will address these similarities and differences in our discussion.

Assessment is essential in the process of determining appropriate courses of action in dealing with child murderers. Ideally, information gained from the assessment includes personality measures; intellectual functioning; information on functioning in the home, school, and community; health states; and physical, moral, and social development.

There are three major considerations in the assessment of children, and each consideration has unique features and complications. The first assessment issue is the establishment of the child's competence. This involves the competence to waive Miranda rights, the competence to stand trial (related to intellect, emotional condition, and developmental maturity), and level of competence at the time of the murder. A second assessment concern is the potential for further harm to others (risk assessment), and the third area is the ability to benefit from treatment and to be rehabilitated (or habilitated).

It is not our intent to provide a comprehensive statement on assessment of all juveniles. We will focus on preteens and provide references to extended sources that will provide the evaluator with more detailed procedural information. For extended coverage the reader is referred to the previously mentioned sources (Heide, 1992; Grisso, 1998; Hoge & Andrews, 1996; and Sattler, 1998).

ASSESSING COMPETENCE

In competency determinations with adolescents, a major issue is the waiver of Miranda rights. This focuses on competency to understand all the issues relating to the criminal act and to make the appropriate self-protective responses when facing pressures in the inquiry by police officers. Officials dealing with preteens have assumed that such young offenders are not competent to make the necessary judgements to waive their rights to remain silent and to have counsel present. As we have indicated in chapter 4, these assumptions no longer apply in the cases of preteens who commit serious offenses.

Preteen vulnerability to coercion and suggestion are well documented, and examples abound of preteen confessions discounted by courts, contested by defense lawyers, and contradicted by subsequent evidence. Should this issue arise, the psychologist's role becomes one of establishing the child's competency to waive rights. Grisso (1998) provides a comprehensive description of the appropriate course of evaluation and assessment necessary to provide answers to this question. Grisso points out that children under 12 are rarely judged to be competent to waive their rights. Given the seriousness of their offense, murder, pressure to obtain answers by law enforcement driven by pressure from the community and the press might permit waiving of rights even in the case of younger children.

In assessing both competencies to waive Miranda rights and to stand trial, Grisso (1998) provides the examiner with detailed and clear procedural instructions for each aspect of these competency issues. A number of measures are available to the examiner attempting to assess the juvenile's understanding of Miranda: the Comprehension of Miranda Rights (CMR), the Comprehension of Miranda Rights-Recognition (CMR-R), the Comprehension of Miranda Vocabulary (CVM) and the Function of Rights in Investigation (FRI). Although instruments have been widely used for juvenile offenders as young as 12, those 14 and younger perform significantly poorer on these measures (Grisso, 1988). The preteens' inability to understand what is requested of them in order to waive rights underscores Grisso's point that their tests are inappropriate for this age group.

Both Grisso (1998) and Hoge and Andrews (1996) provide procedures and instruments useful in assessing competence to stand trial. In most instances the techniques and measures are the same for all competency issues whether the individual is a child or an adolescent. The questions to be answered often differ, however, because of language and cognitive differences between younger and older juveniles.

Grisso describes four components of both Miranda and competence evaluative inquiries: the child's level of functioning, causal factors, the child's interactions with others, and the child's judgmental decisions (moral, social, and cognitive). In the case of Miranda the questions to be answered are the juvenile's understanding and appreciation of the warnings; the juvenile's ability to exercise free choice regarding the waiver; and in the cases of obtained confessions, the reliability of the data. For competency to stand trial, additional questions consider whether the juvenile understands the charges and the potential consequences, understands the trial process, possesses the ability to work with the attorney or advocate assisting in preparing a defense, and has the ability to function in the courtroom (e.g., to testify, to deal with the stress, and to exhibit behavioral constraints).

Several aspects of the competency process require mention. Malingering and other attempts to deceive the examiner are noted most often in older juveniles. Preteens are often transparent in their attempts to exaggerate or conceal symptoms. Although lying may come easily and naturally to some, other offenders consciously and awkwardly feign symptoms of mental illness or even try to cover pathological ideas and thought processes, and these deceptions should be recognized by all but the naive or inexperienced examiner.

During training, graduate students assessing incarcerated delinquents seldom question statements made by juvenile offenders. Our graduate training facility has placed many of our students in a juvenile correctional facility at which graduates averaged three or four evaluations of juveniles per week for one year and occasionally a second year as well. Initial problems in the training of these students most often occurred in their uncritical acceptance of the juveniles' statements, usually rich in denial and external-ization of responsibility. After several evaluations and the observations of similarities among the juvenile's statements, the trainees developed greater critical judgment.

Preteen offenders may attempt to present a distorted picture to the ex-aminer based on instructions from other juveniles, suggestions from friends or family, or even coaching by persons representing them (in in-stances where representation is provided or available). Lacking a fuller awareness of clinical syndromes, they are typically incapable of maintain-ing the consistency or variability of behavior necessary to effect the appear-ance of mental illness or pathology.

Although assessing the child's competence in waving Miranda rights is currently of less concern, there is little question that this will be of increas-ing importance even for the very young murderer. Court and statutory con-cern for due process has resulted in a willingness to lower the age of accountability. Grisso's (1998) work provides an excellent procedural model for the assessor. Most of his presentation is geared to the adolescent, although most issues addressed also speaks to issues relevant to the pre-teen. Assessment of the preteen presents a somewhat more difficult prob-lem because instrumentation suitable for the younger child is lacking, thus producing a deficit in predicting future behavior. In addition, as opposed to adolescents and adults, children seldom have an extended and traceable re-cord, resulting in the assessor having to rely heavily on the interview pro-cess with the child, family, and informants.

RISK ASSESSMENT

In addressing the issue of assessment of violence, Monahan (1996) pres-ents four tasks for the clinician attempting to determine level of risk: (1) achieve an understanding of relevant risk factors, (2) develop adequate methods for gathering relevant information, (3) use this to determine the level of risk, and (4) then communicate this information to the decision makers or inform others of the basis of the decision should the clinician have the decision-making responsibility. Unfortunately, no clear guide-lines exist either in the literature or in graduate training programs. Much of what exists today is the result of assessment experiences by individual cli-nicians who have then presented their experiences to others (e.g., Grisso, 1998). The difficulties recognized for risk assessment of adults and adoles-cents and documented in Borum, Otto, and Golding (1993), Borum (1996), and Monahan (1996) are multiplied when attempting to assess risk in pre-teens.

When assessing adults, the evaluator has clear guidelines as defined in the California Supreme Court decision in the case of *Tarasoff vs. the Regents of the University of California* (1976). This requires that a counselor (and presumably an evaluator) must protect third parties against patient violence. As expressed, this requires action once a therapist has established under applicable standards that a serious danger of violence to others exists. For our population it is difficult to perceive a 7- or a 9-year-old as having lethal intent or possessing the capacity or knowledge to carry out a homicidal act. Yet the assessor may be confronted with children who attempted to strangle or drown younger siblings or even those who succeeded in their attempt. What techniques are available to determine or predict future actions by these children? What can serve to predict response to therapeutic interventions?

THE ASSESSMENT PROCESS

A complete assessment of any person—preteen, adolescent, or adult—contains a series of steps or aspects necessary if meaningful insights are to be reached. The absence of any of these key ingredients weakens the report and reduces the accuracy of predictions. The following component parts are those identified by forensic psychologists as essential parts of the assessment process.

PREPARATION FOR THE INTERVIEW

The assessor should be familiar with all structural aspects of the juvenile court system in the state where the assessment is to take place. Although most examiners are thoroughly familiar with their own states laws and local variations, it is not unusual in high-profile cases, those involving extreme violence or murder, for consultants to be drawn from other areas of the country.

Of extreme importance in the assessment process is access to all records on the child being evaluated. These data include academic records and evaluations, mental health evaluations, records of prior offenses, and police reports of the crime for which the child is being examined. This seems both reasonable and necessary. In many instances, whether employed by the juvenile justice system or as contract evaluators, evaluators function with less than full access to this information. In South Carolina the press for the results of psychological evaluations has at times resulted in the evaluation sessions being scheduled before all records have been received and before reports from other staff (e.g., the social worker's histories) are available. Under these conditions it is possible to provide only limited recommendations. This situation also raises ethical issues for the psychologist, especially in cases of major crimes or when serious dispositional issues arise.

THE INTERVIEW

Sattler (1998) provides an excellent primer for the beginning assessor and a refresher for those experienced persons who may over time have failed to include materials useful in the interview process. Sattler's detailed descriptions and approaches to minority issues, psychological disorders, pediatric health–related disorders, brain injury, and abuse provide excellent guidelines and suggestions for communicating interview findings. These insights are of great value to assessors at all levels. Sattler's study represents a major work in the field and is of critical importance to those who assess preteen offenders.

We cannot emphasize the interview process enough. Data gathered through this process from parents, the child, and observers represent the primary source for understanding the child's personality and social interactions. Personality measures, especially in the younger preteens, have produced disappointing results. Thus, the interview, intellectual assessment, developmental and health data, and psychophysical evidence provide most of the supporting information for treatment, risk assessment, rehabilitative possibilities, and causal inferences.

The functional goals of the interview are clear and well defined. Sattler (1998) provides a detailed description of the entire process with elaboration of the special requirements for specific populations (e.g., minority clients, children with psychological disorders, and forensic cases) in his monumental work on the clinical interview.

From the interview, these data come from the history as reported by the child and the family, the child's rapport with the examiner, behavioral observations during the evaluation that, when compared with other data, lead to the further questions to be answered through assessment of personality testing, cognitive evaluation, and measures of social and behavioral competency. The behaviors most often noted in the evaluation, often as a result of the evaluation, are distractibility, tolerance of frustration, impulsivity, level of cooperation, and demeanor (e.g., bravado, hostility, or counterdependent responses).

INTELLECTUAL ASSESSMENT

The goals for intellectual assessment of the preteen offender (as with adolescents) are to establish the present level of intellectual functioning, which is related to competency to stand trial, to understand Miranda rights, and to assist in determining what forms of intervention are likely to be effective. Further, distorted thinking, judgmental deficits, and ability to follow instructions may appear during the assessment process, at least in instances where the intellectual assessment is an interactive process between the child and the examiner (e.g., Wechsler scales and Stanford Binet).

Group tests offer limited value because they do not stand up well when challenged in court and are frequently at variance with findings of individual tests administered by fully trained professionals. Given the seriousness of the offense, group tests should serve only as further validation of functioning level determined by the individual examination.

It should also be noted that the results of individually administered tests are often unreliable. Many institutions utilize examiners who lack full professional credentials or whose formal training did not include individual intellectual assessment training. When functioning in an advocacy role, a careful searching for who performed previous examinations may reveal results and conclusions drawn by an unqualified and unlicensed person. Procedural variations such as a partial administration rather than a full-scale intellectual examination presents a further opportunity for challenge or question.

Given these concerns and limitations, intellectual assessment of preteens is most often conducted using the *Wechsler Intelligence Scale of Children—III* (WISC-III) typically used for children 6 to 16 years of age. In some instances with our population the choice may be the *Wechsler Preschool and Primary Scale of Intelligence–Revised* (WPPSI-R) or the Stanford-Binet. Many examiners utilize the *Kaufman Assessment Battery for Children* (K-ABC) and the *Peabody Picture Vocabulary Test–Revised* as primary or supplementary assessment tools.

Experienced examiners working with culturally diverse and special populations typically develop a favorite battery of measures they feel more adequately evaluate their subjects. One of the authors of this volume (Hecker) assessing subjects from the rural South from 1955 to 1964 found some tests were less culturally fair and over time developed strategies that more adequately reflected the abilities of this population.

PERSONALITY ASSESSMENT

Personality assessment involves answering essentially the same questions raised in the total assessment picture: competency to stand trial, competency to waive Miranda rights, risk to others, potential for responding to treatment, and potential for rehabilitation. Each question has a personality component, though in differing degrees. Each offers a special challenge for adequate evaluation further complicated by the age of the child and the developmental issues common to our special population.

Objective Measures

Unfortunately, of the most popular measures for examining adolescents, the Millon Adolescent Personality Inventory (Millon, Green, & Meagher, 1982), the Millon Adolescent Clinical Inventory (Millon, 1993), and the

Minnesota Multiphasic Personality Inventory–Adolescent (Butcher et al., 1992), are not suitable for assessing the preteen offender. Reading level and understanding of the questions exceed the level of virtually all preteen children. For those few who are be able to read and understand items adequately, norms are not available.

Several behavioral checklists have been widely used with positive results. The Jesness Inventory (Jesness & Wedge, 1984, 1985) and the Revised Behavior Problem Checklist (Quay & Peterson, 1987) have been used extensively in juvenile correctional facilities for classifications and assignment. Both are affected by limitations of the rater. In the case of the Jesness limitations are those of self-report. For the Quay, results are affected by the degree of sophistication and awareness of the rater. Each assessment tool, however, can enrich the assessment profile when available.

The three Achenbach scales are popular in general clinical usage and provide a multidimensional picture. These behavioral checklists are rated by the parents, the Child Behavior Checklist; by the teacher, the Child Behavior Checklist—Teacher Report Form; and by the child, Youth Self-Report (Achenbach, 1991a, b, c). As with other instruments, successful usage favors the older child, especially with self-report. The parent forms and the teacher forms have proven to be invaluable regardless of the child's age.

The Achenbach scales are especially useful because they address a series of highly relevant issues in their scales, among them ratings of thought problems, attention problems, social problems, delinquent behavior, aggressive behavior, somatic complaints, and anxious, depressed and withdrawn behaviors. Examiners seeking to establish the presence of ADHD typically include the Achenbach scales as part of their assessment battery.

Of importance also is the Eyberg Child Behavior Inventory, a 36-item inventory especially useful with conduct-disordered, acting-out children. Filled out by parents, the scale includes data from minority and low-income populations (Eyberg & Robinson, 1983). Recommended age range is 2–16 years.

Despite their limitations from the reporting source (child, parents, and school), these tests offer the best predictive measures available. When linked with evaluation results, a comprehensive and valid profile of the child emerges.

Projective Measures

Projective personality measures are more controversial. Interpretation is difficult with adults, even more complicated when exploring the responses of young children from diverse and often disadvantaged backgrounds. Proponents of projective testing list several potential benefits of this approach: (1) they present subjects with a relatively ambiguous stimuli to which there are no clear right or wrong answers; (2) they tap into the unconscious and fantasy world of the subject; and (3) they provide an enriched picture of the subject's cognitive tempo and organization and contents of thought. Opponents of projective testing cite, in the case of children, a lack of adequate norms, a lack of validity and reliability, and little predictive value except in cases when the performance is so distorted as to be obvious even to the casual observer of the impairment of the subject. In our view the major test value is as a source of ideas, hunches, and leads for further inquiry through the interview. At the very least projective materials are by their nature entertaining and engaging, making the assessment task playful and gamelike. Given the stress experienced by the murderers or violent child, projectives may be the best way to gain access.

Projective Drawings

Many assessments of children begin with drawing tasks, such as drawing a person or drawing a house, tree, and person, both of which have an extensive literature purporting to predict personality and behavior. Research studies have consistently reported low interrater reliabilities, low predictive scores, and low levels of reliability and validity (see Anastasi & Urbina, 1997, for an extended discussion of these issues). The failure of studies to find significant results were based on a variety of adult and juvenile subjects, many with stable and established patterns of behavior. Even in these studies, predictive value was lacking. It appears that with preteens, the results of drawing tests would be even less predictive.

Examiners, including the authors, frequently begin the assessment of children with a simple drawing task, typically drawing a person; a house, tree, and person; or some favored object. This serves to establish rapport with the child and to provide awareness of the child's interaction with an adult in a strange situation. The drawing often becomes the topic of initial conversation with the child. The objective scoring of the drawing of a person for intellectual level (see Goodenough & Harris, 1963) provides modest correlations with individualized intelligence tests. As a vehicle for developing a dialogue with the child, it remains a useful tool.

Questions of Fantasy and Imagination

Falling somewhere between the interview and the paper-and-pencil personality test are projective tests that require the child to supply answers to open-ended questions. Originally developed by Arthur Jersild for the structured interviewing of children and also by Carl Rogers in his Test of Personal Adjustment (1934), these questions have become part of the lore of psychology. Asking the child to give three wishes or answer the question, "If you were to go to a desert island and could take only three persons with you, who would you take?" provide interesting and occasionally revealing answers. For the assessment process these questions, as with incomplete-sentences tests (of which there are a number), provide the examiner with hunches or leads but little solid data relating to the questions of risk and competence. As with drawing tests, however, they may reduce stress and help create the feeling that the assessment procedure is a game or fun rather than an adversarial process.

Rorschach Test

In its 70+ years of use, the Rorschach has never been without controversy. Other attempts have included an alternative set of inkblots (Holtzman, 1961) and a set of cloud pictures developed by Stern. An improved and more objective scoring system for the Rorschach was introduced by Exner (1974, 1993) to offset limitations of the older Beck and Klopfer systems. However, this new system has done little to increase confidence in the Rorschach. Research studies have not produced levels of validity or interrater reliability similar to those found for more objective measures such as the MMPI or Millon. For example, the study by Greco and Cornell (1992) reported that the Rorschach could not distinguish between violent and nonviolent adolescent offenders. They did find a distinction between those children who committed homicide as part of a crime, and those whose murder involved a conflict with another person. As an ambiguous stimulus the Rorschach offers the subject an opportunity to provide content, often culturally determined: a response style involving whole or partial responses; the use of or failure to use color; the number of responses provided; the use of movement; presence or absence of humans or animals. These responses form a profile that, at least for adults, identifies rare, unusual, or unique response patterns that may be viewed as deviant when compared with the response patterns of other persons, especially those regarded as "normal."

When applied to preteens, the Rorschach appears to have even more limitations. Normative studies of children's responses to the cards have been published, but there is little evidence of predictive or diagnostic value. As was the case with drawing tasks, the Rorschach may provide interesting suggestions to the examiner but little support in the major goals in the assessment of preteen offenders.

Picture Story Projective Tests

One picture test developed 50 years ago, the Rosenzweig Picture Frustration Test (Rosenzweig, 1948), presents the child with 24 pictures in which a frustrating or anger-producing scene occurs. The child provides the verbal responses for one of the participants, usually the victim. Responses are scored as introporitive (turning blame inward), extraporitive (blaming others), or impunitive (making a neutral response). Responses using the standard directions allow the child to project what a person might say or do in the situation presented. One of the present authors found the test useful by asking the child to tell what he would actually do in the scene presented. This has provided helpful information in probing risk potential.

The Thematic Apperception Test and its variations, (e.g., the Children's Apperception Test) present a picture for which the subject creates an explanatory story, describing what is taking place, what led up to the event, and what the outcome will be. There exist many scoring and evaluative systems with somewhat similar foci. Most seek to determine the needs of the characters or the forces acting on them, their environmental pressures. The fate of the hero (or antihero) plays an important diagnostic role in this dynamically based method.

When used with children, these approaches lack meaningful norms, have little predictive validity, and show limited reliability. Younger children engage in simple card descriptions and even story productions that appear rich in content but offer limited insights into the child offender and limited in answering questions related to competency or risk. When considered in the light of research studies wherein "blind diagnoses"—those based only on written responses by a respondent with no personal contact with the rater—resulted in limited accuracy regarding characteristics of the subject. The test itself appears of limited value as a result. When coupled with the clinical interview, however, the test provides an additional behavioral observation in response to an ambiguous stimulus, which may have some value.

ASSESSING MORAL DEVELOPMENT

As indicated earlier, issues of moral behavior are central to understanding, assessing, treating, and rehabilitating the child who murders. Although many assessors and researchers acknowledge the presence or absence of appropriate moral behaviors in the offender, they make little mention of methods for assessing this area and have little discussion of it in the evaluation process. Several experienced assessors, in personal communications, said they judged the Kohlberg stages and levels of violence in children they were examining but rarely if ever used formal scales such as those developed by Jennings, Kilkenny, and Kohlberg (1983) because of their cumbersomeness, because of their inapplicability, or simply because time demands gave priority to other measures. More recently several brief scales have been developed with easy scoring procedures that offer the examiner more ready access to this information.

Index of Empathy for Children and Adolescents

Designed specifically for use with children and adolescents, the Index of Empathy for Children and Adolescents (IEC) a 22–item scale developed by Bryant (1982), is a modified version of Mehrabian and Epstein's (1972) widely used self-report measure of empathy. The IEC utilizes a dichotomous "yes" or "no" format to measure the degree to which respondents experience feelings of sadness in the presence of another's distress (e.g., "It makes me sad to see a girl who can't find anyone to play with"), anger or upset at perceived injustice (e.g., "I get upset when I see an animal being hurt"), and acceptance of or appreciation for individual differences in emotional expression (e.g., "It's hard for me to see why someone else gets upset"). Higher scores on this measure are thought to reflect greater empathy.

The IEC was refined by factor reliability analyses and has internal consistency scores that range from .68 for fourth graders up to .79 for seventh graders (Bryant, 1982). Test-retest reliability scores between .81 and .83 have been obtained for the same age range (Bryant, 1982). Overall, the IEC is identified as one of the most frequently used self-report measures of empathy in children (for a review, see Eisenberg & Miller, 1987).

The Social Reflection Measure—Short Form (SRM-SF)

Designed specifically for use with children and adolescents with limited reading and attention skills, the Social Reflection Measure—Short Form (SRM-SF) is an 11–item production measure of moral judgment (Gibbs, Basinger, & Fuller, 1992). Based upon Kohlberg's hierarchy of moral development, the SRM-SF assesses reasoning skills involving decisions about social contracts (e.g., "How important is it for people to keep promises, if they can, to friends?"); affiliation concerns (e.g., "How important is it for children to help their parents?"); normative value of life (e.g., "How important is it for a person, without losing his or her own life, to save the life of a stranger?"); and property, law, and legal justice (e.g., "How important is it for people to obey the law?"). Respondents are instructed to rate the relative importance of these questions on a three–point Likert-type scale ranging from "very important" to "not important." Following each rating, respondents are asked to write a brief rationale for their decision.

Item responses are then evaluated by the examiner according to the standardized scoring procedures outlined by Gibbs et al. (1992). Several overall scores are produced, including (1) the Sociomoral Reflection Maturity Score (SRMS), which is simply the mean of the item ratings; (2) the Global Stage score, which is a 10-level scale that represents the developmental vicinity in which the SRMS is located; and (3) a Moral Type (A or B) score, which distinguishes the degree to which the respondent's prosocial moral reasoning values are balanced, universalistic, and internalized. Higher SRMS and Global Stage scores are thought to reflect more advanced stages of moral development, and the Type B classification is believed to represent a more thoroughly balanced and internalized sense of moral reasoning.

Gibbs and colleagues (1992) report that the SRM-SF evidences acceptable levels of reliability. Specifically, a test-retest reliability score of .88 was obtained from a sample of 509 individuals ranging in age from less than 10 years of age to greater than 50 years of age. In addition, the measure boasts impressive interrater reliability scores (between .94 and .99). Finally, the present authors report acceptable concurrent, convergent, and discriminant validity. This measure has recently been used with success in a study examining moral reasoning patterns in delinquent versus nondelinquent youth (e.g., Palmer & Hollin, 1998).

PHARMACOLOGICAL FACTORS IN ASSESSMENT

Several factors relating to drugs play a significant role in the assessment process: the presence of prescribed medication in the system of the child; a history of substance abuse and the possibility of drugs in the child's system at the time of testing; and residual drug damage in the child, particularly as it may affect brain function. Because of the high incidence of drug use and abuse, it is of critical importance for the examiner to be thoroughly informed about drugs of abuse, resultant changes in cognitions and behavior, and potential long range effects. Similarly, an understanding of prescribed medications, including appropriate dosages and short-term and long-range effects, is important. Although somewhat rare in preteens, steriods have been identified as having a profound effect on mood and behavior and should not be overlooked in establishing drug histories. Recognizing the need for this knowledge, clinical training programs frequently require a course in psychopharmacology and encourage trainees to participate in drug and alcohol certification programs. This course of study is strongly recommended for persons intending to work with juvenile offenders.

Frequently younger adolescents and preteens who engage in homicide and other violent behaviors are prescribed heavy doses of pharmacological agents for disordered thinking, anxiety, and aggression to reduce their stress and their risk to others. Significant behavioral and cognitive changes may result. If examiners are unaware of the presence of these drugs, they may draw conclusions that result in an inaccurate picture of the child. Detailed descriptions of popular psychotropic drugs and their actions and effects are available to the examiner. One work useful as a brief detailed source is that by Bezchlibnyk-Butler and Jeffries (1998). The present authors have observed many instances of a blunting of affect and reduced cognitive functioning in heavily medicated children. Subsequent evaluation under reduced medication resulted in a clearer diagnostic profile and improved performance. Other prescribed medications (e.g. Ritalin) can also affect performance by their presence or by their absence.

Illegal Substances

As with legal and prescribed medications, an understanding of illegal drugs and their short- and long-term effects is highly desirable when assessing juveniles, even the very young. Case studies of violent juveniles report high incidences of substance abuse (Ewing, 1990; Heide, 1992), which have been reported as contributory in violent acts. Whether such claims are authentic or represent an attempt to place blame on an external reason—drugs, for example—may be difficult to support or establish. There is no question that substance abuse impairs cognitive functioning and lowers the threshold for the release of emotion.

Permanent drug damage may be seen in preteens who regularly engaged in inhaling (huffing) a series of substances, among them glue, gasoline, gasoline additives, and aerosols. A preteen's abuse of these and other substances may require the evaluation to make a neuropsychological evaluation in order to more completely understand the area and level of impairment in the child.

ADHD AND ASSESSMENT

Attentional and hyperactivity disorders represent significant factors in the history of children who have murdered or attempted murder. The assessment process is difficult, especially when attempting to separate minimal brain dysfunction from contextual factors leading to observed inattention or restlessness. The subjectivity involved in parental and teacher reports may describe the behavior but offers little insights into probable cause. Most often ADHD symptoms are seen as features of the child's behavior. It is rare that the "full-blown" hyperactive child is encountered. When such a child is encountered, however, the assessment situation is not soon forgotten. Even the most secure and unstimulating testing environment can be ravaged by the truly hyperactive child.

Most cases fall in the gray area, meeting some of the criteria for hyperactivity or an attentional disorder, but there is little solid data in test performance to allow the evaluator to make a definitive decision as to the presence or absence of brain dysfunction.

The diagnostic information regarding preteens indicates that a significant number of preteen murderers were identified as having ADHD. Both types, inattention-disorganization and overactivity–impulsivity, fall within this classification, although the latter most often describes our population. Research has indicated that those children who meet strict criteria for the diagnosis of ADHD—3% to 4% of elementary school males and 1% to 2% of same-aged females—share many common diagnostic features: accident proneness, academic underachievement, rejection by peers, conflicted families, and low levels of self-esteem (Hinshaw, Klein, & Abikoff, 1998), all fertile ground for the development of anger and aggression.

Following criteria from the American Psychiatric Association, assessment of ADHD, is based on reported and observed behaviors of the child over a period of at least six months for both inattention and for hyperactivity. The following are the diagnostic criteria and requirements for both forms of the disorder based on the DSM-IV of the American Psychiatric Association.

The criteria for diagnosis of inattention are:

1. often fails to give attention to details and makes careless mistakes in schoolwork or other activities
2. has difficulty sustaining attention in tasks or play
3. does not appear to listen when spoken to
4. often fails to follow through on instructions and does not finish chores, schoolwork or duties
5. often has difficulty organizing activities
6. dislikes and avoids activities requiring sustained mental effort
7. frequently loses items necessary for tasks and activities (books, toys, etc.)
8. easily distracted by external stimuli
9. frequently forgetful in daily activities.

The criteria for hyperactivity and impulsivity are:

1. often squirms and fidgets in seat
2. leaves seat and moves about when remaining in seat is expected
3. runs about and climbs excessively in situations which are inappropriate
4. has difficulty in "quiet" leisure or play
5. is frequently "on the go" and unable to relax
6. may talk excessively

The criteria for impulsivity are:

1. often blurts out answers before questions completed
2. frequently unable to wait turn
3. frequently interrupts or intrudes on activities of others.

In both inattention and hyperactivity/impulsivity symptoms should be present for at least six months and at least six criteria met for each.

NEUROPSYCHOLOGICAL ASSESSMENT

Neuropsychological assessment is a complex and difficult process requiring extensive training and experience, typically beyond the level to which most psychologists are trained in their graduate programs. This process is further complicated by the developmental changes occurring in preteens and by the relative lack of well-standardized instruments and approaches for the assessment of younger children. Even the experienced examiner may face difficulty in differentiating developmental lag, cultural impoverishment, and subtle brain dysfunctioning when variations from expected levels of performance occur in perceptual, language, memory, sensorimotor, and cognitive functioning.

Most of the child murders described in the literature do not show extremes of brain damage. The ability to commit a violent act requires a level of energy and strength that most seriously brain-injured children would not possess. More likely, contributing factors are more subtle forms such as hyperactivity, which could be caused either by brain dysfunction or the environment. Neuropsychologists report a high incidence of misdiagnosis and medication for "minimal brain dysfunction" far exceeding the 3% to 8% of ADHD professionals have identified as actually attributable to brain dysfunction. Many researchers have strongly cautioned that attentional disorders and hyperactivity do not necessarily involve central nervous system (CNS) damage (see Gomez & Samson 1994). Many other factors produce similar behaviors: physiological problems; nutritional, motivational, and environmental factors; and even parasitic infestation can be contributory or causal.

Despite limitations, a series of instruments are available for use with preteens in addition to those signs derived from individually administered child and adolescent scales such as the Wechsler scales.

The Halsted-Reitan Neuropsychological Test Battery for Older Children (Reitan & Wolfson, 1986) is a comprehensive battery of tests similar to the adult form and is used with children from 9 to 14 years of age, the age range of most of the violent preteens. The Reitan-Indiana (Reitan, 1987) extends the lower limits and provides neurological assessment for children from 5 to 8 years of age.

The Halstead-Reitan Battery for adults and that used with older children contains tests that examine ability to abstract (Categories test), factual performance, rhythm, perception of speech sound, finger tapping, trail making (connecting dots sequentially), strength of grip, sense perception, tactile perception, and a screening task for aphasia. With young children (5–8 of age) tasks include motor function, sensory perception, memory, language abilities, visual-spatial skills, and organizing ability. The child is tested for lateral dominance because of its impact on comparisons to be made of the two sides of the body.

The limitation of the two Reitan batteries for juveniles is that they are considered to be fixed test batteries to be given in complete form. Some neuropsychologists, such as Lezak (1995), support a more flexible, individualized approach tailored to the person being evaluated. Her testing follows a more clinical model, whereas fixed test batteries follow a psychometric approach. For cases in which results of testing are to be presented in court, many neuropsychologists feel that the fixed battery is more credible and less open to challenges.

Questions are raised by a series of researchers regarding neuropsychological testing with young children. Validity, reliability, appropriateness, test complexity, and the skill of the assessor present complications when evaluating younger subjects.

In addition to the Reitan test, other scales such as the Quick Neurological Screening Test are available. The Quick is an individually administered scale that assesses 15 areas of neurological functioning, including motor development, spatial organization, attention, and auditory perception. For other testing materials and approaches, the reader should refer to Lezak (1995).

As compared with standard test batteries, neuropsychological testing emphasizes adaptive functioning. What is of greatest value is how the individual approaches a task or attempts to solve a problem. Child murderers with neuropsychological impairment may commit a violent act because they fail to recognize a viable response alternative. This inability to shift or to consider other options can be seen in their persistence with one approach in sorting tasks and problem solving even when their approach does not work.

Much of neuropsychological testing examines what has been called executive functioning—namely, formulating goals, planning, executing goals, and performing successfully. Even in the very young the presence or absence of these abilities will play a vital role in the assessment of competence, risk, and capacity to respond to treatment and rehabilitation. In children not suspected of having neuropsychological deficits, these answers are provided through other testing procedures. For the impaired child, evaluation by one expert in neuropsychological testing is a must.

OTHER DIAGNOSES

Other identified disorders associated with violent and murderous behavior represent a small portion of this population. Conduct disorders and ADHD represent the great majority of diagnoses: singly and in combination, these disorders are present in 85% of violent juveniles. Precise rates are uncertain because the studies cited earlier (e.g., Myers & Kemph, 1990) have a limited numbers of subjects.

Evidence suggests that psychosis in preteen murderers also appears to be quite rare (Ewing, 1990). For example, Busch et al. (1990) and Zagar et al. (1990) report a history of hallucinations in only up to 3% of homicidal children. Conversely, the study by Myers et al, (1995), though not meeting DSM criteria for a psychotic disorder, found that a majority (71%) did present some psychotic symptoms. As suggested earlier, this points to a need for further careful investigation of the role of thought disorder in the treatment and evaluation of homicidal children. As a cautionary note, many normal children report occasional perceptions and behaviors that would be regarded as psychotic or prepsychotic in adults, such as "seeing or hearing things." Such experiences take on importance if they played a role in the violent behavior of the child or had a significant role in day-to-day behavior.

Most examiners are cautious about labeling the behavior of preteens categorically, following DSM-IV criteria. Judges, law enforcement personnel, and other professionals who must deal with the child offender want and hope for prescriptive diagnoses. This permits the mandating of treatments for those judged mentally ill or emotionally disabled. Conversely, in the absence of such diagnoses, punishment and rehabilitative training become the focus.

SUMMARY

Preteens present the assessor with a series of difficulties not encountered when evaluating older juveniles or adults. These include a lack of either objective or projective personality measures with adequate or appropriate norms for answering the basic questions of the evaluative process: competency to waive Miranda rights, competency to stand trial, prediction of risk for violence, and potential to benefit from treatment or rehabilitation.

Answers to some of these questions can be supplied through intellectual assessment, which can predict the child's capacity to benefit from educational and training efforts. Motivation to make use of intellectual assets cannot be gained or inferred from the test results, however. The adversarial nature of inquiry taking place following the commission of a violent act and subsequent detention creates levels of stress, anxiety, and anger that make rapport difficult to achieve. The child's failure to respond positively during testing may reflect this stress and not indicate a lack of motivation.

In assessing the preteen, the examiner is able to provide at least partial answers to critical variables when assessing competency to waive rights or to stand trial, and when evaluating future risk and amenability to treatment and rehabilitation. Grisso (1998) lists nine critical factors in assessing risk: Past behavior, substance use, peers and community, family conflict and aggression, social supports and stressors, personality traits, mental disorders, opportunity, and future residence. Most of these factors are salient in the lives of preteen offenders. Although answers to these factors can be provided in part by psychological testing, the burden for the examiner will be that most of the answers will be based on past history and the examiner's ability to infer these factors from school records, court records, family report, personality tests, and the information gained through personal interviews with the child.

Assessing competency follows much the same pattern. Intellectual factors related to competency present a solid base, as do many developmental factors relating to cognitive development and physical maturity. Personality testing may offer some limited help, primarily in identifying distorted or disordered thinking, much of which will be apparent from the interview. Use of the tests related to the understanding of Miranda are an important part of the assessment, particularly underscoring the fact that most preteens will not fully comprehend the issues presented.

The clinical judgment of the examiner of the preteen is the essence of the assessment process. (We have indicated that personality testing for this group is at best limited, neuropsychological issues are affected by developmental issues, and there is limited instrumentation for evaluation. The intellectual assessment, the history, and the interview provide most of the working material for providing answers to the questions raised in the referral.) In the end it is the clinical judgment of the examiner that will address and answer most questions.

Chapter 8

Treatment and
Rehabilitation

INTRODUCTION

As the writing of this chapter is reaching its conclusion, 11-year-old twins face sentencing for the murder of their father and the shooting of their mother and sister. They also face certain release because of existing statutes against retaining juvenile offenders past their eighteenth birthday. The dilemma facing the judge is "what can be done to treat or rehabilitate two violent children in the remaining six years under court jurisdiction?" How can the values of two young boys very knowledgeable about and fascinated with guns undergo changes that would provide the boys with alternative responses to violence and impulsive action?

Do we have the knowledge to modify violence? Do we have sufficient resources (and time) to change the behavior of violent children? If so, can available interventions transform the child murderer sufficiently to function successfully in society? If the child murderer is transformed, will the public allow the now grown offender to rejoin society in a meaningful manner? Whereas questions are many, definitive answers are few. We will nonetheless address these issues, citing research evidence and experientially based judgments to support the answers that can be given.

TREATMENT

Preteens who commit murder are invariably referred for treatment. Conversely, adolescents who commit murder may follow a very different path through the justice system. Younger adolescents may go through procedures similar to those preteens encounter: charges dealt with in juvenile or family court, extensive evaluation, extended observation in a juvenile facility, and mandated treatment and rehabilitation. Older adolescents today are increasingly tried as adults, with treatment and rehabilitation of minimal concern. In April 1999, for example, an older adolescent waived to criminal court and there tried and convicted as an adult for the murder of a preteen was sentenced to 42 years without possibility of parole. This sentencing reflects the changing judicial attitude toward violent crime. No treatment recommendations were made. Similarly, in August 1999 in Conyers, Georgia, a 15-year-old murderer was waived to criminal court and now faces the possibility of imprisonment for life.

Treatment approaches vary enormously based on age alone. Verbal therapies for a young offender whose thinking and cognitive processes operate on a precausal or primitive level are both inappropriate and ineffective. Other factors such as psychiatric disorders, developmental disabilities, cultural factors, and dysfunctional families add to the complications involved in any approach to treatment.

Were that insufficient, the mandating of treatment imposes further constraints on developing the therapeutic environment for successful psychotherapy. In many cases the treatment may be attempted by in-house staff in a juvenile correctional facility. Viewed as part of the punishing system, staff members may find rapport excessively difficult, if not impossible, to establish. Staff members face the further dilemma of being unable to offer confidentiality as part of any therapeutic alliance. In many instances staff members lack the training to provide adequate treatment. Several state facilities employ workers and education specialists who have had no supervised therapeutic training.

Ideally, in cases involving homicide any treatment must offer confidentiality, preferably by someone outside the correctional system. For lesser offenses, research shows, the use of a variety of behaviors and cognitive approaches by in-house therapists has been effective (e.g., Hendrix & Heckel, 1981). A "Clockwork Orange" approach in which total behavioral modification is undertaken on an intensive "24 hours a day, everyday schedule," or the brainwashing model, has been proposed, described, and largely abandoned. The effectiveness of such an approach appears to have had contextual validity. Prisoners of war (POWs) when subjected to torture and brainwashing often complied with their captors' request, signing confessions, admitting their "crimes," and even propagandizing for the enemy. Less clear is whether any of these opinions were carried forward once prisoners were released and no longer brainwashed. Personal statements by prisoners of war indicate no attitudinal changes. Similarly, whereas behavior modification programs have shown high levels of success in modifying neurotic behaviors, habits, and phobias, modifying cognitions—making us more honest, more loving, or less impulsive—has typically met only limited success. What is lacking especially with regard to therapeutic interventions with preteens is a research base indicating what works and what does not.

Some articles are available, primarily case studies in which the therapist's opinion of success or failure provides the database. As far as treatment is applied to modify a psychiatric disorder such as schizophrenia, the evaluative criteria are clear and defensible. When attempting to evaluate treatment designed to produce the cessation of asocial, aggressive, or homicidal behavior, therapists have limited markers of improvement at their disposal. When determining whether the child is to be returned home, decision makers must rely on the patient's words or the therapist's judgments. The patient's statements of regret and of a desire to "do better" may represent nothing more than socially desirable responses made to gain favor with authorities. Other disorders, such as ADHD, etc. may undergo modification through a combination of medication and psychotherapy, as well as through developmental maturity.

The issue for treatment is that with few exceptions those factors that we described as significant in the backgrounds of children who murder speak to a vulnerability and are not in and of themselves causal. Psychiatric disorders, personality disorders, cognitive factors, adverse family factors, abuse, negative environments (including peer influence, and media effects), all contribute. Not any or even all represent that sine qua non for the occurrence of murderous behavior.

GOALS OF TREATMENT

For the adolescent murderer, the first and perhaps most difficult aspect of treatment is the determination of the goals of therapy. If the aim is simply the control of murderous behavior, long-term incarceration is an effective solution. Very few individuals are released from custody at an age when and in physical condition such that recurrent murder is highly probable. Similarly, in cases of diagnosable mental disorders, release is contingent upon clear cessation of symptoms, demonstrated manageability, and adequate community caretaking resources.

For the child who murders, therapeutic goals are even less clear. Is the goal to aid the child in institutional adjustment, to demonstrate repentance and remorse for the pain caused to others, to seek a path of atonement, to gain self-control, or to move from amoral values to a higher level of moral development and to become an achieving adolescent and adult imbued with the values of mainstream culture? Can any of these goals be achieved in an institutional setting? Can they be achieved by these children, given the identified limitations of their lives and capacities? Finally, how can success be measured for even the most advanced and skillfully applied therapeutic interventions, given the contextual limitations of incarceration?

Despite these questions and limitations, some goals are clear. A primary goal of treatment is to develop adequate levels of impulse control to prevent the recurrence of murderous behavior and other violent behaviors. Of equal importance is demonstration of moral development and values to offset and overcome a lack of empathy with and dehumanization of others. Other specific goals exist: raising self-esteem, maximizing use of personal abilities, developing effective communication skills (e.g., listening to others and, expressing oneself clearly), developing a more objective, deeper understanding of one's life experiences, and exgendering a sense of acceptance and understanding of one's role in life events. The degree of importance of these goals will vary considerably depending on the age and circumstances of the child. In our opinion the two issues of impulse control and moral judgment are fundamental to all children who murder, and treatment goals must address these to be successful.

Impulse Control

Self-control, translated as impulse control, represents one of the more difficult problems addressed in therapy. How is it learned? How is it taught? Most important, once found lacking at a particular age, how are the existing cognitions and values replaced? Make no mistake, it is not that these lacking values can simply be added or instilled in what was once an amoral vacuum. The child murderer has a values system—real, existing, and functioning. For this child the controlling value may read as "whatever it takes to meet my needs," "I wanted it and he wouldn't give it to me," or "I didn't know him. He was nothing to me." However stated, it is essential that whatever constraints exist in most persons that cause them to stop before committing violent acts must be added to the violent child's behavioral repertoire. Could it be as simple as the "folk psychology" of "Count to ten before doing anything" or some other related self-talk or instruction? Unlikely. Examination of the histories of children who murder almost without exception reveals a seemingly endless series of abusive episodes, double binds, mixed messages, environmental deficits, and familial and peer models who lack impulse control. In addition, there is a reinforcement history that which makes the impulsive response dominant in the juvenile's response hierarchy. While recognizing the powerful control of past experience, we are aware of equally powerful interventions that modify and shape impulsive and unconsidered responding when carried out fully by trained professionals in combination with family and community resources.

A second critical cognitive area is related to the development of moral values and appropriate levels of guilt, remorse, and regard for others, which is demonstrated in interactions with others.

Moral Development—New Values

The inclusion of our chapter on moral development speaks to our belief that this area is of critical importance in the treatment and rehabilitation of the murderous child. Combined with poor impulse control, poor moral judgment represents the action system that permits the lack of empathy, the dehumanization of others, and inevitably the expression of violence.

Therapists whose treatment aims at raising the level of moral judgment and behavior must first assess where the child is in this developmental process. In an environment where the most commonly held view is that "nothing works," the attempt to change and instill more appropriate moral values appears to be a daunting task. It is not difficult to perceive the violent child as living in a moral vacuum with no redeeming values, nothing to build upon through therapeutic interventions. Is this really the case, or are there incidents and experiences that demonstrate the child's ability to make higher-level moral judgments? As we have indicated, research has shown that levels or stages of moral development are not rigidly fixed, with children capable of operating at diverse levels often determined by contextual factors. Examination of individual cases may reveal that the child who lacks empathy for others or dehumanizes others has a caring, empathic response to younger siblings or feels loyal enough to a gang or peer group member to take blame or endure punishment to protect that person. These behaviors indicate to the therapist or evaluator a capacity to relate at a higher level of concern. Group and individual therapy may be able to shape, extend, and broaden the child's perceptions and proclivity to show empathy to others.

What of the child who appears to be totally lacking in empathy and concern for others? What treatments are available to create values where none presently exist? Can children who are driven only by self-serving motives and needs, who have no limitation on what they are willing to do to satisfy those needs, and who show no concern for others learn to feel guilt and remorse for their actions? Can they develop a desire for atonement and come to recognize that they merited society's retribution because of their behavior? Can they deal constructively with their feelings, rather than responding with alienation and rage?

As our exploration of treatment and rehabilitation unfolds, it will become apparent that our present skills are insufficient to deal with this extreme case. Fortunately, few of our child murderers are so bereft of empathy and human concern.

For most of our murderous children, effective therapies do exist and have, through research, been shown to result in behavioral change. These therapies are most effective only when the juvenile possesses those qualities that permit behavioral change. In the following sections we will examine therapeutic approaches and identify those types of individuals for whom they are most efficacious.

INDIVIDUAL PSYCHOTHERAPY

Individual psychotherapy takes many forms, from classical behavioral modification to cognitive behavioral and dynamic approaches. Each has demonstrated success with violent children, with behaviorally based approaches having the largest body of research support.

To be effective all approaches to treating preteens are dependent upon at least five factors.

1. The child must possess the ability to communicate verbally and be capable of understanding causal links.
2. The child should have reached a level of cognitive development sufficient to engage in problem solving. Functioning at a level of precausal thinking would limit the ability to perform factor 2.
3. The child should have the ability (and willingness) to form a therapeutic alliance with the therapist, recognizing that "willingness" may require much time and patience to be achieved.
4. The therapist who would treat the violent child should have sufficient skill and experience to form a therapeutic alliance and reach a level beyond defensive responses, socially desirable answers, and externalization of blame and causality.
5. The child should be free from disruptive psychotic thought, severe mental incapacity, retardation or brain injury, which would prevent the child's fulfilling the four previous points.

Treatment may be optimized if the child is highly verbal, intelligent, and high-achieving; recognizes and accepts responsibility for his or her behavior; has a regard for the rights of others; is capable of experiencing guilt; does not externalize responsibility for his or her behavior; and actively seeks to change. These factors and characteristics have been identified as those that predict successful psychotherapeutic outcomes for both individual and group approaches.

It is obvious that few, if any, of the children who murder meet these criteria. Most will have some of these qualities and may possess the capacity for developing other positive attributes. In cases where the level of functioning precludes group or individual therapy, alternative treatment approaches such as play therapy, combined drug and behavior therapy, and socialization programs may be applied to the child to shape behavior even in the absence of cognitive awareness.

PLAY THERAPY

Many of the children who murder fail to meet the criteria for effective use of verbally based psychotherapy as described earlier in this chapter. Treatment under these constraints has most often taken the form of individual or group play therapy or of family-based interventions such as family therapy or systems that train parents to modify their child's behavior.

Once violent children are incarcerated, family-based approaches are not suitable. Even individual or group play therapy may be out of the question for most children. Security considerations and lack of trained and skilled play therapists may work against use of this approach.

Despite these problems, play therapy provides the intervention of choice for the violent child who lacks the ability and maturity to solve problems and communicate verbally. Play is also useful as a catalyst and adjunct when working with children whose emerging communication problem-solving skills limit their ability to sustain an extended verbal interaction. These same issues and limitations are found in adolescents who have been culturally and educationally limited.

Play therapy takes many forms; unfortunately, the extensive literature (we found 373 entries for the last five years) fails to provide definitive research that indicates the approaches most suitable for treating various conditions, psychological states, or problem areas. Few of the articles we examined were research based; most were theoretical or case studies.

Most approaches can be reduced to two forms, one in which the focus of play is controlled by the therapist by limiting the child's access to play materials and by selecting the item(s) to be used (e.g., a sand tray, amputee dolls, or paints). The degree of direction by the therapist provides an additional dimension, with some therapists offering a theme or other structural inputs. At the other extreme is the approach that offers open access to all materials in the playroom, permitting the child to select those items to be used during the session.

Most play therapists fall somewhere between the extremes, limiting choices but allowing the child to have several options; and these therapists apply limitations based on age appropriateness and identfied therapeutic goals. Unfortunately, no clear or prescriptive guidelines exist to link approaches to specific behaviors manifested by the child. Age, intellect, and problem-solving abilities are all considered by play therapists in selecting or eliminating some types of activity, although most determinations are made selectively case by case.

Therapists tend to use similar approaches to materials whether working with groups or with individual clients. The added dimension for group play therapy is, of course, the interactions between group members, providing rich data on socialization, response style, regard for self, and regard for others.

Schaefer (1993) lists 14 therapeutic factors found in play therapy and identifies the benefits with their successful outcome. Although not exclusive to play therapy in every instance, they are necessary components: (1) overcoming the child's resistances leads to the formation of a therapeutic alliance; (2) effective communication is a prerequisite to understanding; (3) increasing the child's sense of competence increases self-esteem; (4) developing and reinforcing creative thinking increases problem-solving skills; (5) Catharsis provides emotional release; (6) abreaction, like catharsis, relieves emotional stress by reliving past events; (7) role play provides the opportunity to learn and try out new behaviors; (8) fantasy and visualization give the child the opportunity to explore untried behaviors and experiences; (9) metaphoric thinking helps the child develop "belief systems that structure, energize and give meaning to life"; (10) attachment formation with the therapist may serve as a vehicle for leading the child to a secure attachment style; (11) relationship enhancement experienced through play is transferred to others in the environment; (12) the experiencing of positive emotion through play reduces stress and increases a sense of well-being; (13) mastering development fears follows a process of systematic desensitization, with play the means of approaching and coping with those fears; and (14) game play with the therapist, or with other children in group play therapy, helps the child experience an interactive social process and deal with rules. These potential benefits of play therapy obviously represent desired ends for any therapeutic process and would be especially useful in dealing with the problems presented by preteen murderers unsuited for exclusively verbal therapies. Few of the benefits, however, have specific techniques associated with their use. Research support, other than case studies, and anecdotal evidence are still largely lacking. It is incumbent upon professionals to fill this research gap and provide the necessary documentation for techniques that are passionately felt to work. Today demand for accountability and the demonstration of effectiveness makes this a priority. Otherwise techniques that may be extremely valuable in resocializing the violent child may be dropped from use or may not be fundable by sponsoring agencies.

Once the young offender is incarcerated and treated away from the family setting, living in a highly controlled environment and surrounded by others with serious delinquent histories, one might question whether any therapeutic gain would be adaptive and beneficial to the child. If therapeutic gain is beneficial to institutional adjustment, would that gain be in any way transferable to the community? The central question raised at the beginning of the chapter regarding the goals of any treatment apply equally to play therapies—treatment for what?

For the child murderer, continuous treatment and rehabilitative efforts in various age-appropriate forms will be necessary if hope of successful adjustment can be reached. The lessons from the experiences of Mary Bell as described by Sereny (1999) provide both caution and confidence that successful postincarceration adjustment is possible despite the horror of two infant murders and incarceration marked by serious errors in treatment and management.

As with other therapeutic interventions, play therapy is most effective at the preventive level where parents are separately trained in effective management skills and the child has the opportunity to vent violent and aggressive behaviors while acquiring appropriate responses and prosocial behaviors through therapeutic play.

FAMILY THERAPY

Family therapy as a major treatment intervention following the commission of murder or attempted murder appears to be of limited utility. Most of the family therapies would prove of value as a preventive measure, however, if the family is not changed by legal intervention and the child removed through placement or incarceration. Similarly, at the point of the offender's return to society and possibly to the family, family therapy might provide the returning adolescent (or adult) with a means of access and could play an important role in rehabilitation.

Family therapy during incarceration might be of limited supportive value, though extremely handicapped because of a lack of doing contact, the child's removal from the home community and school environments, and contextual issues within the family and in the correctional facility. In several states programs being developed to provide comprehensive interventions involving incarcerates and their families give promise of providing support and reducing problems of reentry into the family and community.

The greatest benefits from family therapy lie in at the preventive and postincarceration rehabilitative efforts. Family therapy as a preventive measure requires the recognition of potential threat of violence by those able to suggest, urge, or insist that treatment be undertaken. Typically, this function falls to schools, juvenile authorities working with delinquent and predelinquent children, or parents themselves. Many parents are slow to acknowledge their child's problems and resist suggestions for treatment, especially those requiring their active participation. Authorities may provide the impetus for parental participation, but resistance may remain high and any therapeutic intervention handicapped.

Additional Considerations

It is not our intent to discuss the various approaches to family therapy and the techniques they employ. We believe that well-trained family therapists can be effective regardless of their theoretical orientation, with skills being the critical variable. In the case of our homicidal or potentially homicidal juvenile, two approaches have been shown to be effective when working with children whose symptoms are those typical in most children who murder—conduct disorders and attention deficit disorders, which we will describe in separate sections of this chapter.

Family therapy interventions with short-term incarcerates offers greater promise. A child whose violent act is charged as a lesser crime with a consequent lessening of jail time may also benefit. Problems in these instances relate to disinterested dysfunctional families, travel constraints of distance and cost, and the unavailability of fully trained professionals. Even when professionals are available, some families are unavailable except on weekends, a further complication. This problem has been addressed in some settings by extended or marathon approaches.

SUMMARY

In short, family therapy as a treatment modality for the preteen offender is of limited value except as an occasion of family support for the child. Even this cannot be guaranteed, as both the family and the community are changed by the child's behavior, and the family's distress may be brought to the therapy session and thus increase the stress on the child, resulting in further distancing between the child and the family. Yet, the potential good from these activities suggests that they be tried if possible.

The most serious limitations to family-based treatment for the violent child include both parents being employed outside the home, single-parent families, limited community support, poverty, negative peer influences, and distrust of professional services. These factors are overrepresented in statistics describing juvenile delinquents regardless of socioeconomic status (poverty being the exception with middle- and upper-middle-class offenders).

To be effective, a multisystemic, concerted effort by all parties involved is necessary in preventive as well as rehabilitative efforts. This involves the family, the child, the therapist, the community, and the juvenile (or adult) correctional system. Any missing component reduces the possibility of therapeutic effectiveness and increases the potential for future offenses.

GROUP THERAPY

Questions regarding group therapeutic interventions are related to the type of group therapy provided, how often it is provided, what diagnostic mix is used, and what offenses should be included. Also considered are racial and gender issues. No research-based answers exist for most of these questions. Some of the answers available address only outpatient findings. Almost without exception, juvenile murderers will be seen in an institutional setting. Most will be in a juvenile facility; those with severe psychological symptoms may be in a hospital setting in a high-security ward. Most will stay in a controlled environment until attaining their majority (18 to 21 years), with some facing blended sentencing, which may extend their incarceration beyond this point. Therefore, at least six years are available for treatment of the preteen offender, and for many youth, a much longer period is available. The importance of this time frame is that a variety of group therapeutic treatment approaches are both appropriate and necessary (these aspects apply equally to individual therapies as well).

For very young offenders whose verbal and cognitive skills are undeveloped, a play-based approach, described earlier, may be appropriate. Later when communication skills are more advanced a dynamic or cognitive behavioral approach would be in order. Still later, skills-training groups and prerelease groups would provide for the transition from institutional life. It is important to note that preteen murderers, like other violent children subjected to long-term incarceration, will have been denied, to a large degree, the normal experiences of later childhood and adolescence. These have been replaced by an institutional setting that could at its worst, produce similar isolation effects to those seen in the classic studies by Harlow (e.g., 1958) of infant monkeys reared by "wire and cloth" mothers, a social misfit incapable of making normal affectionate and caring responses.

Studies of conduct-disordered juveniles, primarily adolescents, treated through group techniques have revealed mixed results. Research noted negative results most often when homogeneous groupings were utilized (c.g., Dishion & Andrews, 1995). These studies were conducted on an outpatient basis in most instances. Whether group psychotherapy with a homogeneous group of conduct-disordered juveniles enables group members to develop prosocial attitudes and increase self-esteem or encourages them to "feed off" one another and increase delinquent potential is a question we must consider.

Success has been reported for a mixed group of conduct-disordered and nonantisocial juveniles (Feldman, Caplinger, and Woldarski, 1983). Such groupings would be impossible for incarcerated violent children. Finding prosocial role models among peers also appears unlikely. Institutional staff, especially staff conducting psychotherapy, could provide such a role model, however.

As we have indicated, many treatment approaches are well suited as preventive interventions and as such warrant our attention. Two approaches that fall into this category are parent training and skills training for solving cognitive behavioral problems. Both appear in the literature under various descriptions such as Parent Management Training (PMT) or the Parent Training Model. They share a common approach, which is the training of parents in behavioral methods for modifying the behavior of their child. Similarly, behavioral modifiers have been applied to providing at-risk children with new problem-solving training to replace maladaptive responses. These also are presented under a variety of labels, but they share much in both content and approach.

TREATMENT OF CONDUCT DISORDER

Unless their act is the result of self-defense or an attempt to protect others, all children who murder may receive a primary diagnosis of conduct disorder. Conduct disorders are by definition antisocial behavior that is both clinically significant and outside the limits of normal behavior. Other qualifications include frequency, intensity, chronicity, connectedness with other deviant or delinquent behaviors, and whether in the judgment of others, there is significant impairment (Kazdin, 1998). The DSM-IV describes two subtypes of conduct disorder: childhood onset and adolescent onset. Most of our subjects would be classed as childhood onset, in which symptomatic behaviors appear before age 10. As to severity—mild, moderate, or severe—again by definition our preteen murderers or attempted murderer would be classed as severe, the criterion being behavior causing considerable harm to others. Less severe behaviors would also qualify in this category: forced sex, physical cruelty, breaking and entering, and so on.

In a series of reviews (Kazdin, 1988a, b; Weisz & Weiss, 1993) there have been consistent research findings supporting the positive benefits of certain forms of child and adolescent psychotherapy. Its appropriate application can result in a reduction of symptoms as compared with children who do not receive treatment. Kazdin (1998) points out many limitations to those studies, among them a relatively short treatment period of 8 to 10 sessions, with limited followup, averaging five months. Given the severity of issues facing the child murderer, there is little research suggesting which approaches and what level of intensity are required to produce behavioral change.

Kazdin (1998) reports that over 230 psychotherapeutic approaches have been identified and applied to children and adolescents. By far the majority have not been researched, and effectiveness is based on clinical judgment rather than controlled studies. For those approaches to treating conduct disorders, the most effective have been cognitive problem solving skills training interventions.

Parent Management Training

Eyberg et al. (1998) and Kazdin (1998) describe PMT as an important dimension in the treatment of the conduct-disordered child. PMT primarily consists of the therapist's training parents to manage the childs' behavior in the home more effectively. The parents develop greater ability to understand problem behaviors, apply alternative responses, and become effective in delivering prompts, giving reinforcement, and withholding reinforcement. A variety of reinforcing parental responses and mild punishment may help the child in developing prosocial behaviors and positive interactions with others. Although some variations exist among the approaches to PMT, they all involve these basic factors. As a therapeutic and a preventive intervention. PMT has resulted in short-term measurable gain. Evidence for long-term gain has largely been limited to one-year followup. Given conduct disorders' stability through the developmental process, to say that a return to former patterns has not occurred it is not possible.

Unfortunately, as a treatment for the child who has murdered, PMT has many limitations, even when combined in a multimodal approach. First, the child will not be under the direct care of the family until he or she is an adult, and given current sentencing trends, the child may be a mature or even older adult when released. Second, the ability of the family to attend training sessions regularly may be limited by distance and cost, if not by willingness to attend. Finally, the spirit and substance of parent training lies in equipping the family with enhanced skills in dealing with the problems presented by the child. As a result, parent management training may be a major intervention for preventing violence, but rarely, will it have a place in the treatment of the incarcerated violent child. The likely exception would be very young children who have limited awareness of their crime; in their case the court has permitted them to return to the care of the family under careful scrutiny by juvenile authorities.

Other issues limiting the use of PMT are mentioned by Kazdin: the failure of families to respond to treatment, a limited numbers of trained professionals, and a lack of opportunities for training in PMT techniques.

Family Therapies

Approaches to family therapy for the conduct-disordered child, as with PMT, are most appropriate at the preventive level. Use with the incarcerated violent child serving a long sentence would be virtually impossible for the reasons persented as deterrents to use of PMT for violent juveniles. Even were arrangements possible, little evidence exists supporting traditional approaches to family therapy as a means for modifying the behavior of the conduct-disordered child.

TREATMENT OF ADHD

A comprehensive summary of treatment for ADHD including pharmacological, nonpharmacological, and combined (multimodal) approaches is presented by Hinshaw, Klein, and Abikoff (1998) and Greenhill (1998). Recommendations in both articles represent a summary of treatments validated through extensive research with demonstrated effectiveness.

Conclusions drawn by both authors indicate that the most effective treatment for ADHD is stimulant medication, with behavioral contingency management adding an important dimension, provided that contingencies are enforced within school settings and by the family.

For the preteen who has attempted or committed murder and has been appropriately diagnosed as ADHD, effective treatment to modify cognitions must first or concurrently treat the ADHD. Unless attentional difficulties are reduced, other therapeutic interventions will be unachievable or unnecessarily lengthy. For the incarcerated child, stimulant medication will be readily available. It is less certain that programs of contingency management or cognitive behavioral treatments can be adequately provided even if recommended by the court.

As we have indicated, the two most frequently noted diagnoses for child murderers are conduct disorders and ADHD. In our view, the major task of therapy for this population is to instill appropriate social concern (moral judgment and reasoning) and proper impulse control. The linkage of these diagnoses and treatment goals coupled with appropriate behavioral interventions offers hope for successful treatment and also speaks to issues of prevention.

PSYCHOTIC BEHAVIORS

The incidence of juveniles reaching the DSM-IV criteria for a psychotic diagnosis is very low. Most of the diagnoses of psychosis among juveniles are applied to adolescents, not preteens. Those preteens diagnosed as psychotic tend more often toward extreme withdrawal, depression, and autistic features. Murder by this population is unlikely, though not unknown. Discussion of treatment for childhood schizophrenia and depression are beyond the scope of this work, but we will describe issues relating to children with psychotic symptoms.

Treatment of child murderers with diagnosable levels of psychotic behavior are relatively rare, although our earlier review indicated that experts were sharply divided on both frequency and severity. In any case, the numbers are limited and homicidal acts directly related to psychosis (e.g., "voices told me to do it") are rare. Although also rare, attempts at malingering through a claim of psychotic thinking do occur.

Many violent children having psychotic features or symptoms and have a history of contact with mental health agencies, schools, community resources, and other agencies such as social service. Treatment for some may have been extensive, including hospitalization; others may have remained identified as problems with no treatment history. Very few of these children would have escaped awareness. There appears to be very few instances of sudden, recent onset of symptoms. However, family denial or minimizing of psychotic symptoms is quite common.

The point of onset of psychotic symptoms plays a significant role in treatment plans. Acute recent onset, in some cases as a reaction to the homicidal act, are in the main more accessible to psychotherapeutic interventions. In most cases this also involves drug therapy.

Another dimension often overlooked in children involves internalized problems that could reach psychotic levels and increased risk of suicide. The child murderer may manifest strong or extreme levels of depression that may, to the untrained observer, seem to be an appropriate expression of guilt and thus go unreported. Loss of support systems further add to the distress.

Ironically, incarcerated juveniles who display psychotic symptoms are far more likely to receive professional treatment than those children judged to be conduct disordered. Children with ADHD, though medicated, tend to remain in juvenile correctional facilities with little of no psychotherapy. When psychotic behavior is present juvenile authorities in most states defer to state mental health facilities, to whose care the child is transferred until "cured" or until symptoms subside sufficiently to allow return to the juvenile facility.

In our experience when the child exhibits low level or intermittent psychotic symptoms, decisions as to who will deal with the child result in a struggle with neither side, juvenile facility or mental health facility, wishing to assume responsibility. In many instances the final decisions are reached by the adult or juvenile court judges.

SUMMARY OF TREATMENT ISSUES

The two primary goals of treatment for violent children are the gaining of impulse control and the development of moral values. Other goals are significant also, but in our view they depend on achieving some success in the attainment of personal control and respect for the rights of others.

Impulse control is gained from many sources. Incarceration may serve as a restricted environment requiring the learning of new, adaptive responses. Medication may help those with ADHD, psychotic ideation and behaviors, and various forms of anxiety. Cognitive behavioral therapies have been effective in providing the child with adaptive responses to deal more actively with confrontations and to become less reactive. Skills training, behavioral rehearsal, role playing, and anger management techniques can, when available, play a major role in acquiring new responses.

In therapies that seek to change moral values, the role is less clear. Even in normal development a myriad of influences shape the child. In instances when the dominant behaviors of the child are aggression, disregard for the rights of others, dehumanization, and impulsivity there are clear antecedents in the form of parental inconsistency, abuse, inattention, and defective role models.

Do we have suitable techniques to reprogram a child's lifetime of experience and learning? Can this be accomplished in institutional environments? Can this be achieved once the child has committed murder or attempted murder? The literature does not provide us with long-term outcome studies on young children who have murdered. None except Sereny's study of Mary Bell address the changes that occur in moral reasoning.

To say that most of our efforts at treatment are effective for the violent child would be premature. To confirm this in the case of children who murder would require a lifetime of careful observation and scrutiny. The child's verbal responses can be modified to imply guilt, remorse, or other socially desirable responses, but do these words represent real attitude changes? Those of us who have observed incarcerated children are aware of how quickly they learn to say the "right" responses to gain favor with staff persons.

This occurs without treatment. Is it possible to remove the social desirability factor and probe the real or underlying feelings? In a treatment context, whether in group or individual therapy, the skilled therapist can tap underlying feelings and attitudes in the child. Rarely can children conceal feelings and at the same time permit the therapist to delve deeper into their history. Some children will remain superficial and nondisclosing; others will present a story that may impress the inexperienced therapist. Still others, especially those incarcerated at an early age, may be unable to express themselves verbally. This is also true for those of limited intellectual resources, though this is not always the case. Some children of borderline abilities have been able to express themselves effectively and to benefit from therapeutic interventions.

In cases where treatment can be assessed through behavioral means, unobtrusive behavioral measures of social interactions and individual behavior assessed through behavioral rating scales offer somewhat greater assurance. Gathered over time, they provide a baseline of observations that when combined with incidence reports, test scores, and academic achievement can verify the success of treatments. How well treatment efforts will stand up when the child, now an adolescent or young adult returned to society, is at best uncertain. A return to the same community may represent a return to Garbarino's (1995) "toxic environment." It may involve a return to a hostile community, a hostile family, or both. Thus the context is, if not everything, at least extremely important. One of the most difficult issues facing the juveniles in the Jonesboro, Arkansas, murders will be the response of others to their presence in the community. Even the most successful treatment while they are incarcerated may not afford the juveniles the level of insulation necessary to protect them from the rage of the community. Anonymity and name changes or the expunging of juvenile records is no longer possible in most states. Communities demand to know when dangerous persons of any age are placed in their community.

The enormity of the issues and problems should not result in giving up the idea of rehabilitation and treatment. This has occurred in many states in adult corrections where a philosophy of "nothing works" has lead to a complete absence of rehabilitative efforts and where getting tougher is the only policy. To some degree this same philosophy is found increasingly in juvenile institutions. It seems inevitable that if treatment is not provided, life sentences for preteens are likely to follow, either by legislative action or through a subsequent offense upon release.

REHABILITATION

In this section we will address habilitative and rehabilitative interventions for children who have murdered or whose behaviors have involved attempted murder or extreme violence. Interventions for those children are intertwined with legal, environmental and media interest and public concerns, which influence what options are open to the rehabilitative therapists, what time frame is involved, and what outcomes are possible. The course of rehabilitation for an 11-year-old murderer, tried and convicted at age 13, to be released by state law at age 18, may be drastically and dramatically different from that of another 11-year-old, tried as an adult, who may be given a life sentence and released to the community at age 38. It is also possible that revised sentencing with blended sentencing could result in a child's facing a true life sentence never to be released regardless of age. This outcome was faced recently by a 15-year-old convicted of murder.

Of critical importance when considering the rehabilitation of children who murder are the criteria for determining what constitutes rehabilitation? Does it involve the expression of remorse or empathy for the victim or victims? Should the child develop a life plan that involves a continuing appearance of penitence—such as working in a helping role with the disadvantaged? Might that plan involve higher levels of education? What vocations are available and what vocations are closed forever for the child who murders? Given the seriousness of the offense, will society accept the offender in a functional role? Many occupations and roles will be denied the rehabilitated murderer despite the passage of years since the crime. What are the real options that are available? Given the social, occupational, and sometimes criminal penalties for failure to disclose information regarding one's criminal history, can the child murderer, now adult, ever establish a secure place in society? Obviously, contextual issues are important. Children who murder because of neglect, abuse, or sexual exploitation may be granted redemption through justification of their act. Those who murder out of anger, revenge, or exploitation may face a hostile and unforgiving society. What recommendation can be offered as part of their rehabilitation?

Satisfactory answers to these questions are not readily forthcoming, and no general principles appear to address most cases. Instead, each case presents its unique features, problems, and circumstances. Because we are dealing with an incomplete developmental process in all areas—physical, intellectual, personality, moral, and spiritual—all that is certain are that changes will occur. Each child is unique, and planning must be designed for the child's characteristics and modified over time.

When considering settings for rehabilitation, requirements for adolescents may differ sharply from those for the preteen. For the adolescent often the question is whether the time to release is sufficient to rehabilitate. Two years may be insufficient to provide the interventions to unify the identified areas for change. For the preteen whose developmental process is incomplete in the physical, social, and cognitive areas, rehabilitation becomes a matter of how to provide the opportunity to acquire experiences that approximate the developmental experiences of "normal" children.

Without providing positive growth experiences, incarceration could result in the release of an individual unable to cope with society. There is a high probability that the individual released would have been educated by others in the correctional facility to be amoral, asocial, and predatory.

Most juvenile facilities offer containment, control, education, and vocational training. Few, if any, are equipped to provide the total rehabilitative process necessary to modify the offender's cognitions, perceptions, moral values, and behavior sufficiently to convince the judicial system and the public that the preteen murderer has been restored or directed to normal impulses and values with no further threat of violence to others.

In some states rehabilitative process centers are struggling to decide who will provide the primary services. The juvenile system has primary charge; yet in cases of serious mental illness or evidence of retardation, most juvenile systems do not have the resources or the physical facilities to deal with these children. Conversely, state developmental disabilities programs and state mental health programs frequently attempt to block dually diagnosed offenders, again because of the need for greater security and the problem of providing care in already burdened systems ill-equipped to deal with the diagnosed illness and the threat of violence.

In seeking to recommend appropriate rehabilitative services, the evaluating psychologist may find recommendations ignored or beyond the juvenile agencies' capacity. In the golden days of juvenile correctional rehabilitation efforts, recommendations for a variety of services, including group or individual psychotherapy, were provided by staff or through consultants. In most states today consultative services are limited to psychological evaluations. Staffs, limited in numbers, and agencies' "no frills" policies have limited rehabilitative services to basic educational programs, boot camps, or other paramilitary corrective efforts based on adult models. It is not our purpose to evaluate these efforts. Rather, it is to point out to the evaluator that observed deficits suitable for rehabilitative efforts that may appear in recommendations may be beyond the capability of the juvenile system. Given that our subject population represents the extreme in seriousness of offense, perhaps exceptions may be made and services provided. In some instances, this may be the case. There is also the counterargument that the seriousness of the offense places the child "beyond the pale," and thus the child is viewed as beyond redemption. Waiving such children to trials in criminal court further reduces the possibility of therapeutic or rehabilitative intervention because of the generally punitive nature of criminal court decisions regarding serious offenses.

Regardless of the states policy relating to release from custody, many children who murder will at some point have been directed to treatment with a therapist. The presiding judge frequently mandates this, especially when the child is tried in juvenile and family court settings. Once treatment has been undertaken, and assuming the establishment of a therapeutic alliance between therapist and child, at some point treatment is concluded or sufficient progress has occurred for a consideration of habilitative or rehabilitative efforts. Involved in rehabilitative efforts is a process of unlearning or a giving up of present response patterns and the substitution of new responses, a more difficult task, as can be observed in older offender's difficulties in giving up substance abuse and long-standing criminal behaviors. For habilitation, the task is teaching new, adaptive behaviors to expand the child's response repertoire and to provide for more effective coping.

Once the child is ready for rehabilitative services, will the system be prepared to provide these services at an adequate level? Most children who murder will be released as young adults, at least 18 years and older in many cases (e.g., in Arkansas, where the juvenile may be retained until 21 years of age if appropriate facilities are available). State and federal programs geared to working with the disadvantaged to provide career and job counseling and vocational rehabilitation are available, and many states offer regular services to juveniles while they are still in institutions, and increased services upon release.

Agencies, however helpful and willing, face serious limitations. Children who murder carry a stigma that may prevent them from enjoying many of the rights and privileges of citizenship: the right to vote, hold public office, serve in the military, teach, or work for state or federal agencies. Even in the private sector, knowledge of their past may cause employers to bar the offender from most positions. Civil rights could be restored by a pardon, but the pardon process is frought with objections that often result in denial of the request for pardon. When murder is involved, families and interested citizens come forward to object in much the same manner as occurs with parole requests.

Reaching adulthood and release, violent children may face almost impossible barriers in their attempt to make a full return to society. These difficulties only add to the problems resulting from early development deficits and the limitations imposed as a result of incarceration. To this point, our comments have focused on the problems, suggesting that perhaps little may be available and not much hope for true rehabilitation. We will address what might be possible in rehabilitating the violent child.

Guidance

One positive force available, even in the schools in juvenile correctional facilities, is the school guidance counselor. These schools must confirm the state regulations regarding offerings, and guidance is a mandated service in most states.

Guidance by school counselors once consisted of a vocational interest test and a talk on careers by an assistant principal. Today a comprehensive guidance system has evolved and extends from elementary school through high school. Young children today are exposed to programs that describe career opportunities and duties and through films present a wide range of careers ranging from those requiring limited training to professional careers involving years of preparation. Focus in these programs is not elitist but geared to the expectations and limitations of the target population.

These programs form a vital link in the shaping or habilitation of the child and are found in most public and private systems in the country. What the violent child, and especially those children who have murdered or attempted murder, will be able to do or be permitted to do should be a major concern by juvenile authorities and the community at large. At present, no models exist for confronting this problem. Whereas the numbers of children who murder are relatively few, those who are violent, with a high probability for committing murder, are many. Guidance should be viewed as part of the preventive, treatment, and rehabilitative process.

Coordinated efforts among the guidance counselor, the therapist, the prerelease counselor, and the probation officer, with the added involvement of community resources such as vocational rehabilitation and mental health services, can provide the resources for behavioral change necessary for helping the once violent child to survive in the community. Those children who are not offered the corrective measures or those who are so damaged as to be unwilling or unable to change face a bleak future with a high probability of additional incarceration (though not necessarily for additional murders).

Chapter 9

Prevention

Chapter 5 presented the research that identified those characteristics of children, families, and communities that were predictors of violent and homicidal behaviors. In this chapter we will examine measures that have been identified as of value in preventing the expression of violence. Our discussion will cover the major problem areas, which have been identified as causal or contributing:

1. Adjustment disorders (personality disorders, psychiatric disturbances)
2. Cognitive problems (intellectual difficulties, learning disabilities, neurological impairment)
3. Violent behavior (displayed by child)
4. Adverse familial factors (physical abuse, sexual abuse, unstable homes, absent fathers, parental problems, alcohol abuse, criminality, psychiatric problems, violence)
5. Environmental factors (school, neighborhood, community)
6. Media influences

There are no secrets as to what should be done to prevent violence and murderous potential in our children. Liberals and conservatives alike correctly identify the problems: negative changes in the structure, role, and authority of the family; loss of the sense of community in most areas; and the movement of schools from a philosophy of in loco parentis to one of a besieged institution lacking in control over its charges.

What to do about these problems leads liberals and conservatives in somewhat different directions. Liberals retain some belief that a part of the solution lies in the exercise of governmental regulation and intervention. Conservatives seek a return of empowerment to the family and the community.

What liberals fail to consider is that government does not have the knowledge or skill to restore families or communities. Conservatives, conversely, do not consider that neither families nor communities have the capacity or knowledge to take back the responsibility, which was given up in the years following World War II. The controls once offered by extended families, smaller closely knit communities in which neighbors served as part of the extended family network, and schools where authority was vested in principals and teachers and vigorously supported by families no longer exists.

Is restoration possible? In a word, no. In this chapter we will attempt to address what is possible and some indication of interventions, which have been developed to address the social ills contributing to our present culture of violence. We will cite the works of major contributors to our understanding of these issues, who have long recognized the problems and have sought solutions in the form of education and interventions at all levels of prevention.

The remedies for preventing violence and murder are broad, sweeping, inclusive, and are those features that support a better world: fewer single-parent families, less poverty, supportive and protective neighborhoods, and respect for diversity. On an individual basis, helping all children develop a sense of personal worth, empathy for others, appropriate channels for reducing anger, and acceptance by others both in the family and in the community. Garbarino (1992, 1997) has written extensively regarding the impact of toxic environments on the development of children and adolescents and has proposed careful solutions, which can feasibly be employed on a neighborhood, community, state, and national basis. In this chapter we will not attempt to describe in great detail those preventive interventions that involve legislative action on a national or state level. Rather, our major effort will be to describe group and individual interventions by mental health professionals, teachers, community caretakers, and family members to increase the child's options to act in nonviolent manner.

ADJUSTMENT DISORDERS

Adjustment disorders (conduct disorders) comprise the largest diagnostic category for children who murder; such disorders are the primary explanation for delinquent behavior in general. As a result, most of the treatment and research efforts aimed at modifying the behavior of violent and potentially violent children have focused on the adjustment disorders. In approaching preventive measures, most professionals conceptualize three levels of intervention. Primary prevention seeks to identify vulnerable children, those at risk for delinquent behaviors, and provides interventions to remove or reduce risks. Mulvey, Arthur, and Reppucci (1993) describe a series of primary preventive interventions: family-based interventions, parent training, family support interventions, school-based interventions, preschool programs, cognitive behavioral interventions, and social process interventions. Not only do these interventions focus on the child and the family, they also address primary prevention on a community level with emphasis on recreational programs and neighborhoods or community-wide projects.

Secondary prevention involves children who have been identified as exhibiting some of the symptoms described earlier but who have not been adjudicated or formally charged. They are viewed as high risk but salvageable. Programs for these children may involve alternative school placement, family-based interventions, and community-based juvenile counselors who intervene at a variety of levels prior to formally charging the child at risk. Many states have undertaken this approach to reduce the numbers of children adjudicated and institutionalized. This has occurred because of the established negative effects of institutionalization on the subsequent behavior of the child and as a cost-effective method for reducing delinquent potential.

At the tertiary level treatment and interventions are focused on the child who has already engaged in delinquent behaviors and has been adjudicated. In the case of our population, children who have attempted or committed murder, issues of treatment and the process of adjucation are more serious and complex. As a result we address them in separate chapters.

At the primary and secondary levels of prevention our potentially homicidal children share much in common with other delinquent and at-risk children. Once children have engaged in extremes of violence, their treatment and disposition deviates significantly from that afforded other delinquent children. As described earlier, the commission of a serious crime will involve the child in criminal court proceedings. The probability of what would be thought of as preventive interventions will be limited at best. The general rule will be blended sentencing (i.e., long-term incarceration for the offense involving both juvenile detention followed by placement in adult facilities). Isolation and some form of restraint will occur in cases where there is a threat of harm to others or to one's self. These represent preventive measures; they do not remove cause for the child's behavior but only hold cause an abeyance.

Preventive therapeutics are typically utilized as secondary or tertiary levels of intervention. They are applied to children identified as at risk or following the commission of delinquent acts. Intervention can occur at the individual, group, or family level. Those interventions applied to the individual child or to the group require family involvement as collateral in parent training or in individual psychotherapy. Ultimately the child at risk is viewed and treated as part of a system that itself requires modification.

To be effective, preventive therapeutics require several components: (1) early detection, (2) early application, (3) recognition and family acceptance of the problem, (4) a willingness to cooperate in the proposed interventions, (5) a coordination with schools, (6) awareness on the part of those who would treat the child of contextual issues (the community or neighborhood and its resources).

Examination of the histories of child murderers and those committing violent acts reveal that despite professionals' early awareness of risk or difficulties in the child's behavior, absence of one or more of the necessary conditions resulted in minimal use of therapeutic interventions. In many instances repeated attempts to provide services were ignored and the child's negative behavior denied.

Once adjudicated, families and children have shown greater compliance with recommendations for treatment. Unfortunately, by the time cases are adjudicated, behavior patterns may be deeply entrenched and therapeutic efforts less successful. In the case of a violent act or murder, efforts are no longer open to preventive measures. Instead, the course of action is a trial, often in adult court, with therapeutics acquiring a minimal role as compared with the requirements of punishment.

COGNITIVE FACTORS

Observers have identified the role of the family, the environment, and the physical and nutritional history of the child as causal or at least contributory to development of cognitive problems. A major assumption of the kindergarten and preschool movements and the Head Start program was that unless interventions relate to the cognitive (intellectual) development of the child, some segments of our society would be unable to benefit fully from the universal educational experience (35 years after the first program was launched in 1965). Despite success in preparing children at risk for entering the educational system today, only 40% of eligible children are served; 11 states (Alabama, Idaho, Indiana, Kansas, Mississippi, Montana, New Mexico, North Dakota, South Dakota, Utah, and Wyoming) do not yet have preschool programs, and 3 others are only in the planning stage! Ironically some of the states lacking programs are among the poorest in the nation (Ripple, Gilliam, Chanana, & Zigler, 1999).

The importance of cognitive development as a preventive intervention for delinquency in its many forms lies in means by which the child learns the rules of the culture and how to solve problems. If the acquisition process is conducted or guided by competent parents, teachers, and other influential figures, the child's encounters with the larger culture may be addressed with knowledge, understanding, and adaptive responses. Although competency does not guarantee prosocial responses, it does afford children more options in meeting their needs. The imitation of prosocial models and the internalizing of their values and behaviors further enhance this process.

When there is a cognitive developmental lag, whether because of parental neglect, indifference, a lack of resources, an unfavorable environment, or deficient and inadequate school systems, options are reduced and alternative and often undesirable models and situations are accepted and embraced. Therefore, maximizing educational opportunities as early as possible, preferably by age 3 for children who are underserved (Zigler, 1998) is fundamental in addressing issues of violence. Fostering cognitive skills in problem solving coupled with modeling appropriate moral values can result in constructive rather than destructive solutions, but only if all parties involved are at a similar level of cognitive awareness.

VIOLENT BEHAVIOR

Significant progress has been made in identifying initiatives that have been demonstrated as effective in preventing or reducing violence. The Center for the Study and Prevention of Violence (CSPV) at the University of Colorado at Boulder has identified 10 prevention and intervention programs that meet scientific standards of proven effectiveness. Proof is based on four criteria: use of an experimental or quasi-experimental design with matched controls or random assignments; evidence of a statistically significant effect of deterrence in violence, drug usage, or other delinquent behaviors; replication of results; and evidence that the effect has been sustained for at least one year. Given high of recidivism rates that occur mostly within the first five to six months, these finding are impressive.

The 10 programs, called Blueprints, will form a basis of training and technical assistance to community organizations and program providers sponsored by CSPV and the Office of Juvenile Justice and Delinquency Prevention (OJJDP).

The identified programs and their description are reported in the OJJDP Fact Sheet in June 1999:

Prenatal and Infancy Nurse Home Visitation is a program that sends nurses into the homes of at-risk pregnant women bearing their first child. Home visits promote the physical, cognitive, and emotional development of the child and provide general support and parenting instruction to the parents from the prenatal period to two years after the birth of the child.

The Bullying Prevention Program is a school-based initiative designed to reduce bullying problems among primary and secondary school children. The program identifies and addresses incidents from teasing and taunting to intimidation and physical violence; it also attempts to restructure the school environment to reduce opportunities and rewards for bullying behavior.

Promoting Alternative Thinking Strategies is a multiyear, school-based prevention model for elementary school youth designed to promote emotional and social competence, including the expression, understanding, and regulation of emotions.

The Big Brothers Big Sisters of America mentoring program primarily serves 6– to 18–year-old disadvantaged youth from single-parent households. The goal is to provide a consistent and stable mentoring relationship. A mentor meets with his or her assigned youth at least three times a month for three to five hours.

Quantum Opportunities is an educational incentives program for disadvantaged teens. It provides educational, developmental, and service activities combined with a sustained relationship with a peer group and a caring adult during the high school years. The goal of the program is to help high-risk youth from poor families and neighborhoods to graduate from high school and attend college by improving basic academic skills.

Multisystemic Therapy (MST) targets specific factors in a youth's ecology—that is, family, peers, school, neighborhood, and support network—that contribute to antisocial behavior. MST is a short-term, intensive program by credentialed therapists that has been proven effective for decreasing antisocial behavior of violent and chronic juvenile offenders.

Functional Family Therapy (FFT) is a family treatment model designed to engage and motivate youth and families to change their communication, interaction, and problem-solving patterns. FFT has been applied successfully to a variety of youth with problems ranging from conduct disorder to serious criminal offenses such as theft or aggravated assault.

The Midwestern Prevention Project is a comprehensive, community-based program designed to prevent the use of cigarettes, alcohol, and marijuana among junior high and middle school students. The program introduces five intervention strategies in sequence over a five-year period; the strategies involve mass media, school, parents, community organizations, and health policy change to combat drug use in the community.

Life Skills Training is a three-year primary prevention program that targets the use of cigarettes, alcohol, and marijuana (the initial year includes 15 lessons; booster sessions are provided in years 2 and 3). The program provides general life skills and social resistance skills training to junior high and middle school students to increase knowledge and improve attitudes about drug use.

Multidimensional Treatment Foster Care is an effective alternative to residential treatment for adolescents who have problems with chronic delinquency and antisocial behavior. Youth are placed in well-supervised foster families for six to nine months and undergo weekly individualized therapy. Foster families receive weekly group supervision and daily telephone monitoring. Biological parents learn behavior management techniques to ensure that gains made in the foster setting are maintained after the youth return home.

Another significant intervention has been in progress for several years. Sites in Colorado and Florida are investigating the potentials of assessment centers that combine the often fragmental efforts of multiple agencies to deal with children at risk. Too often agencies are completely unaware of efforts other than their own, or they learn too late of service duplications, failed efforts, or even successful interventions. Although results are not available as of this writing, four key elements have been identified as having an important role in the prevention of violence and other delinquent behaviors: a single point of entry for all agencies; immediate and comprehensive assessment, including academic, physical, and psychological measures; integrated case management with all appropriate agencies involved; and a comprehensive and integrated management information system.

This idea is not new. It has been discussed and tried (somewhat tentatively) in a number of settings with mixed success and most often abandoned after a trial period. Stories of jurisdictional battles over delinquent children no agency wants are legend in most agencies (and in the experience of one of the authors of this volume). What is different at present are mandates at the national and state level that something must be done because the present system is not working. These initiatives and the support, advice, direction, and encouragement of the OJJDP offer a potential for success not possible in the past.

ADVERSE FAMILIAL FACTORS

In our chapter on the family, we have detailed changes in the operation and function of the family. Originally it was an extended family model, in a relatively stable environment, that offered some support to families at risk. Today the nuclear family for many children at risk for violence is a single-working parent, living close to if not below the poverty level, with minimal extended family support and virtually no support from the community or the schools. Even when the family is intact, with two parents, and has an above-average income, adverse family factors may be present in the form of neglect or simply lack of awareness. In the Littleton, Colorado, tragedy for example, the media marveled that two well-to-do adolescent boys could accumulate weapons, paraphernalia, and other ominous artifacts without raising parental concern. Were the parents of these boys unique, or do they represent the norm at this social level, where solutions are often reached by following the popular adage "Throw enough money at it and it will go away"?

At all levels of society, from the very poor to the extremely wealthy, children at risk are most often dealt with at the tertiary level, that is, after they have engaged in delinquent behavior and their cases have been adjudicated, rather than being engaged in the preventive activities that would protect most children from reaching the levels of anger, dehumanization, and alienation that prompt to kill or attempt to kill another person.

Many of the well-intentioned solutions currently offered really miss the point. Requiring a valid ID to be able to buy a ticket to an R-rated movie, installing a blocking chip for the TV, maintaining control of internet access, establishing curfews, and passing and enforcing loitering laws, each in its way represents a giving over of control and authority to some external force, when the answer must be a resumption of family authority and responsibility. Given the complexity of today's world, applying limits and controls will not be easy. Dysfunctional families and those unable to cope will need strong external help and support. Early identification of problems by day care facilities and schools will play a significant role. In addition to work training, parenting classes should be offered to persons receiving welfare.

For advantaged children whose deviant behaviors come to the attention of authorities, involving parents presents other problems. "Successful" parents often feel they do not have the time to attend family therapy sessions. They are often more willing to buy their child out of difficulties until the problems reach a level where a buyout is not possible. How to restore responsibility to a family uninterested in investing the time and energy needed to prevent behavioral disasters by their children is an issue without easy solution. However, competent models and functional families do exist, and most children have benefit of such families. Although, unfortunately many children do not, even among at-risk children there are those who thrive and develop moral and prosocial values.

Preaching at, condemning, pointing fingers of shame, and legal mandates have failed to be sufficient incentives to produce change. What can be hoped for in such instances is at best a neutralizing of the negative impact of a parent or of parents; interventions with the child can provide identifiable rewards to aid in behavioral change.

Lest our comment regarding external controls be misconstrued, we do not oppose regulatory statutes or appropriate research-based interventions by local, state, and national governments. We recognize that these programs alone are insufficient in dealing with the violent child. There is no substitute for the support, monitoring, and controls offered by the family and the community.

ENVIRONMENTAL FACTORS

In this section we will address the school, the neighborhood, and the community and their role in preventing violence.

The School

Some of the evolving changes in school operations will positively affect the school climate. Emphasis on preschool and kindergarten programs will identify social and adjustive difficulties earlier than is possible today in many school districts. Focus on all children reaching certain achievement levels and proficiencies could reduce the performance differences between children from advantaged and disadvantaged backgrounds. Smaller class sizes will permit fewer students to be lost or ignored. All these presently existing negative factors combine to create an environment for our children at risk which reduces self-esteem, creates despair and resentment, and in many instances leads to anger and violence. In our work through the years with incarcerated children who have displayed violent behavior, we have seen profiles that reveal an unrelenting series experience in failure. Burdened by limiting family environments such as single-parent families, poor housing, and poverty; by moderate levels of intelligence that restrict academic success; by limited social skills; and by limited sports success either because skills are lacking or prevented from or because participation is restricted as a result of poor grades or poor conduct, these children often have no area in which they have received recognition, acceptance, praise, or other reinforcements. School changes that focus more on individual needs and promote growth can reduce the toxicity of the environment and help the young child to work for socially acceptable goals with some hope of achieving those goals. At least more children will stay the course rather than adopting delinquent solutions for their problems.

Working against these positive efforts has been the movement to strip school systems of special services and activities other than those mandated by state and federal law. Many districts that offered culturally enriching activities such as art, chorus, band, and drama offered for credit, have removed special services offerings. For the advantaged students lack of special services has never been a problem. Soccer moms, ballet moms, music lessons moms, drama class moms (and even occasional dads)are much heard of in the media. Unfortunately, those children who suffer most from restricted services can ill afford to be deprived of activities wherein they could receive recognition and develop "braggable" skills in their interactions with more advantaged students. In adolescence, a number of advantaged young persons choose to become part of a counterculture. For many of the children whose experiences lead to participation in a delinquent subculture, there may be no choice.

What course of action is open to school officials, legislators, concerned ·parents, and concerned citizens? First would be the restoration of authority to the schools through an alliance between parents and teachers and school authorities. Too often today the relationship among these groups is adversarial. Teachers today are unable to take the social and behavioral control once regarded as part of their responsibility as a teacher. Fear of lawsuits by parents or censure by school boards or legislators has deprived teachers of their authority.

Can teachers reassume the role of in loco parentis once held by their predecessors? Doing so would provide an important link in the prevention process. A series of steps would be necessary to achieve this role readjustment. First, legislatures and school boards would have to agree on the desirability of empowering teachers and school authorities. Parents and parent groups would have to concur and then actively support such a position. Teachers would have to accept the added responsibility. Finally, teacher training would have to shift focus to include training for their expanded role. Further, as these roles are expanded, the demands for additional interventions and services provided by school counselors, nurses, and social workers will grow. Teachers will need to actively direct at-risk children to these sources or inform parents of their child's needs. This is not to suggest that teachers do not take these actions today. Indeed, they are taken through the efforts of dedicated teachers and school officials. However, these actions represent individual efforts, not school policy. It is worth considering whether coordinated efforts between schools, parents, and the community might have prevented the tragedies of Jonesboro, Arkansas, or Littleton, Colorado. Would early signs of disturbance or deviance led to proactive actions by teachers or school officials? Deviance in children in the form of dress or behavior may not lead to violence or homicide, but it also should not be ignored. Determining why students exhibit deviant behavior or dress is the first step in prevention.

Garbarino (1992) stresses the need for building a strong home-school mesosystem (linkage) and the necessity for schools to meet families halfway. To do this involves the return of the model of school-family relationships in which partnerships between the two are established and encouraged.

Mulvey, Arthur, and Reppucci (1993) classify school-based interventions into three categories: preschool programs such as Head Start; cognitive behavioral interventions consisting typically of individualized interpersonal problem-solving or behavioral social skills training; and social process interventions, which most often attempt systems-level interventions such as modifying school procedures and processes to more adequately address the needs of the child at risk. Although promising, these approaches have yet to produce research findings indicating their effectiveness in reducing violence and delinquent behaviors.

Changes in the Neighborhood and Community

We have explored in detail changes in the family that have resulted in a dramatic shift in how communities function. Before World War II communities were highly functional as preventive entities. Communities were small, peopled by intact families whose familiarity with one another spanned many years. Even in larger cities, neighborhoods did not reflect high mobility and were not "a gathering of strangers." In many urban places the neighborhood operated in loco parentis or as an extended family, giving additional supervision, interventions, and care.

What constitutes a family has changed dramatically since World War II, producing further community restructuring. Fewer households contain children (45.3% in 1970, 37.6% 1990, with even lower expectations for the year 2000). Households with a married couple are down from 70.5% in 1970 to 56.0% in 1990, still lower projected for 2000. Numbers of households with three or more children are down from 18.5% in 1970 to 7.0% in 1990; again projections for 2000 should be even lower. More persons are living alone, up from 17.1% in 1970 to 24.6% in 1990. These figures represent a few selected statistics that reconfigure the family and households and produce a picture of a community vastly different from that of even a single generation ago.

Not all statistics are negative, however. Families living below the poverty level in 1960 were 22.2% of the population. That figure dropped to 13.5% in 1990 and was projected by the Bureau of Census to be 13.3% in 1997. Specific, rates for African Americans and Hispanics have, however, remained high since these statistics were first available: 32% for African Americans, 25.7% for Hispanics in 1980, with 1997 projections of 26.5% and 27.5% as compared with 11.0% for whites. These inequities present a major problem for government at all levels. Effective legislation must find a way to address these issues if the family or household is to regain a meaningful and functional role in the community.

Acknowledging that the makeup of families has changed and has as a result affected the nature of the neighborhood and the community in general, several excellent studies have examined the relationship between the community and the incidence of delinquent behavior. How communities are structured and organized (or disorganized) plays a significant role in the development of delinquent behavior that extends beyond family composition, poverty, crowding, and the schools. Research (Elliot et al., 1996; Sampson, 1997) has identified the presence or lack of strong informal and formal community support systems as perhaps the key variable in the development or prevention of delinquency. The mandate from these works (Elliot et al., 1996; Sampson, 1997) is that to prevent delinquency the community must provide children with formal and informal resources, and this effort must be made especially in communities where resources are lacking and the community is disorganized. Ideally, in the high-risk community, efforts should be directed toward enhancing community resources and improving family interactions by means of parent training and education programs.

Prevention in the community is an interactive process involving parents, schools, public officials, and community resources. Prevention efforts must begin early, as research evidence indicates that unless programs are applied during early and middle childhood years, fostering the development of prosocial and nondelinquent behaviors may be difficult, if not impossible (Sampson, 1992).

MEDIA INFLUENCES

The role of the media in prevention has received less attention than the perils related to unrestricted viewing of television, the internet, and pornography. The possible effects of video games, CDs, and certain magazines and books have also been explored. These investigations have led to an agreement that for some children, the stimulating effects of engaging with these materials result in increased aggressive and violent behavior. Even these relationships appear to diminish, however, when long-term observations have been made. Other studies have revealed a negative relationship between the amount of TV viewing and academic performance, creativity, and problem-solving ability (Lefrancois, 1995).

Yet media can play a positive role in children's development. Our goal at this point is to examine the role of the media, primarily television, as a positive force in the prevention of violence and delinquency. Many are television shows aimed at young children emphasize prosocial values, education, and achievement—for example, *Mr. Rogers*, *Sesame Street*, and *Barney*. Unfortunately, these shows compete with the more sensational offerings that involve violence, adventure, and heavy product marketing aimed at the young consumer. Studies have shown generally positive outcomes from viewing the prosocial presentations; though without adult supervision and involvement, passive viewing by children may be of only limited value (Shaffer, 1996).

Media campaigns against violence, drugs, alcohol, and the impact of nonattendance of school reach the attention of adults and children alike. Whether these campaigns reduce the possibility of involvement with these negative behaviors is less clear. Supporters suggest that at the very least they alert parents and certainly "do no harm."

That the media have an enormous impact on shaping children is of little doubt. What remain unclear are the specific techniques that are effective and for which children. Until we can reach that level of research sophistication, we are left with a prophylactic approach in which we recommend parental control and monitoring of television and the internet, as well as the encouragement of reading and school achievement, with the hope for positive outcomes for doing what seems to be appropriate and appears to work.

CONCLUSIONS

The broad stroke of prevention involves interventions at three levels. At each level established approaches seek to provide several buffering effects.

The specific aims include promoting the general health and well-being of families, reducing the potential for violence, providing for success experiences and outlets for frustrations, maximizing educational success and achievement, and fostering a positive self-image and self-esteem. Such efforts can reduce the incidence of murders by children and adolescents, but these measures will not remove the possibility entirely. Even the most effective and intensive programs of prevention are not totally successful. Too often, successful programs reduce problems, then suffer cutbacks because of reduced incidence reports, complacency, or the rise of new priorities. The unfortunate reality is that to deal effectively with the problems of children and their potential for violence, the programs must be ongoing. This involves maintaining leadership, funding, and staffing and, most important, building in flexibility for organizational change as neighborhoods evolve, cultures change, and political shifts occur—all services and difficult issues that must be addressed if our culture of violence is to be modified.

In addition to taking preventive approaches, communities need to identify and understand how some children survive and achieve at high levels despite being reared in a toxic environment. What accounts for their resilience and indestructibility when all indicators suggest dramatically opposite outcomes: educational dropouts, violence, gang membership, and criminal behavior. When both efforts are combined, there may then be a possibility of success in reducing violence and murder. We believe that the essential element in preventing violence and murder by children is appropriate moral development and judgment. All measures the form of external controls—gun control, electronic screening, stated prohibitions, and more severe penalties for rules violations will offer only limited containment of violence and murder. What must occur for those children and adolescents at risk is to internalize values that include respect for the rights of others, to develop empathic responses regarding others, and to be able to humanize others even in the face of anger and frustration. Can this be done? We have no alternatives. We must find ways to help the angry, amoral child to internalize a prosocial moral value system and to behave in keeping with that system. This must occur at a point in time before other less acceptable responses become dominant.

Large-scale interventions aimed at prevention may at first seem either impossible or highly unlikely, yet in the history of this country prevention on a national and state level has not only occurred but been highly successful. First and foremost has been the requirement for education for all children. Second has been the requirement for inoculation for the prevention of disease, first for smallpox, later for a series of contagious diseases, and most recently the virtual eradication of polio. Project Head Start has been a successful program seeking to prepare children experientially to deal with problems stemming from poverty and to prepare them to benefit from public education. Thus in the United States the forces necessary to prevent illiteracy and disease have been successfully mobilized. These same forces can be organized now to cope with gun control, violence in children, media excesses, and internet abuse, empowering communities and helping restore them. Between the extremes of no legislative restrictions and heavy handed controls lies a more reasonable position. The tragedies of Jonesboro and Littleton may have signaled to all of us that preventive measures must be undertaken. Granted that the issues underlying violence are complex and that research is relatively sparses, but contributing factors have been identified and professionals have a clear understanding of what needs to be done to deal with preventing such tragedies. What is presently lacking are established procedures informing legislatures and other concerned parties how these goals may be achieved. Public reaction to the events in Jonesboro and Littleton has resulted in alerting the public in general and families in particular to be more aware of the needs and behaviors of children at risk. Efforts must be undertaken to sustain this interest and to increase awareness of the more subtle signs of violence in children. Values are in place. This learning, however, often occurs at inopportune times. The ideal time is early childhood, when other children are incorporating these values in their functional home environment. Ways and means must be developed to instill values for at-risk children in dysfunctional families and delinquent subcultures.

Summary and Conclusions

In this work we have attempted to provide insights into the behavior, motivations, attributions, and uniqueness of preteen murderers as differentiated from adolescent murderers. Although their numbers are few in comparison with adolescent murderers, they do represent a significant group about whom little is known. Access to needed information is limited by the age of the child, how data are collected, and a relative lack of evaluative instrumentation, which can provide authoritative information about mental status, personality, and amenability to treatment and rehabilitation.

Observation of juveniles in the post–World War II era reveals a continuing drop in the age of first offense for a variety of chargeable offenses such as drug abuse, sexual abuse, and crimes against persons. With that trend, if society hopes to stem the increases in juvenile crimes, especially those involving violence, we must develop fuller understanding of causal and contributory factors, make effective diagnoses and identify problem areas, and apply treatment measures successful in modifying undesirable thoughts and behaviors.

As part of our summary and recommendations, we will examine what can be stated affirmatively. The first three chapters, which report on published research, provide demographics, personal characteristics, problem behaviors, family dynamics, and the environments of preteen murderers. The reviewed literature suggest preteen homicide is a rare occurrence that does not appear to have mirrored the increase in juvenile homicide observed over the past 15 years. Perhaps because of its rare nature, this population has been the subject of relatively little research. Furthermore, the majority of studies in this area have relied on small and/or marginal samples, reducing the generalizability of their findings and in some cases spawning inaccurate assumptions about this population.

Recognizing the high degree of heterogeneity across cases, the present review closely examined studies that have attempted to classify this population. These efforts were separated into three general categories, including classification systems based on psychiatric constructs, specific characteristics of the offense, and the victim-offender relationship. Although there is evidence to support the utility of all three approaches, it was argued that classification systems based on specific characteristics of the offense (including the victim-offender relationship) possess several advantages that make them the most logical choice for future efforts. Most important, they allow researchers to use a greater range of developmental factors in attempts to establish their validity. In addition, because these systems were originally developed for criminal and judicial purposes, they do a better job of facilitating interdisciplinary communication. Finally, this classification approach makes sense conceptually. Preliminary data suggest that preteens who murder an acquaintance family member in the course of a dispute may have a different presentation and prognosis as compared to preteens who commit murder in the course of other criminal activity.

In terms of predictors, the present review found that preteen homicide offenders are likely to have psychiatric histories characterized by high rates of conduct disorder and impulse control or hyperactivity deficits—two factors with strong connections to psychopathic behavior in adulthood. Although less certain, there is also evidence to suggest elevated rates of psychotic symptomatology, separation anxiety disorder, polysubstance abuse, enuresis, and depression. In terms of cognitive functioning, though there is conflicting data regarding the intelligence of this population, there is substantial evidence indicating an elevated rate of neurological abnormalities and learning disabilities. Perhaps the clearest finding, however, pertains to this population's family background. Specifically, a high percentage of preteen homicide offenders come from homes characterized by abuse, domestic violence, poor or absent parenting, and overall instability. Finally, there is qualified support for advocating that gun availability is a homicide predictor. The relationship between the remaining environmental factors (gangs and media) requires further investigation.

Overall, although this pool of predictors closely resembles that of adolescent homicide offenders, it would be incorrect to assume an identical etiology between preteen homicide and juvenile homicide. Indeed, what appears to distinguish preteens is not the range of risk factors that can contribute to their offense but, instead, the sheer number and combination of risk factors that affect an individual before the murder. That is, by virtue of their more limited physical and cognitive abilities, preteens clearly have a higher threshold for committing murder than do adolescents. In a select few cases, however, this threshold will be reached when a certain amount, combination, or intensity of these predictors is present. The case-study comparison provided some preliminary support for this hypothesis through its discovery of a slightly elevated number of risk factors in pre-teen cases as well as differences in the prevalence of certain predictors. The challenge for future researchers, however, is to begin to tease apart the specific combination(s) of risk factors that will cause a preteen to murder and to develop models of offending that coherently explain these dynamics.

To assist in this process, the authors call upon the field to make greater use of the literature on the development of juvenile offending. Thanks to the contributions of many researchers, including Rolf Loeber, G. R. Patterson, David Farrington, and Scott Henggeler, the general study of ju-venile offending has made significant advances in terms of methodology and knowledge regarding predictors. Although there are most likely key differences between preteen murderers and their peers who are involved in less serious crimes, youth homicide researchers have perhaps assumed too many differences between these populations. In the process, potentially useful information on issues like "the dynamics behind the escalation from relatively minor to more serious crimes" as well as "the developmental constitution of 'early-starter' criminal offenders" has been ignored. Even-tually, through a combination of studies that focus exclusively on preteen homicide offenders and those that look at juvenile offending in general, the field should reach a point where comprehensive models of preteen homi-cide offending are proposed akin to Hardwick and Rowton-Lee's (1996) model of juvenile homicide.

As we have expressed earlier, several apparent goals for future research include (1) a need to more carefully separate and study preteen violent of-fenders from the adolescent juvenile violent offenders; (2) examination of the developmental evolving of violence from early offenses to more serious crimes by preteens; (3) further exploration of differences between male and female preteen murderers; (4) development of assessment techniques for predicting violence in preteens; and (5) enhanced understanding of moral judgments and their role in violence in preteens.

The most significant impression that emerges from research on this pop-ulation is the high degree of individual, familial, and environmental defi-cits and stressors present across cases. The popular notion that extreme conditions will give rise to extreme behavior appears to ring true in the phenomenon of preteen homicide. Thus, although some preteen homicide offenders may have a better prognosis than others, if one operates from the perspective that society has failed these children (as opposed to the view that these children have failed society), then perhaps an even greater sense of urgency will be instilled in those individuals charged with the much-underappreciated but highly important task of rehabilitating child offenders.

THE INTERVENTIONS

Research has clearly identified the factors that contribute to acts of murder by children. Causality is less clear, though it does appear certain that acts of extreme violence occur only in children who possess some or many of the identified problems presented in our review of research: family alcohol and drug problems, family psychiatric problems, child physical and emotional abuse, unstable home environment, domineering mother, negative relationship with father or male caretaker, unfair treatment by others, isolation, lying, enuresis, rebellious and oppositional behavior, fire setting, stealing, cruelty to other children, fantasy and daydreaming, truancy, cruelty to animals, unhealthy sexual experiences, and murderous thoughts. Although these factors apply to both child murderers and adolescent murderers, several stand out as significant for child murderers: physical and emotional abuse, negative relationship with father or male caretaker, rebellious and oppositional behavior, unstable environment, cruelty to other children, isolation, and family psychiatric problems.

Whether any single factor or combination of factors is causal cannot be established with certainty. As we have observed, attributions by perpetrators often take the form of justifying their behavior or in attempting to lay blame on others. Recall is often shaped by the events of the present and can be highly inaccurate. Investigative interviews with children often provide interpretive suggestions, further confusing the conclusions to be drawn. Finally, the cognitive processes of children may be such that logic and causality are not well developed; impulse may account for many of their acts.

For appropriate remedy and rehabilitation, high specificity of causality is not necessary. Contributions are sufficient. We base this conclusion on the techniques available for prevention; treatment and rehabilitation are broad and rather inclusive. For example, we cannot treat a child for rebellious and oppositional behavior without affecting relationships with others, lying behavior, and abuse. Similarly, other symptomatic behaviors have linkages that must all be addressed for successful outcomes.

MORAL DEVELOPMENT

We have emphasized the importance of moral development as a key in the control of violence and the establishing of empathy and concern for the rights of other persons. We have also presented the clear indication from a variety of research studies that the violent or murderous child lacks empathy and depersonalizes other persons, with the further suggestion that these qualities give violent children license to do violence.

Both remediation and prevention require appropriate measures to ensure that children grow up embracing the prosocial values of empathy and concern for others and, ideally, a level of altruism. Unfortunately, with regard to the teaching of moral values and the modification of deficient moral development, suitable methods are little understood and unknowns far exceed knowledgeable approaches. Whether it is even possible to connect faulty moral judgments with development has been in question. Public policy today is too often guided by the philosophy that "nothing works" and incarceration is the only approach.

We are convinced that with few exceptions, these values are learned responses and as such subject to the laws of learning and learning principles that indicate that it is feasible to replace an undesired response with a positive or prosocial response, given sufficient and appropriate reinforcement. Does this rule also apply to higher cognitive processes? If so, what represents a sufficient level of reinforcement to replace a pattern of responding that is a culturally determined support of violence and a lack of empathy and concern for others?

At this point it is not possible to affirm or deny that murderers or violent children lack any capacity to demonstrate empathy or altruism. This is the current research focus of one of the authors (David Shumaker) of this volume. It is contended that modification and extension of an existing prosocial and moral response is less difficult and complex than creating moral values when none presently exist. These and other questions must be researched to determine the state of moral development in violent children, how moral values can be inculcated, and which methods might be appropriate, given the large individual differences found in these children.

Garbarino and Eckenrode (1997) propose three mandates that represent the minimal level of care for all children: first "access to preventive health care, education, immunization, clothing appropriate to the weather, dental care, adequate nutrition; second, adult care and supervision on an age appropriate level; and finally each child should have an enduring relationship with a responsible caring adult." These requirements are a triad for the prevention of abuse. They are no less appropriate as goals for the prevention of violence and its ultimate consequence—murder.

In our chapter on prevention we have described a series of successful programs sponsored by the OJJDP occurring in selected cities across the country. The implementation of the techniques and lessons of these efforts by states and communities would represent a major step in the prevention of violence. These efforts provide a ringing disclaimer to those whose approach and philosophy is "Why bother? Nothing works."

TREATMENT

Treatment has two distinct categories: (1) treatment directed at preventing the expression of violent behaviors and (2) treatment aimed at restoring the violent child to a meaningful role in society. Efforts at prevention are described in the chapters on treatment and prevention and consist of interventions aimed at providing the child with more effective ways of coping with problems, promoting the development of prosocial attitudes and behaviors, helping the family to use more effective behavioral management and reduce dysfunctional interactions, and supporting community-based efforts that seek to provide protection, support, and the development of prosocial behaviors in this broader context. As noted, much effort has been given to each area and outcomes are promising. What remains is for communities and states to adopt effective programs, that is, those that have demonstrated their success in reducing violence and delinquency.

In the second instance, restoring the murderous child to society presents a complex and vexing series of problems that to date have little evidence of successful solution. Because of variability in public reaction, media attention, projected age at release, and mental state of the offender; differences in sentencing and waiving to adult court; and the presence or lack of treatment and rehabilitative services in each state and each correctional facility, each case requires complete and careful long-range planning by experienced professionals in order to have some hope of a successful outcome for the child murderer. Left to the routine of most correctional facilities, isolated and segregated, treatment or rehabilitative effort would remain inadequate. Costly? Perhaps. But what are the potential costs for returning the untreated violent child (or an adult) to society?

PREVENTION

A myriad of possible childhood experiences have been suggested as causal or contributory to violence in children: video games, movies, drugs, action comics, television, the decline of the family, ineffective schools, and on and on. Certainly each of these may contribute in some cases. Yet, the most significant factors emerging from the latest intervention projects fall into two areas: the dynamics existing in the family and the lack of formal and informal supports in the community. These are the larger issues that must be addressed and implemented if violence is to be reduced. The cosmetic effect of media cleansing will allay the concerns of many and provide potential figures with tangible evidence of change. It will remain for the barod-based restoration of effective communities rich in support, in formal and informal control, to create measurable change and thus progress. Educational programs for parenting and therapeutic interventions for advanced cases, coupled with community efforts, form the core of the prevention of violence.

We have dealt with the treatment of conduct-disordered children and have reported limited successes in dealing with this population of children who display persistent patterns of aggressive antisocial behavior involving opposition to authority, truancy, disobedience, physical aggression, lying, and stealing in younger children, with substance abuse, violent crime, school dropout, and other behaviors added as they reach adolescence. Central to the prevention of conduct disorders (Webster–Stratton & Martin, 1994) is how much of this disorder is rooted in family violence and child abuse. Intervention strategies, which have been successful, have been behaviorally based parent-training approaches applied early in the child's life. Traditional approaches have been demonstrated to be less successful (Kazdin, 1998) as well as more costly.

Behaviorally based family-training approaches require participation in the full programs in order to be effective. Ideally, these programs, should start with the young child, as later attempts with adolescents have proven less successful. Other factors such as the intractability of parental problems—depression, substance abuse, and violence, for example—reduce chances of success and compliance with the treatment plan. The result is that 30% to 50% of children with conduct disorders are reported by parents as still having difficulties following treatment (Webster-Stratton & Herbert, 1994). Whether these children, whose reaction to treatment has fallen short of complete remission of symptoms, have reduced their potential for violence sufficiently to preclude lethal responses is not clear from available data. The data do suggest, however, that research for more effective treatment approaches, as well as better methods for ensuring compliance to treatment for both parents and children, should continue.

For children with other diagnoses, such as ADHD, depression, or psychosis, treatment typically combines drug therapies with cognitive behavioral methods, with increasing support for multimodal approaches for optimum treatment results. As with conduct disorders, additional research on all aspects of treatment are essential for developing effective treatment, prevention, and rehabilitation.

REHABILITATION

The most vexing problem facing legal authorities, communities, and parents is to determine what can be done for or with the child who murders. Most preteens who murder will be released from custody, although the period of incarceration may vary from seven or eight years to a longer period in states where blended sentencing is available. Teenage murderers, increasingly tried in adult criminal courts, will with occasional exceptions also be released, though at ages considerably older than for preteens. Because of the high incidence of teen murders, adolescent offenders are much more likely than preteens to be released with little notice. Preteen murderers, conversely, are almost invariably high-profile cases of great media interest. Their release and the accompanying publicity only further complicate the preteen's reentry to society. Effective postincarceration adjustment must be based on extensive planning and education for the child, the family, and the community. The possibility that members of the community may react as they do to the presence of child molesters or rapists is very possible. Many community members may fear that the act of murder could be repeated, and thus they may show extreme hostility.

Finally, research on prevention, treatment, and rehabilitation has resulted in major gains for professionals dealing with the violent and potentially homicidal child. Federal and state agencies have implemented research-based approaches and have demonstrated at least limited success in each area. What remains, to be undertaken is the dissemination of this knowledge and the provision of the resources necessary for its implementation. The OJJDP has provided leadership and incentive, as have the professionals such as Ewing, Garbarino, Grisso, Heide, and Sampson. It is vital that these efforts continue. Prevention is the best, if not the only, course.

References

Achenbach, T. (1991a). *Manual for the Child Behavior Checklist/4–18 and 1991 profile.* Burlington: University of Vermont Department of Psychology.

Achenbach, T. (1991b). *Manual for the Teachers Report Form and 1991 profile.* Burlington: University of Vermont Department of Psychology.

Achenbach, T. (1991c). *Manual for the Youth Self-Report and 1991 profile.* Burlington: University of Vermont Department of Psychology.

Adam, B.S., & Livingston, R. (1993). Sororicide in preteen girls: A case report and literature review. *Acta Paedopsychiatrica, 56,* 47–51.

Adams, K.A. (1974). The child who murders: A review of theory and research. *Criminal Justice and Behavior, 1,* 51–61.

Anastasi, A., & Urbina, S. (1997). *Psychological testing* (7th ed.). Upper Saddle River, NJ: Prentice-Hall.

Andreasen, M.S. (1990). Evolution in the family's use of television: Normative data from industry and academe. In J. Bryant (Ed.), *Television and the American family* (pp. 3–55). Hillsdale, NJ: Lawrence Erlbaum Associates.

Bailey, S. (1996). Adolescents who murder. *Journal of Adolescence, 19,* 19–39.

Bandura, A. (1991). Social cognitive theory of moral thought and action. In W.M. Justines & J.L. Gewirtz (Eds.) *Handbook of moral behavior and development* Vol. 1, pp. 45–103. Hillsdale, NJ: Lawrence Erlbaum Associates.

Bartholomuew, K., & Horowitz, L.M. (1991). Attachment styles among young adults: A test of a four-category model. *Journal of Personality and Social Psychology 61,* 226–244.

Baumrind, D. (1971). Current patterns of parental authority. *Developmental Psychology Monographs, 4* (1, part 2).

Bender, L. (1959). Children and adolescents who have killed. *American Journal of Psychiatry, 116*, 510–513.

Bender, L., & Curran, F. J. (1940). Children and adolescents who kill. *Journal of Criminal Psychopathology, 1*, 297–322.

Bernstein, J. I. (1979). Premeditated murder by an eight-year-old boy. *International Journal of Offender Therapy and Comparative Criminology, 23*, 47–56.

Bezchlibnyk-Butler, K.Z. & Jeffries, J.J. (Eds). (1998). *Clinical handbook of pyschotropic drugs* (8th rev. ed.). Seattle: Hogrefe & Huber.

Bjerregaard, B., & Lizotte, A.J. (1995). Gun ownership and gang membership. *Journal of Criminal Law and Criminology, 86*, 37–58.

Blasi, A. (1980). Bridging moral cognition and moral action: A critical review of the literature. *Psychological Bulletin, 88*, 1–45.

Blatt, S.J., Brenneis, C.B., Schimek, J.G., & Glick, M. (1976). Normal development and psychopathological impairment of the concept of the object on the Rorschach. *Journal of Abnormal Psychology 85*, 364–373.

Block, R., & Block, C.R. (1993). *Street gang crime in Chicago*. Washington, DC: U.S. Department of Justice, National Institute of Justice.

Blumstein, A. (1995). Youth violence, guns, and the illicit-drug industry. *Journal of Criminal Law and Criminology, 86*, 10–36.

Borum, R. (1996). Improving the clinical practice of violence risk assessment. *American Psychologist, 51*, 945–956.

Borum, R, Otto, R., & Golding, S. (1993). Improving clinical judgement and decision making in forensic evaluation. *Journal of Psychology and Law, 21*, 35–76.

Bowlby, J. (1988). *A secure base: Clinical applications of attachment theory*. London: Routledge.

Bryant, B.K. (1982). An index of empathy for children and adolescents. *Child Development, 53*, 413–425.

Busch, K.G., Zagar, R., Hughes, T.M., Arbit, J., & Bussell, R. E. (1990). Adolescents who kill. *Journal of Clinical Psychology, 46*, 472–485.

Butcher, J.N., Williams, C.L., Graham, J.R., Archer, R.P., Tellegen, A., Ben-Porath, Y.S., & Kaemmer, B. (1992). *Minnesota Multiphasic Personality Inventory—Adolescent*. Minneapolis: University of Minnesota Press.

Capaldi, D.M., & Patterson, G.R. (1996). Can violent offenders be distinguished from frequent offenders: Prediction from childhood to adolescence. *Journal of Research on Crime and Delinquency, 33*, 206–231.

Cook, T.D., & Campbell, D.T. (Eds.). (1979). *Quasi-experimentation: Design and analysis issues for field settings*. Chicago: Rand McNally.

Corder, B.F., Ball, B.C., Haizlip, T.M., Rollins, R., & Beaumont, R. (1976). Adolescent parricide: A comparison with other adolescent murder. *American Journal of Psychiatry, 133*, 957–961.

Cormier, B.M., Angliker, C.C., Gagne, P.W., & Markus, B. (1978). Adolescents who kill members of the family. In J. Eekerlaar & S. Katz (Eds.), *Family violence: An international and interdisciplinary study* (pp. 466–478). Toronto: Butterworth.

Cornell, D.G. (1993). Juvenile homicide: A growing national problem. *Behavioral Sciences and the Law, 11*, 389–396.

Cornell, D.G., Benedek, E.P., & Benedek, D.M. (1987a) . Characteristics of adolescents charged with homicide: A review of 72 cases. *Behavioral Sciences and the Law, 5,* 11–23.

Cornell, D.G., Benedek, E.P., & Benedek, D.M. (1987b). Juvenile homicide: Prior adjustment and a proposed typology. *American Journal of Orthopsychiatry, 57,* 383–393.

Cornell, D.G., Miller, C., & Benedek, E.P. (1988). MMPI profiles of adolescents charged with homicide. *Behavioral Sciences and the Law, 6,* 401–407.

Dill, K.E., & Dill, J.C. (1998). Video game violence: A review of empirical literature. *Aggression and Violent Behavior, 3* (4), 407–428.

Dishion, T.J., & Andrews, D.W. (1995). Preventing escalation in problem behaviors with high risk adolescents: Immediate and 1–year outcomes. *Journal of Consulting and Clinical Psychology, 63,* 538–548.

Douglas, J.E., Burgess, A.W., & Burgess, A.G. (1992). *Crime classification manual.* New York: Lexington Books of Macmillan.

Duncan, J.W., & Duncan, G.M. (1971). Murder in the family: A study of some homicidal adolescents. *American Journal of Psychiatry, 127,* 74–78.

Easson, W.M., & Steinhilber, R.M. (1961). Murderous aggression by children and adolescents. *Archives of General Psychiatry, 4,* 1–9.

Eisenberg, N., & Miller, P.A. (1987). The relation of empathy to prosocial and related behavior. *Psychological Bulletin, 101,* 91–119.

Eisenberg, N., & Murphy, B. (1995). Parenting and children's moral development. In M.H. Bornstein (Ed.), *Handbook of Parenting: Vol. 4. Applied and practical parenting* (pp. 227–257). Mahwah, NJ: Lawrence Erlbaum Associates.

Elliott, D.S., Wilson, W.J., Huizinga, D., Sampson, R.J., Elliott, A., & Rankin, B. (1996). The effects of neighborhood disadvantage on adolescent development. *Journal of Research in Crime and Delinquency, 33,* 389–426.

Ewing, C. (1990). *When children kill: The dynamics of juvenile homicide.* Lexington, MA: Lexington Books.

Exner, J. (1974). *The Rorschach: A comprehensive system* (Vol. 1). New York: Wiley.

Exner, J. (1993). *The Rorschach: A comprehensive system* (Vol. 1, 3rd ed.). New York: Wiley.

Eyberg, S.M., Edwards, D., Boggs, S.R., & Foote, R. (1998). Maintaining the treatment effects of parental Training: the role of booster sessions and other maintainence strategies. *Clinical Psychology Science and Practice, 5,* 544–554.

Eyberg, S.M., & Robinson, E. (1983). Conduct problem behavior: Standardization of a behavioral rating scale with adolescents. *Journal of Clinical Child Psychology, 12,* 347–354.

Farrington, D.P. (1995). The development of offending and antisocial behaviour from childhood: Key findings from the Cambridge study in delinquent development. *Journal of Child Psychology and Psychiatry, 360,* 929–964.

Federal Bureau of Investigation (1997). *Uniform crime reports 1996.* Washington, DC: Author.

Feld, B.C. (1987). The juvenile court meets the principles of the offense: Legislative changes in juvenile waiver statutes. *Journal of Criminal Law & Criminology, 78,* 471.

Feldman, R.A., Caplinger, T., & Woldarski, J.S. (1983). *The St. Louis conundrum: The effective treatment of autisocial youths.* Englewood Cliffs, NJ: Prentice-Hall.

Figueira-McDonough, J. Community structure and delinquency: A typology. *Social Service Review*, March, 68–91.

Freedman, J.L. (1984). Effect of television violence on aggressiveness. *Psychological Bulletin, 96,* 227–246.

Frick, P.J., O'Brien, B.S., Wootton, J.M., & McBurnett, K. (1994). Psychopathy and conduct problems in children. *Journal of Abnormal Psychology, 103,* 700–707.

Friedrich-Cofer, L., & Huston, A.C. (1986). Television violence and aggression: The debate continues. *Psychological Bulletin, 100,* 364–371.

Garbarino, J. (1992). Children and families in the social environment (2nd ed.). New York: Aldine DeGruyter.

Garbarino, J. (1995). *Raising children in a socially toxic environment.* San Francisco: Jossey-Bass.

Garbarino, J., & Eckenrode, J. (eds.). (1997). *Understanding abusive families: An ecological approach to Theory and Practice.* San Francisco, CA: Jossey-Bass.

Gibbs, J.C., Basinger, K.S., & Fuller, D. (1992). *Moral maturity: Measuring the development of sociomoral reflection.* Hillsdale, NJ: Hove and London.

Gill, D.L., Gross, J.B., & Huddleston, S. (1983). Participation motivation in youth sports. *International Journal of Sport Psychology, 14,* 1–14.

Gilligan, C. (1982). *In a different voice: Psychological theory and women's development.* Cambridge, MA: Harvard University Press.

Godow, K.D., & Sprafkin, J. (1993). Television "violence" and children with emotional and behavioral disorders. *Journal of Emotional and Behavioral Disorders, 1,* 54–63.

Goetting, A. (1989). Patterns of homicide among children. *Criminal Justice and Behavior, 16,* 63–80.

Goldstein, A.P. (1991). *Delinquent gangs: A psychological perspective.* Champaign, IL: Research Press.

Gomez, R., & Samson, A. (1994). Mother-child interactions and noncompliance in hyperactive boys with and without conduct disorder. *Journal of Child Psychology and Psychiatry, 35,* 470–490.

Goodenough, F.L., & Harris, D.B. (1963). *Goodenough-Harris Drawing Test.* San Antonio, TX: The Psychological Corporation Harcourt Brace & Compnay.

Greco, C.M., & Cornell, D.G., (1992). Rorschach object relations of adolescents who committed homicide. *Journal of Personality Assessment, 59,* 574–583.

Greenberg, H.R., & Blank, R.H. (1970). Murder and self-destruction by a 12–year-old boy. *Adolescence, 5,* 391–396.

Greenhill, L.L. (1998). Childhood attention deficit hyperactivity: Pharmacological treatments. In P.E. Nathan & J.M. Gorman (Eds.). *A guide to treatments that work* (pp. 42–64).

Griffiths, M. (1999). Violent video games and aggression: A review of the literature. *Aggression and Violent Behavior, 4* (2), 203–212.

Grisso, T. (1988). *Competency to stand trial evaluations: A manual for practice.* Sarasota, FL: Professional Resource Exchange.

Grisso, T. (1997). The competence of adolescents as trial defendants. *Psychology, Public Policy and Law, 3,* 3–32.

Grisso, T. (1998). *Forensic evaluation of juveniles*. Sarasota, FL: Professional Resource Press.

Hagan, M.P. (1997). An analysis of adolescent perpetrators of homicide and attempted homicide upon return to the community. *International Journal of Offender Therapy and Comparative Criminology, 41,* 250–259.

Hardwick, P.J., & Rowton-Lee, M.A. (1996). Adolescent homicide: Towards assessment of risk. *Journal of Adolescence, 19,* 263–276.

Hare, R.D. (1991). *The Revised Psychopathy Checklist*. Toronto, Ontario, Canada: Multi-Health Systems.

Harlow, H. (1958). The nature of love. *American Psychologist, 13,* 673–685.

Harris, G.T., Rice, M.E., & Cormier, C.A. (1991). Psychopathy and violent recidivism. *Law and Human Behavior, 15,* 624–637.

Harris, G.T., Rice, M.E., & Quinsey, V.L. (1993). Violent recidivism of mentally disordered offenders: The development of a statistical prediction instrument. *Criminal Justice and Behavior, 20,* 315–335.

Heckel, R.V., & Mandell, E. (1971). *Crime and delinquency. Social Problems Research Institute Monograph No. 3*. Columbia, SC: Social Problems Research Institute, University of South Carolina.

Heide, K.M. (1992). *Why kids kill parents*. Columbus: Ohio State University Press.

Heide, K.M. (1993a). Juvenile involvement in multiple offender and multiple victim parricides. *Journal of Police and Criminal Psychology, 9,* 53–64.

Heide, K.M. (1993b). Weapons used by juveniles and adults to kill parents. *Behavioral Sciences and the Law, 11,* 397–405.

Heide, K. (1993c) Parents who get killed and children who kill them. *Journal of Interpersonal Violence, 8,* 531–544.

Heide, K.M. (1994). Evidence of child maltreatment among adolescent parricide offenders. *International Journal of Offender Therapy and Comparative Criminology, 38,* 151–162.

Hellsten, P., & Katila, O. (1965). Murder and other homicide by children under 15 in Finland. *Psychiatric Quarterly, Suppl. 39,* 54–74.

Hendrix, C.E., & Heckel, R.V. (1981). The effects of a behavioral approach on modifying social behavior in incarcerated male delinquents. *Journal of Clinical Psychology*.

Hinshaw, S.P., Klein, R.G., & Abikoff, H. (1998). Childhood attention deficit hyperactivy disorder: Nonpharmalogical and combination treatments. In P. E. Nathan, & J. M. Gorman (Eds.), *A guide to treatments that work* (pp. 26–91).

Hoffman, M.L. (1988). Moral development. In M.H. Bowstein & M.E. Lamb (Eds.), *Development psychology: An advanced textbook* (2nd ed.) (pp. 497–548). Hillsdale, NJ: Erlbaum.

Hoge, R., & Andrews, D.A., (1996). *Assessing the youthful offender: Issues & techinques*. New York: Plenum Press.

Hoge, R.D., Andrews, D.A., & Leschied, A.W. (1996). An investigation of risk and protective factors in a sample of youthful offenders. *Journal of Child Psychology and Psychiatry, 37,* 419–424.

Holmes, R.M., & Holmes, S.T. (1994). *Murder in America*. London: Sage Publications.

Holtzman, W. (1961). *Inkblot technique: Administration and scoring guide.* New York: Psychological Corporation.

Howell, J.C., Krisberg, B., & Jones, M. (1995). Trends in juvenile crime and youth violence. In J.C. Howell, B. Krisberg, J.D. Hawkins, & J.J. Wilson (Eds.), *Serious, violent, & chronic juvenile offenders: A Sourcebook* (pp. 1–35).

Huesmann, L.R., Eron, L.D., Lefkowitz, M.M., & Walder, L.O. (1984). Stability of aggression over time and generations. *Developmental Psychology, 20,* 1120–1134.

Hughes, J.N., & Hasbrook, J.E. (1996). Television violence: Implications for violence prevention. *School Psychology Review, 25,* 134–151.

Jennings, W.S. , Kilkenny, R., & Kohlberg, L. (1983). Moral development theory and practice for youthful and adult offenders. In W.S. Laufer, & J.M. Day (Eds), *Personality theory, moral development and criminal behavior* (pp. 281–355). Toronto, Canada: Lexington Books.

Jesness, C., & Wedge, R. (1984). Validity of a revised Jesness Inventory I-level classification with delinquents. *Journal of Consulting and Clinical Psychology, 52,* 997–1010.

Jesness, C., & Wedge, R. (1985). *Jesness Inventory classificaton system: Supplementary manual.* Palo Alto, CA: Consulting Psychologists Press.

Jones, M., & Krisberg, B. (1993). Detention utilization: Case level data and projections (a study of secure detention in five sites). *Focus.* San Francisco: National Council on Crime and Delinquency.

Kazdin, A.E. (1988). Child psychotherapy: Developing and identifying effective treatments. Needham Heights, MA: Allyn & Bacon.

Kazdin, A.E. (1998). Psychosocial treatments for conduct disorder in children. In J.M. Gorman, & P.E. Nathan, (Eds.), A guide to treatments that work (pp. 65–89). New York: Oxford University Press.

King, C.H. (1975). The ego and the integration of violence in homicidal youth. *American Journal of Orthopsychiatry, 45,* 134–145.

Kohlberg, L. (1984). *Essays on moral development: Vol. 11. The psychology of moral development.* San Francisco: Harper & Row.

Krisberg, B., Schwartz, I., & Fishman, G. (1987). The incarceration of minority youth. *Crime and Delinquency, 33,* 173–205.

Lande, R.G. (1993). The video violence debate. *Hospital and Community Psychiatry, 44,* 347–351.

Lefrancois, G.R. (1995). *Of Children: An introduction to child development* (8th ed.). Belmont, CA: Wadsworth Publishing Company.

Lepper, M.R. (1983). Social-control processes and the internalization of social values: An attributional perspective. In E.T. Higgins, D.N. Ruble, & W.W. Hartop (Eds.), *Social cognition and social development* (pp. 294–330). Cambridge, England: Cambridge University Press.

Lewis, D.O., Moy, E., Jackson, L.D., Aaronson, R., Ritvo, U., Settu, S., & Simons, A. (1985). Biopsychosocial characteristics of children who later murder: A prospective study. *American Journal of Psychiatry, 142,* 1161–1166.

Lewis, D.O., Pincus, J.H., Bard, B., Richardson, E., Prichep, L.S., Feldman, M., & Yeager, C. (1988). Neuropsychiatric, psychoeducational, and family characteristics of 14 juveniles condemned to death in the United States. *American Journal of Psychiatry, 145,* 584–589.

Lewis, D.O., Shanok, S.S., Gran, M., & Ritvo, E. (1983). Homicidally aggressive young children: Neuropsychiatric and experiential correlates. *American Journal of Psychiatry, 140,* 148–153.

Lezak, M.D. (1995). *Neuropsychological assessment* (3rd Ed.). New York: Oxford University Press.

Lidz, C.W., Mulvey, E.P., & Gardner, W. (1993). The accuracy of prediction of violence to others. *Journal of the American Medical Association, 269,* 1007–1011.

Loeber, R., & Dishion, T. (1983). Early predictors of male delinquency: A review. *Psychological Bulletin, 94,* 68–99.

Loeber, R., & Farrington, D.P. (Eds.). (1998). *Serious & violent juvenile offenders: Risk factors and successful interventions.* Thousand Oaks, CA: Sage Publications.

Lyman, D.R. (1996). Early identification of chronic offenders: Who is the fledgling psychopath? *Psychological Bulletin, 120,* 209–234.

Maccoby, E., & Martin, J. (1983). Socialization in the context of the family: Parent-child interaction. In P. H. Mussen (Series Ed.) & E.M. Hetherington (Vol. Ed.), *Handbook of child psychology: Vol. 4. Socialization, personality and social development* (pp. 1–101). New York: Wiley.

Malmquist, C.P. (1971). Premonitory signs of homicidal aggression in juveniles. *American Journal of Psychiatry, 128,* 93–97.

Malmquist, C.P. (1996). *Homicide: A psychiatric perspective.* Washington, DC: American Psychiatric Press.

Maxson, C.L., & Klein, M.W. (1996). Defining gang homicide: an updated look at member and motive approaches. In C.R. Huff (Ed.), *Gangs in America* (2nd ed., pp. 3–20). London: Sage Publications.

McGuire, W.J. (1986). The myth of massive media impact: Savagings and salvagings. In G. Comstock (Ed.), *Public communication and behavior:* (Vol. 1, pp. 173–257). San Diego, CA: Academic Press.

Mehrabian, A., & Epstein, N.A. (1972). A measure of emotional empathy. *Journal of Personality, 40,* 525–543.

Mezzich, A.C., Coffman, G., & Mezzich, J.E. (1991). A typology of violent delinquent adolescents. *Journal of Psychiatry and Law, 19,* 63–78.

Miller, D., & Looney, J. (1974). The prediction of adolescent homicide. Episodic dyscontrol and dehumanisation. *American Journal of Psychoanalysis, 34,* 187–198.

Millon, T. (1993). *Millon adolescent clinical inventory.* Minneapolis, MN: National Computer Systems.

Millon, T., Green, C.J., & Meagher, R.B., Jr. (1982). *Millon behavioral health inventory manual* (3rd ed.). Minneapolis: National Computer Systems.

Monahan, J. (1988). Risk assessment among the mentally disordered: Generating useful knowledge. *International Journal of Law and Psychiatry, 11,* 249–257.

Monahan, J. (1996). Violence prediction: The last 20 years and the next 20 years. *Criminal Justice and Behavior, 23,* 107–120.

Mulvey, E.P., Arthur, M.W., & Reppucci, N.D. (1993). The prevention and treatment of juvenile delinquency: A review of the research. *Clinical Psychology Review, 13,* 133–167.

Mulvey, E.P., & Lidz, C.W. (1984). Clinical considerations in the prediction of dangerousness in mental patients. *Clinical Psychology Review, 4,* 379–401.

Murphy, S. (1999). The cheers and the tears: A healthy alternative to the dark side of youth sports today. San Francisco: Jossey-Bass.

Myers, W.C. (1994). Sexual homicide by adolescents. *Journal of the American Academy of Child and Adolescent Psychiatry, 33,* 962–969.

Myers, W.C., & Kemph, J.P. (1990). DSM-III-R classification of murderous youth: Help or hindrance? *Journal of Clinical Psychiatry, 51,* 239–242.

Myers, W.C., & Mutch, P.J. (1992). Language disorders in disruptive behaviour disordered homicidal youth. *Journal of Forensic Sciences, 37,* 919–922.

Myers, W.C., Scott, K., Burgess, A.W., & Burgess, A.G. (1995). Psychopathology, biopsychosocial factors, crime characteristics, and classification of 25 homicidal youths. *Journal of the American Academy of Child and Adolescent Psychiatry, 34,* 1483–1489.

Nuffield, J. (1982). *Parole decision-making in Canada.* Ottawa, Ontario, Canada: Solicitor General.

O'Donnell, C. R. (1995). Firearm deaths among children and youth. *American Psychologist, 50,* 771–776.

Paik, H., & Comstock, G. (1994). The effects of television violence on antisocial behavior: A meta-analysis. *Communication Research, 21,* 516–546.

Palmer, E.J., & Hollin, C.R. (1998). A comparison of moral development in young offenders and non-offenders. *Legal and Criminological Psychology, 3,* 225–235.

Paluszny, M., & McNabb, M. (1975). Therapy of a 6-year-old who committed fratricide. *Journal of the American Academy of Child Psychiatry, 14,* 319–336.

Patterson, G.R., DeBaryshe, B.D., & Ramsey, E. (1989). A developmental perspective on antisocial behavior. *American Psychologist, 44,* 329–335.

Petti, T.A., & Davidman, L. (1981). Homicidal school-age children: Cognitive style and demographic features. *Child Psychiatry and Human Development, 12,* 82–89.

Pfeffer, C.R. (1980). Psychiatric hospital treatment of assaultive homicidal children. *American Journal of Psychotherapy, 34,* 197–207.

Podkopacz, M.R., & Feld, B.C. (1996). The end of the line: An empiricial study of judical waiver. *Journal of Criminal Law and Criminology, 86,* 64–99.

Pope, C.F., & Feyerherm, W. (1993). *Minorities and the juvenile justice system.* Washington, DC: U.S. Department of Justice, Office of Juvenile Justice and Delinquency Prevention.

Post, S. (1982). Adolescent parricide in abusive families. *Child Welfare, 61,* 445–455.

Quay, H.C., & Peterson, D.R. (1987). *Manual for the Revised Behavior Problem Checklist.* Miami, FL: Herbert C. Quay and Donald R. Peterson.

Reitan, R.M (1987). *Neuropsychological Evaluation of Children.* Tucson, AZ: R.M. Reitan.

Reitan, R., & Wolfson, D. (1986). *Traumatic brain injury: Recovery and rehabilitation.* Tucson, AZ: Neuropsychology Press.

Ressler, R.K., Burgess, A.W., & Douglas, J.E. (1988). *Sexual homicide: Patterns and motives.* New York: Free Press.

Rest, J., Thoma, S., & Edwards, L. (1997). Designing and validating a measure of moral judgement: Stage preference and stage consistency approaches. *Journal of Educational Psychology, 89,* 5–28.

Rice, M.E., & Harris, G.T. (1995). Violent recidivism: Assessing predictive validity. *Journal of Consulting and Clinical Psychology, 63*, 737–748.

Ripple, C.H., Gilliam, W.S., Chanana, N., & Zigler, E. (1999). Will fifty cooks spoil the broth? The debate over entrusting Head Start to the states. *American Psychologist, 54* (5), 327–343.

Roberts, D.F., & Macoby, N. (1985). Effects of mass communication. In G. Lindzey & E. Aronson (Eds.), *Handbook of social psychology* (Vol. 2, pp. 539–598). New York: Random House.

Rogers, C. (1993). Gang-related homicides in Los Angeles County. *Journal of Forensic Sciences, 38*, 831–834.

Rosenzweig, S. (1948). *Rosenzweig P-F study*. Pittsburgh: Saul Rosenzweig.

Rowley, J.C., Ewing, C.P., & Singer, S.I. (1987). Juvenile homicide: The need for an interdisciplinary approach. *Behavioral Sciences and the Law, 5*, 1–10.

Russell, D.H. (1965). A study of juvenile murderers. *Journal of Offender Therapy, 9*, 55–86.

Russell, D.H. (1979). Ingredients of juvenile murder. *International Journal of Offender Therapy and Comparative Criminology, 23*, 65–72.

Russell, D. H. (1985). Girls who kill. *International Offender Therapy and Comparative Criminology, 29*, 171–176.

Sadoff, R.L. (1971). Clinical observations on parricide. *Psychiatric Quarterly, 45*, 65–69.

Samenow, S. (1989). *Before it's too late: Why some kids get into trouble and what parents can do about it*. New York: Times Books.

Sampson, R.J. (1992). Family management and child development: Insights from social disorganization theory. In J. McCord (Ed.), *Facts, frameworks and forecasts* (pp. 63–93). New Brunswick, NJ: Transaction Publishers.

Sampson, R.J. (1997). Collective regulation of adolescent misbehavior. Validation results for eighty Chicago neighborhoods. *Journal of Adolescent Research, 12*, 227–224.

Sampson, R.J., & Groves, W.B. (1989). Community structure and crime: Testing social disorganization theory. *American Journal of Sociology, 94*, 774–802.

Sargent, D. (1962). Children who kill—a family conspiracy? *Social Work, 17*, 35–42.

Sattler, J.M. (1998). *Clinical and forensic interviewing of children and families: Guidelines for the mental health, education, pediatric, and child maltreatment fields*. San Diego: Jerome M. Sattler, Publishers.

Schaefer, C. E. (1993). *The therapeutic powers of play*. Northvale, NJ: Jason Aronson.

Scherl, D.J., & Mack, J.E. (1966). A study of adolescent matricide. *Journal of the American Academy of Child Psychiatry, 5*, 569–593.

Sendi, I.B., & Blomgren, P.G. (1975). A comparative study of predictive criteria in the predisposition of homicidal adolescents. *American Journal of Psychiatry, 132*, 423–428.

Sereny, G. (1999). *Cries Unheard: Why children kill: The story of Mary Bell*. New York: Metropolitan Books, Henry Holt and Company.

Shaffer, D.G. (1996). *Developmental psychology: Childhood and adolescence*. Pacific Grove, CA: Brooks-Cole.

Shumaker, D. (1998). Children who murder: A review. Unpublished manuscript. Columbia, SC.

Sickmund, M., Snyder, H., & Poe-Yamagata, E. (1997). *Juvenile offenders and victims: 1997 update on violence*. Washington, DC: Office of Juvenile Justice and Delinquency Prevention.

Singer, J.L., Singer, D.G., & Rapaczynski, W. (1984). Family patterns and television viewing as predictors of children's beliefs and aggression. *Journal of Communication, 34*, 73–89.

Smith, S. (1965). The adolescent murderer: A psychodynamic interpretation. *Archives of General Psychiatry, 13*, 310–319.

Snyder, H. (1994). Are juveniles driving the violent crime trends? *Fact Sheet 16.* Washington, DC: Office of Juvenile Justice and Delinquency Prevention.

Snyder, H., & Sickmund, M. (1995). *National report on juvenile offending and victimization*. Washington, DC: Office of Juvenile Justice and Delinquency Prevention.

Solway, K.S., Richardson, L., Hays, J.R., & Elion, V.H. (1981). Adolescent murderers: Literature review and preliminary research findings. In J.R. Hays, T.K. Roberts, & K.S. Solway (Eds.), *Violence and the violent individual* (pp. 193–210). New York: SP Medical and Scientific Books.

Sorrells, J. (1977). Kids who kill. *Crime and Delinquency, 23*, 312–320.

Sorrells, J. (1980). What can be done about juvenile homicide? *Crime and Delinquency, 26*, 152–161.

Spergel, I.A. (1983). *Violent gangs in Chicago: Segmentation and integration*. Unpublished manuscript, University of Chicago.

Spergel, I.A. (1995). *The youth gang problem: A community approach*. New York: Oxford University Press.

Spreen, O., Risser, A.H., & Edgell, D. (1995). *Development neuropsychology*. New York: Oxford University Press.

Stearns, A.W. (1957). Murder by adolescents with obscure motivation. *American Journal of Psychiatry, 114*, 303–305.

Szymanski, L. (1998). Oldest age juvenile court may retain jurisdiction in delinquency matters. *NCJJ Snapshot*. Pittsburgh: National Center for Juvenile Justice.

Thomas, R. Murray. (1997). *An integrated theory of moral development*. Westport, CT: Greenwood Press.

Tooley, K. (1975). The small assassins: Clinical notes on a subgroup of murderous children. *Journal of the American Academy of Child Psychiatry, 14*, 306–318.

Torbet, P., Gable, R., Hurst, H., IV, Montgomery, I., Szymanski, L., & Thomas, D. (1996). *State responses to serious and violent juvenile crime*. Washington, DC: Office of Juvenile Justice and Delinquency Prevention.

Torbet, P., & Szymanski, L. (1998). *State legislative responses to violent juvenile crime: 1996–97 update*. Washington, DC: Office of Juvenile Justice and Delinquency Prevention.

Toupin, J. & Morissette, L. (1990). Juvenile homicide: A case control study. *Medicine & Law, 9*, 986–994.

VanSchie, F.G.M., & Wiegman, O. (1997). Children and video games: Leisure activities, agression, social integration and school performance. *Journal of Applied Social Psychology, 27*, 1175–1194.

Walshe-Brennan, K.S. (1975). Children who have murdered. *Medico Legal Journal, 43*(1), 20–24.

Walshe-Brennan, K.S. (1977). A socio-psychological investigation of young murderers. *British Journal of Criminology, 17*, 58–63.

Webster-Stratton, C., & Herbert, M. (1994). *Troubled families—problem children working with parents: A collaborative process.* New York, John Wiley & Sons.

Weisz, J.R., & Weiss, B. (1993). *Effects of psychotherapy with children and adolescents.* Newberry Park, CA: Sage.

Whiting, B.B., Edwards, C.P., Ember, C.R., Erchak, G.M., Harkness, S., Monroe, R.L., Monroe, R.H., Nerlove, S.B., & Seymour, S. (1988). *Children of different worlds: The formation of social behavior.* Cambridge, MA: Harvard University Press.

Wiegman, O., Kuttschreuter, M., & Baarda, B. (1992). A longitudinal study of the effects of television viewing on aggressive and prosocial behaviors. *British Journal of Social Psychology, 31*, 197–164.

Wood, W., Wong, F., & Chachere, J. (1991). Effects of media violence on viewers' aggression and unconstrained social interaction. *Psychological Bulletin, 109*, 371–383.

Woods, S.M. (1961). Adolescent violence and homicide. *Archives of General Psychiatry, 5*, 38–44.

Yarvis, R.M. (1991). *Homicide: Causative factors and roots.* Lexington, MA: Lexington Book Company.

Zagar, R., Arbit, J., Sylvies, R., Busch, K., & Hughes, J. (1990). Homicidal adolescents: A replication. *Psychological Reports, 67*, 1235–1242.

Zenoff, E.H., & Zients, A.B. (1979). Juvenile murderers: Should the punishment fit the crime? *International Journal of Law and Psychiatry, 2*, 533–553.

Zigler, E. (1998). School should begin at age 3 years for American children. *Journal of Developmental and Behavioral Pediatrics, 19*, 37–38.

Index

About the Authors

ROBERT V. HECKEL is Distinguished Professor Emeritus in the Department of Psychology at the University of South Carolina.

DAVID M. SHUMAKER is a doctoral candidate in Clinical-Community Psychology at the University of South Carolina, Columbia.